David Bowie in Darkness

David Bowie in Darkness

A Study of 1. Outside *and the Late Career*

Nicholas P. Greco

McFarland & Company, Inc., Publishers
Jefferson, North Carolina

ALSO BY NICHOLAS P. GRECO

"Only If You Are Really Interested": Celebrity, Gender, Desire and the World of Morrissey (McFarland, 2011)

Title page: David Bowie (by and used by permission of Tamara McKenzie).

LIBRARY OF CONGRESS CATALOGUING-IN-PUBLICATION DATA

Greco, Nicholas P., 1973–
    David Bowie in darkness : a study of 1. outside and the late career / Nicholas P. Greco.
    p.   cm.
    Includes bibliographical references and index.

    ISBN 978-0-7864-9410-1 (softcover : acid free paper) ∞
    ISBN 978-1-4766-2194-4 (ebook)

    1. Bowie, David. 2. Bowie, David. 1. outside. 3. Rock musicians—England—Biography. I. Title.
ML420.B754G74 2015
782.42166092—dc23   2015020266

BRITISH LIBRARY CATALOGUING DATA ARE AVAILABLE

© 2015 Nicholas P. Greco. All rights reserved

No part of this book may be reproduced or transmitted in any form or by any means, electronic or mechanical, including photocopying or recording, or by any information storage and retrieval system, without permission in writing from the publisher.

Cover Image: David Bowie © Photofest

Printed in the United States of America

McFarland & Company, Inc., Publishers
  Box 611, Jefferson, North Carolina 28640
    www.mcfarlandpub.com

To Serafina and Antonella.

Acknowledgments

I would like to thank Dr. Susan Fast, Dr. Ken McLeod and Dr. Fred Hall for their guidance when I was writing the earliest drafts of chapters 2 through 6. Critical to my development as a young scholar was the guidance of the music faculty at McMaster University in the late 1990s; in particular, I would like to thank Dr. James Deaville and Dr. Hugh Hartwell for their support and encouragement throughout those early days.

I must mention, with gratitude, my colleagues at Providence University College, especially Dr. Michael Gilmour, whose help, advice and friendship have been invaluable throughout this process. I thank Cameron McKenzie, the academic dean of the University College, for granting me a sabbatical in order to complete this manuscript. He is a superior, but also a colleague and a dear friend. I have added the name of Dr. Randall Holm here because, if I failed to mention him, he would be sad. I am pleased with the drawing of Bowie by Tamara McKenzie, which now hangs in my office.

Finally, I am grateful for the correspondence with Bowie's guitarist, Reeves Gabrels, who was kind enough to respond to emails and messages from a fan-scholar. His insight into Bowie's world is a wonderful resource.

Table of Contents

Acknowledgments vi

Preface 1

Introduction 3

1. The Beginning of the End 11
2. The Descent of Anxiety 67
3. Mugging Demons for Wisdom 85
4. The Culture of Body Modification 106
5. An Analysis of *1. Outside* 129
6. Bowie in Video and Live Performance 164

Postscript 189

Chapter Notes 197

Bibliography 209

Index 217

Preface

This book focuses on the destruction of the early David Bowie persona. That very destruction takes place during his later career; this book explores Bowie's negotiation of his celebrity during this period, with a particular focus on an album that he released in 1995 entitled *1. Outside*. It is the symptom of a break in his career, a break that occurred in or around 1988.

Bowie's later career can be mapped out in the following way, and this is how this book will treat his career. In 1983, Bowie released *Let's Dance*, marking the beginning of a period of unprecedented commercial success. This is also a period during and after which Bowie experienced truly global success, leading to his status as global celebrity. In 1984, the documentary film *Ricochet* was released, packaged with the concert video for the *Serious Moonlight* tour. The documentary focuses on the Asian leg of *Serious Moonlight* in late 1983, which included stops in Singapore, Thailand and Hong Kong. In 1988, Bowie collaborated with guitarist Reeves Gabrels on a remix of the single "Look Back in Anger." The original track appeared on 1979's *Lodger*, produced by Brian Eno. In 1992, Bowie released *Black Tie White Noise*. During this period, Bowie renewed his relationship with Brian Eno and began considering how to approach the creation of future music. In 1995, Bowie released *1. Outside*, an album that acts as a focal point of this later period. Furthermore, more than any other artifact from his career, *1. Outside* characterizes Bowie's state as celebrity during this later period. Theoretically, the album is symptomatic of a deep-seated anxiety, both in the form of Bowie's star image and of Western society at large. What can be read as a reflection of societal anxiety becomes a reflection of a sort of personal anxiety. From 1997 to 2003, Bowie released a group of albums that

Preface

include *Earthling*, *'hours...,'* *Heathen* and *Reality*, marking the end of a period of his career. Some of these albums recall his previous material: while *'hours...'* shows Bowie attending to a dead version of himself, indicating the death of his 1990s persona, *Heathen* revisits some of the darker themes of his *1. Outside* album. In 2004, Bowie became a recluse, with very few examples of artistic production. Unexpectedly, in 2013, Bowie released *The Next Day*, and in 2014, he released the single "Sue (Or in a Season of Crime)" and its companion piece "'Tis a Pity She's a Whore."

Chapter 1 explores the latter half of Bowie's career through case studies that elucidate the notion that Bowie is a celebrity who negotiates this stage of his career in a particular way. Bowie requires an audience for his continuance as a celebrity, but works against that audience in the creation—or, rather, the *destruction*—of his star image. Chapters 2 through 6 look in detail at his *1. Outside* album, an anchor and representative work of this period.

Introduction

David Bowie is a "chameleon," an artist who sheds his present persona to create a new one. This is what keeps Bowie popular, relevant and compelling. Or so one might think. Rather, Bowie is an artist who is able to work with the resources around him to create something new. In fact, he has been extremely successful in doing so, causing many people to see him as a sort of lone artist rather than a collaborator in the creation of the celebrity entity known as "David Bowie." But there is something else: Bowie does not always create. He also *destroys*. And he has been destroying since the middle of his career.

In the early 1980s, Bowie received much commercial success with *Let's Dance*, and continued successes with *Tonight* and *Never Let Me Down*, though the latter two albums were met with less than stellar critical reception. In a way, this forced Bowie to reconsider his musical journey, which is made clear by his collaboration with guitarist Reeves Gabrels and the formation of Tin Machine, a band that produced a trio of albums from 1989 to 1992. He returned to stability—that is, the "mainstream" of popular music—with the jazz-infused *Black Tie White Noise* in 1993. *Black Tie White Noise* afforded Bowie some commercial success, presenting a sanitized and overproduced version of the singer after the rougher-sounding Tin Machine recordings, even if *Black Tie* features Bowie holding a cigarette on its cover. The album also betrays a darker, alienating side of the singer.

The alienation hinted at in *Black Tie White Noise* comes to a head with *1. Outside*, an ambitious project featuring an often disjointed narrative accompanying often disjointed and jarring musical soundscapes. In support of the album, Bowie embarked on a tour he co-headlined with Nine Inch Nails, a band which, at that time, was firmly entrenched

Introduction

in industrial music, a sort of amalgamation of metal and electronic music, and almost anathema to Bowie's *Black Tie White Noise* musical output. This move seemed strange in that the audiences for Nine Inch Nails and for Bowie generally do not intersect (this was certainly the case in the mid-1990s). Furthermore, Bowie's stage presentation at the time seemed to alienate his fans at the concerts. For instance, he would physically turn his back on the audience; play music unfamiliar to many, performing songs coming from the as yet unreleased *1. Outside* album and straying away from any of his hits; and revel in the often atonal and frantic playing of lead guitarist Gabrels. Nevertheless, the album was acclaimed by critics, reactions probably bolstered by Bowie's choice of producer in Brian Eno.

The album is a symptom of a societal anxiety that existed leading up to the year 2000, an anxiety which was ultimately deemed unnecessary: the "wall" of the new millennium brought none of the societal breakdowns suggested by the "Y2K" technological failure (there was rampant speculation that computer systems would not be able to deal with the change of digits—from "99" to "00"—that would accompany a calendar change, and thus fail to operate). Furthermore, the psychological barrier of the new millennium and its unknowns seemed eclipsed by time continuing as it always did. There were even those who subsequently argued that the true new millennium began on the first of January 2001, making the 2000 date less of a marker to pass over and more of a marker to ignore completely.

For Bowie, an important trend in the 1990s was the prevalence of body modification; he felt that this was a return to a primitive religion, a replacement for the pervasive—and, it is assumed, failed—Judaeo-Christian ethic in Western society. The trend of piercing, tattooing and other more extreme forms of body modification were, for Bowie, a symptom of anxiety in late twentieth century Western society, and an attempt to attain a sort of transformation in the face of the unknown of the turn of the century and millennium.

Such anxiety as expressed in the various facets of *1. Outside* was not only a reflection of Bowie's perception of how Western society felt at that point but, it will be argued, was a reflection of deep-seated personal anxiety on the part of Bowie himself. At the very least, it was a

Introduction

symptom of the discomfort that Bowie felt at being in the celebrity spotlight, constrained as a mainstream "pop" star. This unease can be traced back to 1988 (though it can be seen prior to this), ironically at a time when Bowie himself seemed to be "settling down": he experienced global success in the 1980s, was married to supermodel Iman in 1992 and became a father to a second child, a girl named Alexandria, in 2000. The anxiety manifested itself in continued experimentation through *Earthling* in 1997 and *'hours…'* in 1999. The cover for *'hours…'* featured Bowie cradling a supposedly dead version of himself, in a manner reminiscent of religious iconography of Mary and the dead Christ.

In 2002, Bowie released *Heathen*, an album which hearkened back to the darkness and anxiety expressed in his output of the mid-1990s. *Reality*, released in 2003, broke from some of the darkness of the other releases and resulted in Bowie touring extensively. The tour ended in June of 2004 when Bowie suffered from chest pain, which was discovered to be caused by a blocked coronary artery. Bowie then largely left the gaze of the public, only to return in 2013—almost a full decade later—with *The Next Day*.

This book explores the broader evolution taking place during this time period, an almost 30-year period in which the musical expression of anxiety seems to reflect not only the state of the Western world (at least as perceived by Bowie), but also a personal state, one which ultimately results in a decade-long pause of a career beginning in 2004. And even with the release of *The Next Day* and "Sue (Or in a Season of Crime)," his destruction continues.

Chapter 1 maps out his later career by exploring particular cases that demonstrate his negotiation of celebrity. It considers the concert film *Ricochet* from 1984, a curious work that seems to betray some of the later darkness under the sheen of commercial successes and popularity. It continues by exploring the collaboration between guitarist Reeves Gabrels and Bowie in 1988 to produce a remix of "Look Back in Anger." The analysis draws on Roland Barthes' work on fashion and illustrates how Bowie hides himself with the very act of dancing on stage with another person. Chapter 1 goes on to explore the notion of space in David Bowie's music. Victor Turner's conception of liminality will be introduced, and becomes an important element in the analysis of *1. Out-*

side, which makes up chapters 2 through 6. The discussion of space leads to an exploration of a musical moment on stage in 1997, during Bowie's fiftieth birthday celebration. Barthes' notion of "cruising" the singing voice allows Bowie to lose himself in moments of fragmentation, in the space of "signifiance" that opens in the "grain" of Bowie's voice.

Foucault's heterotopia, another sort of space, helps to elucidate the video for "Thursday's Child." In 2003, Bowie released an accompanying film with *Reality*, a rich artifact that demonstrates how Bowie distances himself from his audience through mediation. Chapter 1 looks to the work of Paul Virilio and Roland Barthes in detail in order to understand a contextual space for Bowie's dystopian utopia in the video for "Valentine's Day" from 2013. Finally, it takes Bowie's recent work as a focus, looking in particular at "Valentine's Day" from *The Next Day* and "Sue (Or in a Season of Crime)" released in late 2014, and ends by mapping out where this work can go in the future, and what might come of Bowie's celebrity as time continues. These studies strive to demonstrate Bowie's affinity toward the production of his own destructed, and continually destructing, personae.

Chapters 2 through 6 embark on a detailed analysis of Bowie's mid–1990s album *1. Outside*, a sort of anchor of this latter part of his career, and an excellent example of Bowie's sustained construction of a liminal space within which to disappear. Chapter 2 explores Reeves Gabrels' influences on Bowie; it also addresses the musical and cultural context in which Bowie was working in the early 1990s, which informed his *1. Outside* album.

Chapter 3 builds upon the previous one in that it outlines Brian Eno's compositional processes and philosophies in order to provide context and background to the essential work of *1. Outside*. Reeves Gabrels and Brian Eno can be thought of as architects of Bowie's later career: Gabrels is the songwriter and collaborator who enables and assists Bowie in the creation of the music, and Eno is the philosophical muse that informs *1. Outside* in particular, which anchors the era. In addition to the influence of these two figures, the late twentieth century, and its prevalence of body modification in mainstream society, provided Bowie with a hook: the anxiety of Western society at the end of the millennium. In light of this phenomenon, Chapter 4 explores the world of body mod-

Introduction

ification in late twentieth century Western society. The action of modifying one's body was essential in informing Bowie's thoughts in the conception and creation of *1. Outside*. Chapter 5 shows how the *1. Outside* album creates a space that characterizes societal anxiety at the end of the twentieth century. Chapter 6 continues in this vein, exploring a selection of Bowie's live performance and video output during this period.

The majority of writings on David Bowie have focused on his early groundbreaking work or have presented the life of Bowie in a biographical manner. It is certainly true that Bowie's early work has much merit, as has been made clear by the vast pool of both academic and popular writings regarding his work in the early 1970s. This seems to be the case even in the public imagination: the recent travelling exhibition *David Bowie Is* featured many pieces of ephemera, art and fashion from Bowie's career, but even such a comprehensive project seems weighed toward the earlier part of his career. This might be due to the prevalence of overt theatricality in that part of Bowie's career, manifest in his choice of clothing, for instance. Until very recently, much of the academic writing on Bowie has chosen to focus only on these earlier works and ignores his more recent material, especially once he attained global celebrity status. While much is said of Bowie's various personae, there has not been a work that attempts to map out the evolution of these personae or explore how they are created, transformed, expressed and mediated, and ultimately destroyed.

Martin Roth calls Bowie an "instigator not just of memorable individual pieces—an album sleeve, a costume, a hairstyle—but of a particular zeitgeist that is uniquely his and yet resonates with enormous numbers of people around the globe." What is curious, though, is how this particular zeitgeist *does* resonate with so many when it is seemingly isolationist. Roth continues to suggest that Bowie has contributed significantly to the concept of individuality, that members of society are free to create and further their own look or outward expression of their very being without being concerned by the opinion or attention of others.[1]

In fact, Bowie does indicate an individuality which others follow, all the while seeming to hold on to a rather tenuous line: as a celebrity, he *relies* on his fan following. The star "David Bowie" counts on the fact

Introduction

that people will follow him, and be his fans. But he also moves forward without an overtly or obviously calculated sense of purposefully cultivating that following (but, of course, at some level, this is happening). In fact, once Bowie becomes a global star in the 1980s (along with his most mainstream—and uninspired—musical output), he seems less inclined to cater to fan favor; this is the obvious outcome of commercial success, that is, not relying on continued financial support from others and instead relying on personal, independent wealth. Rather, it seems Bowie *leads* without being concerned with monetary matters. Of course, this is a simplistic view of things: it is impossible for any celebrity to continue her or his agenda, or very existence, without concern for a following, but with Bowie's move to global star, he no longer requires the same sort of cultivation of fandom. Instead, he is assured a following, while at the same time turning his back on it.

Matt McAllester recognizes this shift in Bowie's star image. In his review of Bowie's *The Next Day* in the 13 March 2013 issue of *Time*, McAllester remarks that Bowie mostly disappeared from performing—and, in fact, appearing in public at all—in 2006, a couple of years after suffering a heart attack on stage. But McAllester makes an interesting observation, that Bowie was a star who was a leader in concealing his true self behind what he calls "bizarre, intimidating invented personas."[2]

This is a strange remark in light of what McAllester has to say next. He suggests that Bowie in the 1990s did not "make up" for the commercial success—and thus the critical and artistic failure—of Bowie in the 1980s. To illustrate the 1980s downfall of Bowie, a graphic accompanies McAllester's piece in which Bowie's "Quality of Work" and "Level of Exposure" are plotted on the vertical y-axis and his "Level of Exposure" along a horizontal x-axis of chronological time. In the early to mid-1970s, Bowie's quality of work and level of exposure are both high; the late 1970s (during Bowie's so-called "Berlin" period) show a very low level of exposure but a high quality of work, a relationship that becomes completely inverted as the 1980s continue. And with the release of *The Next Day*, the relationship between the two elements inverts again: Bowie exhibits a low level of exposure but a high quality of work.

And, for McAllester, Bowie's middle period of artistic dread is mapped out quite neatly when one visits the *David Bowie Is* exhibition,

Introduction

as 1983 marks the strong emergence of new fashion for Bowie: he begins wearing the suit, a sort of garish revival of the zoot suit of the 1930s (McAllester calls this "a kind of neocolonialist take"). During the 1990s, Bowie's quality of work (what McAllester calls "hit or miss") was low and his exposure was moderate.[3]

McAllester's reading is acceptable to a point, especially his comment regarding Bowie's personae, at least in the 1990s. It is more of a stretch, though, to consider Ziggy Stardust as one example of "intimidating invented personas," at least in the conventional sense. Certainly, Ziggy Stardust was intimidating in the face of mainstream societal conceptions of gender representation, and to notions of stardom and celebrity itself. It is strange that McAllester would make such a close equation between quality of work and low level of exposure. While Bowie is certainly *deliberately* keeping his exposure level low, it is unclear that this has anything to do with quality of work. It is not necessarily the case that Bowie's artistic output from the 1980s is somehow less artistic, but that the 1980s commercial output—with its high level of exposure—sets the stage for everything that follows. Fundamentally, Bowie walks the tightrope of needing exposure as a celebrity, and shunning that exposure at every turn, post-1988.

Chris O'Leary, in his excellent commentary about Bowie's "Everyone Says 'Hi'" from 2002's *Heathen*, writes that the song is addressed to any companion who has moved on; O'Leary even suggests that it might be a call from beyond the grave, a kind of greeting coming from those who have already died. He mentions a cover of the song by the German singer Claudia Brücken from 2012, suggesting that the song can be read as addressed to a then-departed Bowie, who vanished without anyone realizing that he had gone. This might have been the result of global fame: it is difficult to notice that a celebrity is gone when he or she is ubiquitously "present" in the popular culture fabric.[4]

In an interview with Terry Gross from 2002, aired on the WHYY Philadelphia radio program *Fresh Air* on 19 September 2003 (distributed by National Public Radio in the United States), Bowie claims that he has not manufactured any personae since 1975 (except for the characters that he portrays in *1. Outside*). When he portrayed Ziggy Stardust in the early 1970s, he did so for only 18 months, though he is known among

Introduction

the general public particularly for that persona. He claims that he gets quite bored of performance and makes an important statement: "I don't live for the stage. I don't live for an audience."

This seems a strange statement for Bowie to make, but it sheds light on much of his later career. How can a celebrity be bored by performing or be unconcerned about his audience? Bowie seems to exist in a tension between these forces: he requires an audience to be a celebrity but has made it clear that he has a level of disregard for it. Once the mid–1990s arrived, it became clear that Bowie shows a disdain for the audience; as is the case with all celebrity pronouncements, whether this statement is genuine or not is difficult to ascertain, though his comments in the interview with Gross might suggest that it is.

This tension, though, is part of what makes Bowie such a compelling figure. Consider the following visual metaphor for Bowie's actions: while using his hands to shield himself from the light of the audience, Bowie makes sure that his fingers are slightly apart so that the audience can see him just a little bit. But even what they see is then hidden in shadows

1

The Beginning of the End

Something happened in 1988 to change the trajectory of David Bowie's career. After the release of *Never Let Me Down* in 1987, Bowie worked on a new arrangement of "Look Back in Anger," a song that appeared originally on *Lodger* in 1979. The new arrangement was put together with the help of guitarist Reeves Gabrels, who is one of the most important architects of Bowie's new music throughout the 1990s. The music was specially created for a collaborative dance number with Canadian troupe La La La Human Steps at the Institute of Contemporary Art in London in July 1988. This was the start of an important collaboration with Gabrels but also a marker for a particular turning point in Bowie's career. This chapter explores the roots of this musical expression in the latter half of Bowie's career, beginning around 1988—after the critical failure of the *Glass Spider* tour—to his self-imposed exile (or health-related hiatus) in the 2000s and his return in 2013 with *The Next Day*. These roots run earlier in his career, from his first self-imposed exile to Los Angeles and Berlin in the mid-1970s, and musically in the albums from that period as well. A new arrangement of the song "Look Back in Anger" arguably becomes the inaugural song for the second part of Bowie's career; it is not a surprise that the song comes from the last album of his Berlin trilogy. This second part of his career is notable in that, in it, Bowie is presented as a particularly dark figure, making every move to destroy his past—even while referring to it—without necessarily any look forward to the future. Bowie inhabits and expresses a sort of musical "space of the perpetually present" beginning in the 1990s. Of particular importance is the album *1. Outside* which acts as an anchor point for his later career output, an album that encapsulates much of his aesthetic and informs his subsequent releases. Violence seeps throughout the album, and this theme continues throughout Bowie's later career, in which he employs violence in destroying his very persona with each passing release. But a hint of things to come would, in fact, appear much earlier, in a most unexpected place.

Ricochet

Ricochet is a 1984 documentary film directed by Gerry Toryna. The film was released in an extended version on the 2006 DVD release of the *Serious Moonlight* concert video. The film follows David Bowie on the Asian leg of his *Serious Moonlight* tour in December 1983, in support of his *Let's Dance* album. *Ricochet* features Bowie exploring the local sights and sounds of Hong Kong, Singapore and Bangkok, and shows clips of the singer's performances in each location. Writer Ben Slater points out that this is not the actual order of Bowie's travelling: after performing in New Zealand, Bowie travelled to Singapore for a performance on 3 December, then to Bangkok for a performance on 5 December, and finally to Hong Kong for two performances on 7 and 8 December.[1] Filmed over the span of about a week, the documentary features a sort of narrative thread in each of the locations, constituting three loosely-constructed narrative acts. It is within these narratives that the "documentary" nature of the film is ultimately defeated; it is clear that many of the events are staged and characters appear naïve. In Hong Kong, a couple of members of a Bowie cover band help each other to purchase tickets to the Bowie concert there. In Singapore, a couple of young women are practicing for a performance in Chinese opera. Finally, in Bangkok, Bowie himself searches the city for *something*.

The tour was unrivalled in terms of size at that point, and was only eclipsed years later by tours by Michael Jackson and The Rolling Stones in the late 1980s. For Bowie and his band, though, the tour had become routine: the portion of the tour showcased in *Ricochet* were the last four shows of a 96-show tour, which took place in 16 countries. Bowie is not only a performer on tour participating in all of these activities for the documentary camera, but he is also in the process of destroying his per-

1. The Beginning of the End

sona. This is a subtle action: Bowie manifests Walter Benjamin's notion of the *flâneur* and, as a result, becomes a "hidden man."

Ricochet is a strange film in many ways, showing what the viewer might expect: a peek into the life of a celebrity on tour, engaging with a fascinating culture that is not his own, while performing to adoring crowds at every turn. This film, though, also contains a strange subtext of surveillance, oppression and paranoia. As Bowie arrives, and subsequently explores and performs, in each of the locations, Hong Kong, Singapore and Bangkok, there are moments when a mysterious figure is shown to the viewer. A man, invariably wearing sunglasses (even at night), is shown in the vicinity of Bowie himself. The figure seems to be surveiling Bowie in some way. The man is expressionless and seems somewhat sinister, his eyes concealed by the lenses of his dark glasses. When the camera focuses on this figure, the image freezes on him for a moment, and is then transformed to a grainy still image, as if the still image of the figure is being shown on a malfunctioning cathode ray tube television. It is true that this would have been the type of television on which this documentary would have been viewed. The image is grainy, and marked with "static" noise, something that has almost disappeared with the advent of liquid crystal display and plasma television technologies, which will replace the incoming "static" image of "no signal" with a blue screen. This striking visual transformation of the figure's image is accompanied by a harsh clicking sound. This still image appears for only a brief moment before the narrative of the "documentary" continues as before. These brief interruptions to the narrative of the film add a sense that something will happen to the protagonist of the film, that is, Bowie himself; there is some suspense injected into what otherwise seems a shallow and simple look at a segment of the tour.

In contrast to the sense of foreboding brought upon by the mysterious figure, Bowie himself appears, in some sense, to appreciate the people with whom he engages. Not long after the start of the film, a reporter asks the singer if he always had a fascination with the East, to which he replies that he has. The film shows this fascination: for instance, the singer asks a taxi driver in Singapore about local laws and acceptable ways of behaving. In another scene, Bowie asks an interviewer in Bangkok how people there might manifest rebellion against authority and the law. At a dinner with a group of Hong Kong residents, he wants to know how one of them is anticipating the handover of the British Colony to the Chinese in 1997: the resident seems to be somewhat negative regarding the handover, suggesting that professionals who have the financial means are planning to emigrate, while those in the lower classes are not—this will destroy what she calls the "infrastructure" of the area.

Tempering this sense of concern is the cavalier attitude that emerges at times when it is least expected. Immediately after asking the question regarding the handover of Hong Kong, there is a sighting of the sinister figure sitting close by. Bowie then asks his fellow diners about an Asian pop song from the 1950s, and wonders if the group knows anything about the song. Spontaneously, they all begin to sing it, and Bowie is smiling. Political and economic discussions are over for now.

There is an accompanying narrative in the Hong Kong segment, where a trio of young people, who make up a sort of Bowie cover band, are trying to save up enough money with which to buy tickets to the concert. One of the musicians is having a lot of trouble getting enough money for a ticket, first attempting to sell some of his vinyl records and finally asking his friend's boss for a loan. Interspersed within this story is a moment with Bowie and one of his handlers discussing ticket prices for the concert there, mentioning that they need to balance the price of tickets with a need for a complete "sell-out" of the concert venue—a full house of ten thousand attendees—for the two nights of concerts in the city. They do not lower ticket prices.

Like the earlier juxtaposition of interest in political issues and concern for local residents in anticipation of Hong Kong's handover and the boisterous singing of an Asian pop song, so here is the juxtaposition of a narrative of class difficulties with the discussions between organizers of a tour concerned with making *enough* money to cover costs (exorbitant amounts of money, in any case). Bowie and his entourage need people to buy tickets, but will not lower ticket prices. The young man in the cover band desires a ticket and struggles to obtain one.

The film features a curious four-minute segment in Singapore during which Bowie rides a set of escalators in the night. What seems immediately to be a mundane activity becomes something otherworldly and

1. The Beginning of the End

enigmatic in its presentation. Ben Slater describes the sequence as follows: "A thin white man wanders around a near-deserted shopping mall. It's night. His drift is purposeless, but he keeps moving. What secret rendezvous is he heading towards? Is he being followed or is he following? Eerie sounds in the background."

The sequence begins with Bowie gazing into a mirror and gathering up his blazer in his room. The phone rings unanswered and a television transmits static as the camera surveys an empty hotel room: Bowie has left. The next scene shows Bowie walking outside in the night toward an eerily-lit set of escalators; fluorescent lights mounted below the escalator's travelling handrails cast a bluish tint to the sequence. As he approaches the escalators, the foreboding instrumental piece "Sense of Doubt" (what Slater calls "Muzak from another planet") from *"Heroes"* accompanies his journey.

As Bowie travels on the escalators, which seem to lead to a pedestrian bridge, others pass on the opposite escalators, either ignoring the singer or looking curiously at the camera. Bowie continues to travel up and down abandoned escalators, all touched by the whitish-blue hue provided by the fluorescent lights; the camera focuses on the escalators devoid of any passengers, and on the reflection of Bowie on the mirrored surface of the upper escalators which serve as the ceiling of Bowie's own. The escalators seem to lead to a shopping mall and as it is late, the mall is dark and deserted, with all of its stores closed.

Suddenly, in one moment, what appear to be military or police officers take notice of Bowie as he travels on the escalators and point at him. It is probably no coincidence that they are both wearing sunglasses even though they are indoors and that it is the evening. Seemingly in reply, Bowie momentarily looks back before continuing on.

He is then shown sitting around a sort of fountain formed within three floodlights that are embedded in the high ceiling of the mall. From the circumference of the circular lights come streams of water that create columns, not unlike the opaque "Roman" columns of the *Serious Moonlight* tour stage, as featured in the Vancouver concert which this documentary film accompanies.

Slater describes Bowie as a "walker" who might not be human, but rather a sleepwalking, stateless extraterrestrial, travelling through a "decentred landscape": "He's come down to earth to look for the past, but instead he's found the future. Strip-lit walkways and glittering atria; a musical fountain; a deranged architect's plan for some deluded utopia." But the utopia is deserted and abandoned: the only figures are its patrolling guards and Bowie, the foreigner and alien.

Slater calls Bowie a "misplaced alien," and this last image, Bowie at the fountain, reinforces this: the embedded lights evoke the image of an alien vessel from science fiction, with Bowie occupying a space at its feet, marking its landing site. Also, Bowie is at the foot of its downward columns, as if caught up by its attracting beams. A shopping mall fountain is also a religious site, with its downward flow of water, offering what Jon Pahl suggests is a symbolic baptism, a place of purification and refreshment.[2]

Mostly, though, the sequence indicates Bowie's loneliness, and is pervaded by a sense of paranoia and surveillance, especially with the moment featuring the officers who, unlike the rest of the population on the escalators, take alarmed notice of the solitary figure who is going nowhere in the Singapore night.

The sequence ends with a fade-out, with a lingering moment of black. Bowie is then seen "back in the world," in the rear seat of a taxi in the daytime. Bowie wishes to visit an older part of the city, and a taxi driver brings him to a hotel that appears to be colonial in its architecture and style; Bowie is seemingly not interested in "true" or "traditional" remnants of these areas. It is in the hotel that he crosses paths with another of these sinister bespectacled figures. Later, in what appears as a humorous staging of a scene, Bowie wishes to enter a rehearsal of traditional Chinese opera, but his entry is barred, forcing him to attend the performance in the evening, a feat which, for him, is "difficult." In Bangkok, he sees another figure at the airport who seems to take the car for which Bowie and his entourage were thought to be destined.

The climax of the film seems to come when Bowie enters what appears to be a strip club in Bangkok, in which he encounters the sinister figure again. The singer seems to make the connection that all of these men, with their dark glasses, are versions of himself. Immediately before the live performance, presumably from his concert in Bangkok, the video still of the sinister figure is shown again, as Bowie begins to sing his

1. The Beginning of the End

song, "Fame." The lyrics to "Fame" suggest a kind of love/hate relationship to the lifestyle that Bowie is expressing throughout the documentary film. In the song, the singer asks why one might question his rejection of this fame in the first place. He then immediately confirms that "fame," a sort of embodied figure, is in fact unfazed; Bowie cannot "shake," or get rid of, "fame." The sinister figure in the sunglasses is Bowie's fame, now at one with him and unable to be left behind. It follows him unmercifully, and appears to act as a foil, forcing him to play a fool rather than show any sort of compassion toward local residents with whom he engages.

One of the most interesting portions of a somewhat uninteresting film is Bowie's epiphany (if one calls it such) in the club, when he realizes that these fragments of figures that have been following him are actually himself. This is a crack—a break—in the celebrity to which the viewer is exposed throughout the film. Bowie shows a weakness here, a sort of panic in realizing that there is no escape from the fame that has engulfed him. His performance of "Fame" ends with the singer aggressively shouting the title just before the credits of the film roll on the screen.

Bowie as "Hidden Man"

When Bowie walks the streets of the city, one cannot help but consider the *flâneur*, an urban figure who explored Paris in the eighteenth and nineteenth centuries as recounted by theorist Walter Benjamin. The *flâneur* emerges as a literary figure in the work of Charles Baudelaire and Edgar Allan Poe (Poe's "The Man in the Crowd" is particularly important in the conception of the *flâneur*). In Benjamin's discussions, there are three urban types described in French literature, all related to the city dweller: the *flâneur*; the *badaud* or gawker; and the detective. The *flâneur* is a detached observer, unhurried by the world that surrounds him (note that there is a specific name for the female urban type, the *flâneuse*); Benjamin writes, "In 1839 it was considered elegant to take a tortoise out walking. This gives us an idea of the tempo of flânerie in the arcades."[3] The arcades were Paris' covered streets and alleys, a precursor to the modern shopping mall. The *badaud* or gawker is addicted to images: this figure loses his sense of self in the crowd, and needs crowds in order to function. Benjamin calls the *badaud* a "rubberneck" who disappears in a crowd, "absorbed by the external world," unlike the *flâneur*.[4] The detective interprets the reality with which he engages, unmasking the surface: the detective seeks to see below surfaces, to possess a sort of x-ray image to see how things function, and how things have become the way they have. But the detective is also engaged in a solitary pursuit, an idle self-indulgence in exploring the margins, those behaviors and places at the edges of conventionality. Tom Gunning calls the detective an observer studying the "unfolding images [coming into his field of view as he wanders] for narrative enigmas, testing them with anticipatory schemata, predicting narrative outcomes and processing the image for its relevant narrative information and cues."[5] Gunning conceives of the *flâneur* as a spectator, not unlike one engaged with cinema.

For Benjamin, the *flâneur* seeks to understand a sort of urban history; Benjamin describes the actions of this particular figure in the following way: "The street conducts the flâneur into a vanished time. For him, every street ... leads downward ... into a past that can be all the more spellbinding because it is not his own."[6] Bowie fits into this image quite easily, being a white person on the night streets of Singapore; Bowie explores the darkness of the city with bleached blonde—strikingly *yellow*—hair and an extremely fair complexion. Though Bowie seems tanned (certainly unnaturally so) in other portions of the video, the dark seems to lessen the effect of his somewhat orange skin, a characteristic so obvious in the sunshine, accentuated by his blonde hair, "sun kissed" in the daylight. The almost blue hue of the fluorescent lighting on the escalators upon which Bowie embarks at night only increases the effect: Bowie seemingly glows in the dark. It is obvious that this urban space is not his. While this is not a past *per se*, it is an existing world to which he is certainly only a visitor (and a visitor from another world, it seems, with the otherworldly accompaniment to his strange explorations). In total, the presentation is spellbinding, as the figure moves through an urban history that is certainly not his own, nor ever will be.

The uniformed figures that Bowie encounters seem to understand

1. The Beginning of the End

this fact. As authority figures, as police or military officers, they look upon this visitor with some suspicion, gesturing in his direction, noting his presence. Benjamin mentions the moral character of the *flâneur* as noted by a Paris officer at the turn of the nineteenth century who comments that "it is almost impossible to summon and maintain good moral character in a thickly massed population" in which the crowd allows an individual to hide. Benjamin suggests that the *flâneur* "takes on the features of the werewolf restlessly roaming a social wilderness."[7] It is impossible to deny Bowie's Other-ness during this late night journey up and down the escalators, subject to a sort of deserted nocturnal social wilderness (Benjamin comments that "the city can appear to someone walking through it to be without thresholds: a landscape in the round").[8] It is less clear whether Bowie acts as a werewolf, a monstrous predator with questionable morals in the urban crowd; the suggestion of a glowing predator might be a bit much considering his slight frame and seeming physical control, but he is unquestionably an Other with unknown destination or destiny in this sequence.

This moral disguise continues when Bowie talks to the women with the aim of entering the Chinese opera rehearsal. Benjamin mentions the relations and roles of those in the urban crowd, where "the inferior is disguised as the superior" and vice-versa.[9] This is certainly the case as Bowie negotiates his passage through the city. As a global celebrity, as he certainly is at this point in his career, it is quite reasonable to expect that Bowie would have no problem gaining access to a rehearsal for a local production, no matter how much of a stranger he might be. In the sequence, though, he is barred access to the rehearsal, much to the amusement of the viewing audience, who quite clearly notice that the camera captures the encounter from *inside* the doorway of the building that is presumably holding the rehearsal, and even from perhaps the rehearsal space itself. The episode is obviously staged, complete with Bowie exchanging names with the women, and mentioning how difficult it would be for him to attend the performance of the opera that evening (as he would be performing himself). In many ways this comes off as a colloquial and humorous exchange which provides a sense of realism to the film; no matter how unrealistic it truly is, it might be an attempt at a sort of *cinéma vérité*, inserting a moment of "real life" into the film, when an Other is truly an Other, unknown and disallowed. But it is also a sequence that highlights the notion of the questionable morality of the *flâneur*. He is obviously a superior who poses as an inferior, a disguise that is afforded him because of the character of the urban environment: the crowd and the labyrinthine nature of the urban space. In fact, Bowie's visit to the Chinese opera, as well as to the colonialist hotel, serve to reinforce his role as *flâneur*; Benjamin states that, for the wandering figure, "far-off times and places interpenetrate the landscape and the present moment."[10]

There is an earlier moment when Bowie engages in conversation with the taxi driver, wanting to visit an older part of the city of Singapore, a trip which takes him to the colonial hotel, an unexpected destination considering Bowie's request. Benjamin discusses the possibility of E.T.A. Hoffmann as a type of *flâneur*, quoting biographical notes from a collection of his writings: "What mattered to him more than anything else was the human being—communication with, observations about, the simple sight of, human beings."[11] While his interaction with the women at the Chinese opera rehearsal appears staged, the sequence with the taxi driver does not (perhaps due to the subject matter discussed: Bowie asks about local laws and the use of narcotics). It seems as if, in his wanderings, he is genuinely interested and wanting to understand this urban history. As pointed out by Anke Gleber, Siegfried Kracauer describes something that can be thought of as a sort of "ethics of *flânerie*": "this reporting job is done with unconcealed compassion for the people depicted."[12] For Kracauer, the *flâneur* is a kind of camera, registering the world, which explains his use of the notion of reporting. If Bowie is engaging in an ethical *flânerie* (if there is any other sort), this is the moment in which his ethic is clear.

Walter Benjamin makes a claim regarding the *flâneur* that is paramount to the discussion of Bowie, and seems apt in describing his character in the film. Benjamin describes what he calls the "dialectic of *flânerie*" as follows: "on one side, the man who feels himself viewed by all and sundry as a true suspect and, on the other side, the man who is utterly undiscoverable, the hidden man."[13] This is key to understanding this early example of Bowie's negotiation of his celebrity in the later phase of his career. With worldwide fame, and a monetary fortune to

1. The Beginning of the End

match, Bowie becomes Benjamin's "hidden man," though he is in full view of the police, the women at the opera and, ultimately, the fans who attend the concerts throughout the film. For that matter, Bowie is the object of the film, though the viewer is separated from him by time, space and the nature of the viewer's engagement with the visual medium: Bowie is mediated. He is truly "utterly undiscoverable," ambiguous as an Other, as a sort of werewolf and a superior disguised as an inferior, exploring an urban history that is not his own. This is what is evident in that moment in the film when Bowie is sitting at the interior fountain, a lone figure in the deserted shopping mall in the middle of the night. For Benjamin, the *flâneur* "is always in full possession of his individuality," but this individuality is masked in the "hidden man," Bowie's ultimate presentation here.[14] As per Benjamin's "maxim of the *flâneur*" (which he gets from Daniel Halévy), "it is right here, deep below the surface that we must go. Estrangement and surprise, the most thrilling exoticism, are all close by."[15] Perhaps this is the impulse that Bowie feels as he leaves his hotel room. It is for this reason that the viewer sees the mysterious empty room, strewn with his effects, complete with the television still turned on and a phone ringing unanswered. The room exhibits signs of Bowie's quick, almost manic, departure. But Bowie finds none of this promised exoticism (except, perhaps, his feigned excitement in finding the Chinese opera). Rather, he finds estrangement, resulting in being alone at the end of the sequence. The surveillance and the backward glances between the officers and Bowie on the escalators work to create a sense of unease, building to this final state of being undiscoverable, of being the "hidden man."

This is a precursor to, a foreshadow of, the Bowie of a few years later, when his negotiation of his celebrity persona becomes more explicit, though no less clever. *Ricochet* is an artifact that reveals cracks in a façade of mainstream success—as well as cracks in the façade of *cinéma vérité* documentary. It is through those cracks that the viewer experiences, not a *real* Bowie, but a *different* Bowie. In fact, the Bowie revealed in the film is Bowie as "hidden man": while it is impossible to know the "real" of the mediated celebrity, here the viewer is exposed to the "hidden" of the mediated celebrity. In a way, should one want to discover more about Bowie, to discover what might be in the cracks of the façade, one finds the undiscoverable. This seems an active process, one that shows its functioning here in the documentary film. It is only later, with *1. Outside* in particular, where Bowie's "undiscoverable-ness" is made particularly explicit, with his physical turning away from the audience in live performance. His "undiscoverable-ness" is then made most evident, or thrust into the foreground, with his hiatus from the public eye for almost a decade before the release of *The Next Day*.

This is not to suggest that Bowie was not clever in negotiating his celebrity in ways that obfuscated the public concerning his "real" self, but rather that, in the midst of arguably his most visible period—that is, his period of largest mainstream success—Bowie begins a process of breaking himself down. When he is most visible, he begins the process or the functioning of becoming hidden, a state which he ultimately attains when the spotlight is turned off of his career in the late 2000s.

Like with the *Ricochet* documentary, Bowie hints at the future change in the trajectory of his career with the single "Time Will Crawl." The video, directed by Tim Pope, features Bowie preparing for the *Glass Spider* tour. The video features guitarists Carlos Alomar and Peter Frampton, as well as a group of dancers, practicing, it is assumed, for the upcoming tour. Like *Ricochet*, the video is shot in a documentary style, with the camera acting as an observer, rather than some sort of window into a fantasy. The action of the video takes place in a warehouse, or some sort of nondescript rehearsal space. The video features dancers, moving to the music, and showcasing *avant-garde* movement, both strange and violent. What is most interesting here, though, is that Bowie participates in the choreography. This predates the performance with La La La Human Steps from 1988.

The video begins with Bowie sliding down a rope from a high scaffold, and then the video can be divided into sequences, which, it is presumed, correspond to parts of the *Glass Spider* tour, for which this seems to be a rehearsal. First, Bowie interacts with a male dancer, dancing playfully, though simply. Secondly, and strikingly, Bowie closes his eyes as if blind, and is accompanied by a female dancer wearing dark glasses, who is being carried by another dancer. Bowie is hold-

1. The Beginning of the End

ing on to a crutch. There are multiple levels of disability shown here: the woman is not mobile on her own, but she is reliant on her "carrier" to move her; Bowie himself leans on a crutch and relies on his blind companion to lead him around. This is certainly an example of "the blind leading the blind," the results of which are not generally positive.[16] Is this visual gesture a foreshadowing of the critical reception of the tour itself?

The video continues to another sequence of violent dancing, which does foreshadow the dancing between Louise Lecavalier, her partner and Bowie. The dancing features Bowie being thrown from one dancer to another in a closed group; it is as if Bowie is being beaten, picked up and thrown throughout this sequence. This is a shocking sequence: it is unusual for the star of the music video to be featured violently handled as he seems to be here. He is passed from dancer to dancer, and then flipped over another dancer and moved around again, all at a great speed. His body is loose, like a rag doll being passed around, but he also puts on a striking posture. When he is caught by one of the dancers after the flip, he drapes himself loosely over the receiving dancer's torso. This posture would have made Bowie's dance much safer, of course, but it also foreshadows Bowie as fashion, clothing the dancer. This is a theoretical precursor to the later translation of Bowie into "image-object." After this portion, Bowie observes the other dancers from above, away from the action on the rehearsal floor.

In the fifth and final sequence, Bowie sings to his own reflection in a mirror, echoing the manic nature of the music with his own manic— and mad—posture. That is, he is crouched down, staring at the mirror with his head facing down but his eyes wide open, gazing straight at his reflection. Furthermore, he grimaces, not in pain, but in madness. He wraps his arms around his body as if confined, and then places his hands over his face as if hiding himself, though he looks through his fingers. His seemingly clipped delivery of the lyrics in the video adds to this sense of mania. Thus, "Time Will Crawl," like *Ricochet*, shows a break or crack in the façade of Bowie's star image, the initial chipping away that will lead to destruction. The video is a definitive artifact from near the end of a very commercial period for Bowie, which clearly showcases disability, blindness, immobility and violence.

Dance as David Bowie's Fashion

The first collaboration between Bowie and guitarist Reeves Gabrels, a new arrangement of "Look Back in Anger," breathed new life into Bowie's critical career. For live performances of the new version of the song during 1990's *Sound+Vision* tour, Bowie involved Canadian dance troupe La La La Human Steps, who choreographed a dance routine that not only featured the principle dancers of the troupe, but also involved Bowie himself. At various points in the performance, the troupe soloist Louise Lecavalier seems to carry Bowie, draping him over herself. In a way, Lecavalier literally takes him upon herself: like clothing, *she puts him on*. It is not only in terms of musical sound that Bowie makes a break from his past, but through the "fashion" with which he clothes her, and its "opportunity for self-knowledge," as Roland Barthes suggests.[17] It is through the fashion of dance that he destroys—or obfuscates—his past musical output while performing it, a risky move that enables him to move forward.

Bowie planned to perform with La La La Human Steps at London's Institute of Contemporary Arts (ICA) in July 1988, at a benefit concert called "Intruders at the Palace." The performance, choreographed by La La La Human Steps' Edouard Lock, included Bowie and the soloist dancing together, as well as a component of the performance which included a projected portion of the two dancing on a screen at the back of the stage.

One of the most important people in the creation and cultivation of Bowie's later career is guitarist and co-writer Reeves Gabrels. In a 2003 interview with Gabrels, Billy Donald discusses the beginnings of this collaboration: Gabrels met Bowie in 1988, when Gabrel's journalist wife chose to cover Bowie's tour as a balance to some rather taxing investigative journalism she had done on the subject of child exploitation. Gabrels suggests that he and Bowie would spend time together backstage, and that Gabrels never revealed that he himself was a musician. Rather, Bowie was under the impression that Gabrels was a visual artist, a painter.[18] Chris O'Leary suggests, and with good reason, that Bowie's relationship with Gabrels is unique, in that Gabrels was only one of a few of his creative collaborators (O'Leary mentions

1. The Beginning of the End

Eno and Iggy Pop as the others). Furthermore, O'Leary calls Gabrels Bowie's "loud conscience (or an extended middle finger)."[19] While some consider Gabrels' musical contributions to be somewhat crass, O'Leary points out that many underestimate Gabrels' contributions to Bowie's music in the 1990s; in fact, Bowie of the 1990s would not have happened without Gabrels—or Eno, for that matter. Donald points out that Gabrels co-wrote and co-produced much of the material from this period, and thus was a sort of architect for the sound, more so than simply a session musician. As such, his contribution to the music of Bowie cannot be ignored. In an email to the author on 22 February 1998, Gabrels confirmed this: "it is a much more collaborative situation than most diety [sic] oriented fans/critics seem to be able to comprehend. So, I guess that stuff combined with the fact that I do a lot of the live arrangements does indicate that if I wasn't there it would sound different." In his own way, Gabrels is a key player in allowing Bowie to develop his project: to continually destroy—not reinvent—his persona.

There is a subtle difference being posited here. In popular discourse, Bowie is considered something of a chameleon, able to change his image, to reinvent himself. Gabrels gives insight here as well: in a Facebook message to the author on 12 January 2014, Gabrels suggests that Bowie is not a chameleon, but rather "the constant at the center of a changing cast of producers and musicians." For Gabrels, Bowie was a good art director, gifted with working with the right people, including Gabrels himself. The process was akin to bringing Bowie ideas to which he would react, rather than to dictate the direction: a collaborator would bring Bowie a "basket of ideas" and he would choose what interested him.

Regarding "Look Back in Anger," O'Leary writes that the song, at its heart, reflects the notion of Bowie "considering the prospect of decline and tearing himself up, sampling and dispersing himself."[20] David Buckley calls the performance "dangerously theatrical and arty."[21] In the 12 January 2014 Facebook message, Gabrels states that the troupe needed the song to extend over seven minutes, at the request of Lock, the choreographer. Bowie's sole direction for Gabrels was to build a "gothic cathedral of guitars."

David Bowie in Darkness

The live performance of "Look Back in Anger" features Bowie and a small band performing with La La La Human Steps. Featured at the forefront of the performance is Bowie, the soloist Louise Lecavalier and her partner, with the band being almost completely obscured in the shadows at the back of the stage. The band consists of two guitarists (including Gabrels) and an electric bassist; it is unclear if there is a drummer or percussionist as part of the band. The lack of a drummer is not really an issue, as the band is almost nonexistent, in that they need not be there; they are only really revealed when they come to the front of the stage at the end of the performance. Even Bowie seems to take a lesser role compared to the dancers. The performance begins without any music at all, and Lecavalier dancing alone in the silence. Bowie walks onto the stage and begins to engage with her, mimicking her movements. As he does this, the music begins, and a prerecorded monochrome video of a dance between Lecavalier and Bowie is projected onto a large screen behind and above the band. During the musical introduction of the song, Bowie twice moves toward the microphone to sing. These errors are unexpected and add tension to the performance, but also provide a sense of anticipation: the viewer is waiting for Bowie to "get it right." A viewer might initially think that Bowie has made an error, trying to sing earlier than he is meant to. His second attempt, though, makes it clear that this is part of the performance. The tension here foreshadows the tension that arrives in full as the dance begins in earnest.

Bowie and Lecavalier begin to dance together and there are two points of particular interest: Lecavalier picks Bowie up vertically, by wrapping her arms around his waist and picking him up off of the ground. In doing so, she is practically invisible, covered completely by Bowie's body. Soon after this, Lecavalier crouches down and lays a straight and rigid Bowie across her legs, as if he has died. As she does so, she caresses his face. Both of these gestures strongly evoke Christian imagery. In lifting Bowie up, she perhaps crucifies him.[22] Once Lecavalier drapes Bowie over her knees, they evoke the image of the *Pietà*, with the dead Christ in the arms of his mother Mary. This action also foreshadows the cover of Bowie's *'hours...'* from 1999.

Throughout the performance, but particularly before Lecavalier begins to dance with her troupe partner, Bowie is embroiled in the manic

1. The Beginning of the End

violence of the dance. One of the characteristic movements that Lecavalier employs is a "barrel jump," a sort of horizontal spin, over the crouching back of Bowie. In those moments when Lecavalier shows her extraordinary strength by lifting Bowie in her arms, Bowie becomes something which she ends up putting on; Bowie becomes a sort of covering—a garment or set of clothing—for the dancer.

As Bowie begins to sing, Lecavalier's partner takes his place in the dance, and the dance becomes more manic and violent. Bowie then begins to play the guitar while watching the dancers, remaining at the front of the stage. Both he and the dancers are at the forefront of the audience's attention. Toward the end of the violent and, at times, sexually charged performance, the dancers embrace and kiss each other. Lecavalier also returns to Bowie, caressing him.

Bowie acts as a sort of garment for Lecavalier, and in the translation of the performer into a garment, he becomes something else, an "object-sign," a "similacrum of the real object." For Roland Barthes, fashion is both an "institution and individual act."[23] He speaks of fashion as a "sign system" apart from language, a system akin to photography, film and other expressive arts, "texts" that generate meaning. For Barthes, fashion is an area that he himself invests in, in that he chooses to put on clothing—a sort of expression of an external personal aesthetic—and in doing so increases his own self-knowledge. But also, Barthes claims that "these objects possess an intellectual existence, offering themselves to systematic analysis by formal means."[24] Curiously, Barthes decides that a systematic understanding of "described" fashion is more profitable theoretically as a basis for the study of "lived" fashion. This is what makes Barthes' system so appropriate for consideration in the case of Bowie and the dance: "what one says shifts in some way instantaneously … to what one wears and sees."[25] In other words, the communicative, semiotic act takes place in the visual realm: the message of Bowie is in the very act of how he puts himself on to someone else.

What is further compelling about Barthes' theoretical framework is his claim that, in fashion (which he calls "social objects"), "ideological alienation" is revealed. Here, Barthes is exploring the differences between what he calls "described" or written fashion and the fashion exhibited in "real life," and he bases his analyses ultimately on what he considers the Saussurean semiotic system, the sign made up of the signifier—the physical or graphical representation, the thing one engages with—and the signified—that is, the signifier's referent, what it means. For Barthes, the denotative meaning of something, the ways that the object can be described, can be quite different from its connotation, that is, its cultural and often arbitrary meanings. When those connotative meanings are thought of as denotative or "natural," Barthes calls these things "myths" or ideologies. Thus, for Barthes, fashion and clothing are of the realm of ideology, "objects reified and mythicized by mass culture." Such objects, including fashion, are alienating in that they conceal their true identity with the guise of connotation. As an example, Michael Moriarty explains how Barthes considers red wine as "doubly alienating": "it palliates the exclusion of the North African population from its own environment and culture and debars the intellectual from a whole-hearted uncomplicated relationship with what is after all a 'belle et bonne substance.'"[26] In other words, as Jazmin Rodger suggests, wine condones the exploitation of workers, as well as concealing its true identity as a simple commodity.[27] It is always important, it seems, to consider the narrative in these social objects, the particular combination that is presented in the real world.[28] In a way, the "social object" of dance as fashion—Bowie being literally put on to someone else—is, as Barthes points out, a kind of "dialogue between writings": music, dance, fashion and lyrics, as well as mediated performance. In fact, elsewhere, Barthes suggests that fashion puts into dialogue "material, photography, language."[29] He then suggests that, somehow, the "entire space of history," what here might be simply Bowie's greater project, his own "ideological alienation," returns to the observer "in an entirely new *fashion*."[30] It is in Bowie's new combination of media, or media in dialogue, that the artist projects his own alienation, manifest in his literal putting of himself onto the dancer, her putting on of him in performance, a sort of fashion.

The possibility of Bowie "putting on" the means of his own ideological alienation as performance evokes Judith Butler's notions of performativity of gender: "if I were to argue that genders are performative, that could mean that I thought that one woke in the morning, perused the closet or some more open space for the gender of choice, donned

1. The Beginning of the End

that gender for the day, and then restored the garment to its place at night." Butler qualifies this statement by suggesting that, while the performativity of gender is at work, the subject's existence is "already decided by gender."[31] That is, "performativity must be understood not as a singular or deliberate 'act,' but rather as the reiterative and citational practice by which discourse produces the effects that it names."[32]

More recently, Butler writes, "[the performativity of gender] is a practice of improvisation within a scene of constraint. Moreover, one does not 'do' one's gender alone. One is always 'doing' with or for another, even if the other is only imaginary."[33] The question, though, is whether a figure like Bowie is putting on his own ideological alienation for some (possibly imaginary) other. Barthes is helpful here as well, doubly so.

First, Barthes suggests that fashion ignores—or more properly *erases*—its causes: "such is the trajectory that fashion follows so as to convert its cause, its law and its signs all at once into fact." Second, fashion subverts what comes prior to it: "All new Fashion is a refusal to inherit, a subversion to the oppression left by the preceding Fashion."[34]

Continuing his exploration of fashion in his book *The Fashion System*, Barthes is concerned with the language of fashion, that is, how fashion is described in magazines dedicated to its showcasing and exploration. Barthes needs to make a choice between the analysis of what he calls the "real (or visual) system," and the written discourse of fashion. So, Barthes chooses to discuss *described* fashion, "vestimentary features already constituted ... into a system of signification." For Barthes, this is a "true code," and, most importantly, the study concerns "neither clothing nor language but the 'translation,' so to speak, of one into the other."

It is here that Barthes' ideas come into accord with the present project: if Barthes is exploring the translation of clothing into language, that is, the transformation of clothing into semiotics, then this present work is similar in that it explores the transformation of the *person* "David Bowie" into the *semiotic* "David Bowie," the "object-sign."[35] Barthes explains more of his idea:

> Fashion, like all fashions, depends on the disparity of two consciousnesses, each foreign to the other. In order to blunt the buyer's calculating consciousness, a veil must be drawn around the object—a veil of images, of

reasons, of meanings; a mediate substance of an aperitive order must be elaborated; in short, a similacrum of the real object must be created.³⁶

This is the crux here: the dancer not only physically puts on Bowie as she would clothing, but she puts on Bowie as fashion. But Bowie himself, in the act of being put on the dancer as fashion (physically and actually), becomes fashion, translated into "object-sign."

Barthes' argument is based on the notion of three types of garments: image-clothing, clothing depicted in or represented by images; the written garment, clothing described through writing or in language; and real clothing, the actual garment. These three types of garments *mean* in different ways: image-clothing are iconic; written clothing are translated through verbal "structures"; and actual garments are translated through technological structures, the actions of manufacture.³⁷

In the case of Bowie's performance, then, there are at least two structures in play: the iconic structure of the image-clothing (Bowie's act of becoming the "clothing" of the dancer) and the technological structure of the "clothing" itself. Consider the dance choreography as a sort of "action of manufacture." It is within the context of the dance that the dancer Lecavalier puts on Bowie, and it is only because of the context and performance that Bowie becomes the clothing for the dancer in the first place. In fact, through the process of this present exploration, the image-clothing is being translated into verbal structures, which Barthes suggests "freezes an endless number of possibilities; words determine a single certainty."³⁸

Cruising David Bowie's Voice

The monochrome video of Bowie and Lecavalier emerges again during Bowie's fiftieth birthday concert, which took place at Madison Square Gardens in New York on 9 January 1997. During the performance, Bowie sings "Battle for Britain (The Letter)" from the album *Earthling*, which was released the following month. As Bowie sings, the monochrome dance footage (it appears to be the same material or similar to the footage shown at the London performance in 1988, or featured in the promotional music video for "Fame '90" where a dance between

1. The Beginning of the End

Bowie and Lecavalier also appears) is projected onto a massive screen that hangs in front of the band, and at the very front of the stage. The screen is made of a material that allows the audience to view Bowie and the band, because they are illuminated, as well as see the projection of the dancers (a similar screen was used during the *Outside* tour during the performance of "Hurt" with Nine Inch Nails). It is unclear why Bowie has chosen to use the almost ten-year-old video during the performance of this song; the most obvious reason would be to act as a recognizable reference to the past, as the event was a celebration of Bowie's birthday. The video is a marker of a past moment in the singer's career and its replay brings that memory to the forefront. Interestingly, the song performed is not "Look Back in Anger" or even "Fame '90"; except for perhaps the correspondence between the manic nature of the dance and the manic nature of the rhythm of "Battle for Britain (The Letter)," there are no obvious lyrical—and certainly no musical—links to the earlier performance of the dance.

Gabrels' loud "cathedral of sound" guitars punctuate the first beat of each measure before Bowie begins to sing the verses, along with the frenetic drum beat. At the start of the second verse, the only accompaniment to Bowie's voice are Zachary Alford's drums and Gail Ann Dorsey's descending bass line, which is prominent in the mix. The disjointed nature of the music of the song is compelling, especially in this live performance: the drum beat seems stunted, moving along at a kind of stumbling, yet unrelenting, pace. Certainly in the live performance, Bowie's vocals seem to lag behind the music ever so slightly; the listener is then dragged along as well. In the birthday performance, there is a musical interlude during which Mike Garson, the keyboard player, plays staccato chords, disjointed due to their pointed character (like much of the rhythmic character of the song), but also in terms of harmony: he plays around a tonal centre but seemingly without any teleological movement (except for at the very end). At the end of this interlude is a moment of what can be described as "liminality"—a moment "betwixt-and-between," a moment of timelessness and statelessness, in which Bowie ceases to sing, and physically whirls himself as if out of control. The music stops, and the only rhythm is supplied by Bowie's prerecorded, heavily mediated and processed voice, which has been fragmented into very short, abrupt, pieces. Some of these fragments are recognizable (for instance, the listener can make out fragments of the chorus, in which the narrator of the song tells an unknown listener to not be discouraged by his letter) but, for the most part, the segment is chaotic and difficult. The stuttering arrests the listener, though, and becomes a kind of anchor point that launches the rest of the song, as Bowie begins singing the chorus anew.

What of this moment of rupture, fragment and anchor? Roland Barthes suggests that the answer might come to the listener as he or she "cruises" the song, through the very act of listening.[39] Barthes calls cruising a "voyage of desire," an intentional awareness in pursuit of satisfaction. Barthes, of course, is using the act of looking for sexual liaison or, as he calls it, the "erotic quest"—the idea of "cruising" for a lover—as an analogy and "cruising" a text for pleasure: "Cruising is an act that repeats itself, but its catch is absolutely fresh." It is "the search for novelistic features. What offers itself in the surprise of the 'first time.'" In other words, there is a knowledge of what is found at that site of desire, but there is a novelty to it as well, as if there is a first meeting, a "freshness" to the particular "catch." This literary "cruising" is "related to the catch of sentences, citations, turns of phrase, fragments."[40] Barthes further hints at what he means by "cruising" in the preface of Renaud Camus' novel *Tricks*:

> Repetition is an ambiguous form; sometimes it denotes failure, impotence; sometimes it can be read as an aspiration, the stubborn movement of a quest which is not to be discouraged; we might very well take the cruising narrative as the metaphor of a mystical experience.[41]

Nicholas de Villiers calls this mystical experience "the desire for the new, the unexpected, for difference—thus not 'picking' or 'choosing' but 'cruising.'"[42]

In "Battle for Britain (The Letter)," Bowie's voice is suddenly divided and fragmented at a very particular moment. The listener takes in these fragments, a kind of destruction, and experiences them as "absolutely fresh," no matter how often one might listen to them. In fact, the listener cruises these fragments, these turns of phrase (that is, fragments of Bowie's encouraging words to the unknown listener not be depressed by his letter), these moments of a kind of "happiness of chance, but

1. The Beginning of the End

chance that is wished-for, quite thought-out." As will be explored in the third chapter of this book, this evokes Brian Eno's compositional processes. The first time one listens to the song, the chaotic moment is a sort of "chance" experience, unexpected and relished; once the song has been understood as "ordered sound," after repeated listens (much like an episode during which Eno's repeated listening to the sound of a random recording made the sounds "ordered"), then the moment is transformed into "chance that is wished-for."

For that matter, the listener might expect pleasure in the act of simply listening to the song, especially when one considers the actions of fans and consumers of popular music. While the song was never one of Bowie's singles, it was performed live, including a performance at Bowie's fiftieth birthday concert: thus, the song (in fact, any song by a global celebrity like Bowie) becomes a showcase for the singer, a promotional or advertisement for the album. For Barthes, the text (in this case, the popular musical text) is created in order to be "spied-upon," to be the object of a gaze, in a way. In terms of listening to a single—or, in this case, a new song from a new album played at a birthday celebration for a limited number of fans—the voice can be perceived as subject to an aural gaze, a "cruising" gaze which is looking for pleasure, for chance happiness found in the fragments, a pleasure which is repeated in the "catch" of sentences. If thought of in this way, then, the song seemingly *asks* to be listened to, to become a source of pleasure for the listener.

Barthes' term seems to fit well with the pleasure afforded from listening to popular music. An established way of treating pleasure in popular music is through the notion of the "hook," the musical or lyrical fragment that acts as a base from which—and to which—the listener is "hooked." Gary Burns suggests that even the term itself connotes being caught or trapped, like a fish or an addiction. Furthermore, a casual listener might be trapped by what he or she is hearing, and need to hear the song again (as an addict).[43] Devin McKinney suggests that hooks fall into the category of "jagged musical tool," and that they are "hard sharp implements designed to hold a thing in place."[44] There is the idea, then, that a "hook" is both pleasurable (though it is true that being trapped and addicted are problematic notions) as well as repetitive, conventionally. In some cases—as in the Bowie case here—the repetition comes from an act of repeated listening by the "addicted" listener, seeking the anchoring point of the song. "Hooks" are also, according to McKinney, constrictive and perhaps violent or dangerous; the sharpness of a "hook" holds not only the listener (McKinney's "thing") but also the piece of music. These hook moments are both the ground (stability) and the air (freedom and pleasure), the sites of pleasure for which one searches.

McKinney suggests that the critic's role of analyzing what he calls the "mechanics and mystery of the pop moment" is "cruising a road to nowhere: 'cruising' with its pleasurable associations of ease, adventure, and incidental delight, 'nowhere' with its darker implications of displacement, disarticulation, confusion of identity and idea."[45]

The "hook" can also be a kind of distraction from the mundane of the song itself. The moments of pleasure occur within a musical context that is not necessarily completely pleasurable; the "hook" catches the listener and allows one to continue to listen to a song. The mundanity of the moment itself might also be a source of pleasure. McKinney states:

> One thing we enjoy about the moment is that it's *only* a moment, it *has* no future, it obviates the *idea* of a future. Suddenly we're free to not care what a thing does, where it leads, what good or bad it will do to us, what it will teach anyone about life and how to live it—i.e. free not to care what the thing means.[46]

If Barthes' notion of "cruising" suggests the promise of pleasure, the expectation and repetition of pleasure *in time*, McKinney's notion suggests the pleasure that occurs out of time (remember Bowie's "liminal" moment, spinning while the fragments are playing); Barthes talks about looking for chance encounters as sites of pleasure, while McKinney explores what it means *at* these sites of pleasure. McKinney's notion might be more akin to Barthes' distraction, where one is "free not to care what the thing means," but simply that it would break up the day, and allow one to escape from the mundanity of regular time.

The analog that both Barthes and McKinney use, that of "cruising the text," allows one to begin to understand the process behind the desire for pleasure that comes from the text, which, in this case, is a song. In fact, there is the suggestion in Barthes' other writings that pleasure can come from the singing voice, from the voice's "grain." How the listener

1. The Beginning of the End

engages with that voice, or how the pleasure is "worked out" by the listener is informed by Barthes' concept of "cruising the text."

This part of the song points to the singer at his best, though he is not really present at all. That is, at that fragmented moment, Bowie is not singing in the present, but the audience is hearing a fragmented recording. The well-processed fragment of voice invites the listener to listen, to discover what the voice can do, to spy upon that voice, to subject that voice to the "aural" gaze of the listener. This is the voice in action, and it *will* give pleasure to the listener. But the voice that the listener hears is not Bowie's voice at all: it is a processed, highly mediated version of Bowie, mediated that much more through Bowie's star image. This is striking in that, when the audience entered Madison Square Gardens, they had the impression that they would be experiencing a performance by a very present "David Bowie." At this moment, though, they see Bowie flailing and swirling but *not singing*. He is both present and absent, constituting what Barthes calls a "third term" (more on this later).

This, though, is one way in which desiring in popular music functions. The listener "cruises" the voice of Bowie, though fragmented, spies upon that voice, and expects something from the single, the promotional release, the showcase of the artist's voice. There, in the midst of fragments and repetition, is the "hook," the portion of the song that catches the listener, that acts as a kind of distraction from the everyday, a way for the listener to continue the work of listening to the song.

Space

Bowie is situated within a sometimes bewildering space between being outside the pop mainstream, and being one who very much defines the pop mainstream. If anything, Bowie constantly pushes against the boundaries of what is acceptable as mainstream. Bowie can be thought of as being in a place between various worlds: he is the best-selling performer of *Let's Dance* fame, the singer who has performed duets with Mick Jagger and Tina Turner, but also the co-headliner with Nine Inch Nails and a performer with avant-garde dance troupe La La La Human

Steps. In a way, he embodies a place that intersects these two worlds, both mainstream and not, both safe and commercial and daring and experimental. The place he inhabits is *liminal* which, by its very nature, makes it a difficult place for success: to be uncategorized is to be misunderstood, and those unable to fit into proper categories can end up in no categories at all. In being in a liminal space, Bowie challenges the notion of commercial success at all stages.

Victor Turner, in his theory of liminality, draws from anthropological studies of non–Western (more accurately, preindustrial) rite of passage rituals to create a model for transformative ritual, of which the modern ritual of theatre is a part. From these studies, he theorizes that a rite of passage as a transformative ritual consists of three phases: a preliminal phase, a liminal phase, and a postliminal phase. In the preliminal phase, an initiand is a regular member in some socio-cultural state, although it can be extrapolated from a need for a rite of passage that an initiand in a preliminal phase is somehow incomplete. The initiand needs to be made complete by the passage through a transitional liminal phase; it is through a transformative event that the initiand is made complete—and made into an initiate—which leads to a postliminal phase in which the initiate can be considered a member of an exclusive group. Turner defines the liminal stage as follows:

> Liminality can perhaps be described as fructile chaos, a fertile nothingness, a storehouse of possibilities, not by any means a random assemblage but a striving after new forms and structure, a gestation process, a fetation of modes appropriate to and *anticipating postliminal existence*. It is what goes on in nature in the fertilized egg, in the chrysalis, and even more richly and complexly in their cultural homologues.[47]

Bowie inhabits this sort of liminal space, especially at a time in which he was making some of the most alienating music of his career. As will be argued later, the music of *1. Outside* and the alliance with Nine Inch Nails and the context of Industrial music anticipates a problematized postliminal experience. Considering the nihilistic nature of much of that genre, one can speculate that the "new forms and structure" brought about by the postliminal are of the very character of the liminal phase, that is, chaos and nothingness, whether they be fructile or fertile or not. As keyboardist Mike Garson suggests, Bowie's *Outside*

1. The Beginning of the End

sessions were a product of some of the most creative environments in which Garson had ever participated.[48]

Turner's definition of liminality suggests a *positive* outcome among the "storehouse of possibilities," with the resulting phase being anticipated and compared to the rebirth of a butterfly, or the emergence of life from the egg. If Bowie embodies the liminal, it is unclear if he suggests a positive outcome out of the "storehouse of possibilities" that he also embodies; as suggested above, though Bowie might be, himself, an extremely creative "environment," is the chaos he inhabits fructile or fertile? Because of its lack of the positive "storehouse of possibilities" as a result of the transformation, or even its lack of anticipation of positive transformation, Bowie seems to not *necessarily* fit into Turner's definition of the liminal.

Ian Maxwell suggests that Turner's notion of the performance space as being a potential site for utopian change can be misleading. The utopian nature of the space (or performance space in postindustrial society) is something inherent in Turner's definition of the liminal phase. That is, the liminal phase is followed by a postliminal phase, in which the initiand is "initiated," or "reaggregated," as a complete member of the society. For Maxwell, though, one can "misrecognize" the opposite happening: there is, quite possibly, "something altogether darker and dangerous at the heart of communitas."[49] Communitas, for Turner, is an analog to "community," except that he prefers "the Latin term 'communitas' to 'community,' to distinguish this modality of social relationship from an 'area of common living.'" Also, the notion of communitas contains within is a sense of the sacred, that is, it acknowledges "an essential and generic human bond, without which there could be no society."[50] Maxwell points out that Turner's conception of "an instant of pure potentiality" in the liminal communitas is "at the heart of revolutionary art and cultural movements."[51] But also, for Maxwell, there is a sort of "ethical void" at the core of Turner's communitas, when inhibitions are forgotten and the utopian impulse is embraced. The communitas—or crowd, according to Maxwell—possesses a "fundamental amorality." Maxwell refers to Elias Canetti's *Crowds and Power*, which suggests "the crowd ... 'needs a direction ... it moves towards a goal'—*any* goal."[52] Canetti writes that a crowd "will accept any goal. A crowd exists so long as it has an unattained goal.... The nature of these [that is, the crowd] is often not predictable."[53] Canetti's conception of the crowd is certainly not necessarily a positive one: his work is, after all, a discussion of power and the crowd emerging from post–Second World War European thought on influence and responsibility. It is no surprise that Canetti might be suspicious and wary of crowd activity. The possibility remains, though, that Canetti's crowd can be equated with Turner's communitas, as Maxwell suggests.

Turner's notion of communitas comes from his desire to delineate the rite of passage—the process of being transformed from one societal state to another—from society's "civic" need, if one can use such a crude term, to graduate a member of society from one state to another. Turner's communitas evokes something of the sacred, in that there is something deeper occurring than simply a permission, as might happen in civic situations. Turner suggests that it is not simply "giving a general stamp of legitimacy to a society's structural positions" but instead "a matter of giving recognition to an essential and generic human bond, without which there could be *no* society."[54] Does this sacredness differentiate communitas from Canetti's crowd, though?

Canetti suggests that the crowd has four main attributes: that it always wants to grow; that it embodies equality; that it can never be too dense; and that it needs direction (*any* direction, as Maxwell is sure to point out). Canetti discusses crowds as phenomena that can erupt at any time, possessing equality, direction and unity, all characteristics that might be attributed to the community of the initiated.

The problem occurs when one tries to situate David Bowie as a site for communitas—as postliminal. Maxwell's observation that the liminal can suggest the negative possibilities of Canetti's crowds helps to illuminate how Bowie might be construed in the light of Turner's liminal framework. Bowie does not necessarily evoke the sense of a clear and positive postliminal state; he does not seem to suggest communitas. David Bowie's construction of a problematized liminal phase will be explored in the latter part of this book.

Perhaps Edward Soja's notion of "Thirdspace" is more useful in understanding what might be occurring in the persona of David Bowie, in that Soja suggests a sort of "postmodern spatiality" as it is described

1. The Beginning of the End

by James W. Flanagan. Flanagan suggests that Soja presents a space that embodies a "Thirding-as-Othering," a complex idea which moves beyond the physical notion of space (what Flanagan describes as "materialist" or "perceived space") and the mental notion of space ("idealist" or "conceived space"). Instead, Soja presents a "Thirdspace," or "lived space," a "strategic reopening and rethinking new possibilities." These spaces have been lost and need restoration, which still suggests a sort of positive sense for those spaces; they are also spaces in which the "real and the imagined are intertwined."[55]

Soja builds his model on Michel Foucault's idea of the "heterotopia," and it is his intention to extend those ideas to work in concrete examples, to reveal instances of oppression and abuse of power that are hidden by spaces, both perceived and conceived. And while Foucault's ideas pre-date—and thus inform—those of Soja, and proceed from the general ideas presented in Turner's "liminal space" (though from very difference academic, historic and geographic contexts), Foucault also provides a much more ambivalent presentation of this enigmatic conception of space.[56]

"Thursday's Child" and Heterotopia

An excellent example of the complexity of spaces in David Bowie's later career is the video for "Thursday's Child," the first single from *'hours...'* from 1999. The video features David Bowie in what appears to be a hotel room, standing in front of the sink and mirror. The radio that sits on the counter is turned on and the new single "Thursday's Child" begins to play through it. Bowie mumbles through some of the words, barely singing along to the sound coming through the radio, as he looks at himself in the mirror. He is joined there by a woman, assumed to be his lover. As she removes her contact lenses, Bowie has a sort of otherworldly experience, a fantasy. In some ways, Bowie enters a heterotopia.

O'Leary makes an interesting observation: "'Thursday's Child' wasn't hip; it didn't offer any pretense that it was—it sat in a comfortable present tense and stewed on the past. It felt genteel and a bit shabby."[57] A surface reading of the video suggests Bowie's struggle with the passage of time and the progress of life; after all, he fantasizes of his younger self and has an erotic moment when he kisses what is presumed to be a younger version of his female companion. But there also seems to be an element of darkness in the video: Bowie is presented as a dark figure. As he stares at his reflection in the mirror, it is not only sadness that seems to be reflected, but a particularly sinister stare. The reflection is more angry than simply sad; Bowie's strong stare seems to evoke madness, aggression and a personal interior darkness. There is something somewhat *off* in this otherwise sentimental expression of the passing of time.

The lyrics describe the account of the life of the narrator, looking back on what went on before: the narrator notes that he constantly tried to do all that was possible with what was provided him, but nothing came of any of that effort. His days were monotonous, and his nights were full of sorrow and sleeplessness. Even so, the narrator suggests that there was a glimmer of hope within him, a hope that ultimately came to naught. But in the midst of the darkness and hopeless repetition, the narrator is edified by the smile of the one to whom the song is being sung. The narrator suggests that his life might be split into two: the past, a period full of unfulfilled potential and broken promises; and the future, in which things seem to work out, in which he is successful. The narrator wishes, then, to discard the past for the possibility of tomorrow. While the narrator seems to regret most of the past, he does not regret the person who provided a light in his darkness, a positive to his negative life.

The video seems to illuminate the lyrics of the song, in that there seems to be some regret on the part of the character that Bowie plays; he wonders how his life has passed him by, as he looks at his present—older—self in the mirror. But just as the lyrics suggest that his life can be split into two, he himself inhabits two spaces: the space in front of the mirror (the present time); and the space *through* the mirror (a present and a past in one moment).

Michel Foucault writes of certain spaces that "suspect, neutralize, or invert the set of relations that they happen to designate, mirror, or reflect." He calls such spaces heterotopias; "it exerts a sort of counter-action on the position."[58] An article, "Of Other Spaces," was published in 1986, a translation of Michel Foucault's lecture "Des Espaces Autres"

1. The Beginning of the End

given in March 1967. In the English translation by Jay Miskowiec, Foucault describes a sort of history of space. Of note, he suggests that the "actual" space of the Middle Ages constitutes what he calls a "space of emplacement": "a hierarchic ensemble of places: sacred places and profane places; protected places and open, exposed places; urban places and rural places (all these concern the real life of men)." For Foucault, the Middle Ages demonstrated "this complete hierarchy, this opposition, this intersection of places" in a particularly marked and compelling way.[59] The Middle Ages was an age in which one was strongly placed in a certain space, without possibility for mobility. Each space, also, was marked as what it was, without the possibility of change; categorization of space, and of its occupants, was fixed. As in other areas of Foucault's study, the study of space reveals power relations.

Put simply, Foucault suggests that the spaces that one lives in that define one's life are also defined by society, and other power holders and discourse creators and reinforcers (Judith Butler would agree). The spaces or sites in which one lives are related to each other: it is through these spaces that order is established in society. Foucault states, though, that such mundane sites are not of ultimate interest to him:

> I am interested in certain ones that have the curious property of being in relation with all the other sites, but in such a way as to suspect, neutralize, or invert the set of relations that they happen to designate, mirror, or reflect. These spaces, as it were, which are linked with all the others, which however contradict all the other sites, are of two main types.

The types to which Foucault refers are "utopias" and "heterotopias." For Foucault, then, utopias are unreal, that is, presentations of perfected forms of society. Heterotopias, on the other hand, are *real* spaces, though "absolutely different from all the sites that they reflect and speak about." Between the utopia, which is unreal, and the heterotopia, which is real, is what Foucault calls the mirror. While the heterotopia is reflected or mediated by the mirror, the mirror becomes a sort of heterotopia in itself: "it makes this place that I occupy at the moment when I look at myself in the glass at once absolutely real, connected with all the spaces that surrounds it, and absolutely unreal, since in order to be perceived it has to pass through this virtual point which is over there." The mirror exists in the real world, and thus reflects the unreal idea of utopia in a solid object:

"The heterotopia is capable of juxtaposing in a single real place several spaces, several sites that are in themselves incompatible."[60]

Thus, Bowie's fantasy in the mirror—his gaze upon a younger version of himself and his companion, as well as the kiss between his present self and the younger companion—are both in reality and unreality: the mirror itself acts as a sort of virtual point. The "mirror world" that Bowie's character inhabits for that brief moment, in which he takes the place of his younger self, is a world of both the fulfillment of fantasy (his kissing of a younger version of his companion) and of a kind of deep resentment and betrayal. The Bowie character pines for a time that has passed, and while he is sentimental about that time, he seems also to harbor a sort of anger for his present state in the face (literally) of his past. Furthermore, his tryst with the younger version of his companion—a fact that is only speculative and not confirmed by the narrative at all, in any case—seems to be in spite of the fact that he is with an older version of the woman. His hesitance is only apparent in a moment after the kiss—and before returning to "reality"—when he pulls away, seemingly ashamed and thrust back into the present.

Foucault discusses various principles of heterotopia; one of his principles suggests that "heterotopias always presuppose a system of opening and closing that both isolates them and makes them penetrable." Foucault states, "There are others [that is, other heterotopias] ... that seem to be pure and simple openings, but that generally hide curious exclusions." For instance, Foucault describes what he calls "famous bedrooms" that existed in South America, as containing an entry door that did not lead to the central chambers in which the family lived, but rather to an open bedroom in which a stranger was allowed to stay, but only for a time, that is, for the evening. Foucault makes a compelling observation: he suggests that these South American bedrooms are akin to the "famous" American hotel rooms in which "illicit sex is both absolutely sheltered and absolutely hidden, kept isolated without however being allowed into the open."[61]

Recall Foucault's description of those spaces that are *not* the spaces which define the lives of those in society, but rather those spaces that convey *something else*: they "suspect, neutralize, or invert the set of relations that they happen to designate, mirror, or reflect."[62] Consider

1. The Beginning of the End

Maxwell's criticisms of Turner's liminal here, though: what if the inversion of the set of relations causes more harm, though it be liberating? The potential utopic emancipation offered by these spaces is tempered by the real possibility of damage or harm. For example, Foucault suggests that heterotopias are able to juxtapose "several sites that are in themselves incompatible." Furthermore, these are heterotopias of deviation, what Foucault describes as "those in which individuals whose behavior is deviant in relation to the required mean or norm are placed."[63] While Foucault is suggesting behavior deviant to the norm, there is the possibility inherent in such spaces that deviant behavior—harmful behavior—is a potential result.

The image most closely associated with the heterotopia is a boat, an item at its most comfortable (for lack of a better word) on the sea, in an unfixed position, always swaying to and fro. Foucault states, "the boat is a floating piece of space, a place without a place, that exists by itself, that is closed in on itself and at the same time is given over to the infinity of the sea."[64]

Regarding *1. Outside*, an important Bowie text, the polysemic nature of the text, the labyrinthian levels and layers of meaning, those spaces of emplacement that are also juxtaposed into sorts of networks of manifest utopia, point to a kind of unfixed text, a space which becomes, as Foucault suggests, "the greatest reserve of the imagination." If the *1. Outside* album, the "Thursday's Child" video, and the later career of Bowie itself, present chains of heterotopia, then these might also presents a real (though strange) example of the ideal utopia. Without that "greatest reserve of the imagination" which characterizes that particular album, Foucault continues, "dreams dry up ... and the police take the place of the pirates."[65]

While liminality, thirdspace and heterotopia all provide compelling models to consider for the case of Bowie's inhabited space in terms of expression and creation, none reflect perfectly the ambivalence that seems inherent in Bowie's celebrity persona. Rather, a new model—certainly informed by Turner, Soja and Foucault—is needed. Perhaps Bowie inhabits a space which, like the other sorts of spaces mentioned above, implies utopia, in that it allows for a certain freedom away from the constraints of society at large (though, obviously, informed by those constraints at some level—there is no sense that Bowie lives or expresses an alien space, removed from reality and the known world). But it seems that Bowie's space does not *necessarily* look to the past with any sort of fondness *really*. Bowie destroys the past and, rather than reinventing himself, which is the common discourse surrounding his star image, he destroys himself and moves forward *without looking forward*. The future, for Bowie, at least as suggested by this space that he inhabits and expresses, is dark: there is a void implied by the space—in a way, both in the past and the future. The space itself is not devoid of meaning, but rather, it is rich with meaning. In a way, Bowie inhabits Barthes' neutral. According to Barthes, the neutral is a "third term," that seems to be found between binaries. The "third term" can be thought of in the context of gender (the neuter, or the drone bee in a hive), or in the context of politics (Switzerland as a neutral), or in the terms of sound, that is, "the annihilation of opposition between sounds within certain languages."[66] This third way of conceiving of the third term is probably the most appropriate here: Bowie inhabits that "other place." For Barthes, the neutral is "neither-nor" (not unlike Turner's "betwixt-and-between"). For Barthes, the neutral is a sort of "degree zero," a language without sign, and thus exempt from meaning. Bowie, though, is not exempt from meaning, but now he "cannot be determined [or] arrested." He is "postmeaning," a term Barthes uses in some of his later work.[67] But even the neutral seems to imply the utopic. Bowie's space does not.

Bowie inhabits and expresses a state that seems to stage the present, a present perhaps informed by the past but which ultimately destroys it, and a present which does not look toward the future (analyses of Bowie's work suggests this, though the discourse surrounding him suggests otherwise). If anything, the space that Bowie occupies is a sort of perpetual present but, again, without the liminal promise of the future; it always looks to the present without any regard for past and future, a constant present presence, ambivalent to the core.

It should be noted that David Bowie is considered here more as a concept than a single, living, person. In other words, Bowie is the sum of his many parts: the important biographical information—both published and speculative—that informs how fans and scholars understand the celebrity himself; the totality of his recorded musical work, as expres-

1. The Beginning of the End

sion of both the man and his image; the various manifestations of Bowie as represented by music video, album art, live performance set design and other visual media; and the discourse that surrounds the celebrity. As Sir Christopher Freyling suggests, David Bowie is a myth: "We keep talking about Bowie, and actually we're talking about the 'myth of Bowie.' ... Bowie has played lots of parts, but we always talk about him as if they exist."[68] In that way, all of these elements contribute to what here is being described as Bowie's sense of communitas—or, at least, all of these elements are what are at play when Bowie's sense of communitas is being questioned. Furthermore, Bowie, defined not as a single, actual person but as a combination of all of his various elements, is said here to be inhabiting (or exhibiting, or manifesting) a liminal (not necessarily postliminal) space. This is not to say that the real, actual person is not involved in this negotiation, but rather that the whole celebrity construct must be considered in such an exploration. It is not necessarily the case that Bowie himself, upon questioning, would have any sense that he personifies or exemplifies a space for Turner's liminal phase, but with Maxwell's and Canetti's qualifications attached. Roland Barthes' notion of "the death of the author" gives license to such a reading, where the power to decode the meaning of cultural artifacts—of which Bowie is one—is in the hands of the reader, the cultural consumer.

As is argued in more detail later, an important element in Bowie's *1. Outside* is the idea of body modification in Western modern society as transformative ritual at the end of the twentieth century. Bowie himself, in constructing *1. Outside*, suggests that the album should be read as a kind of account of the period before the dawning of a new millennium. As such, *1. Outside* can be considered a perfect example of Turner's liminal stage, Soja's Thirdspace, Foucault's heterotopia, and Barthes' neutral. It accomplishes the creation of this space through lyrics, album art, music video and Bowie's live performance. As such a constructed space, it presents characteristics similar to these sorts of spaces, such as a recombination of familiar elements (including the *carnivalesque*, which is considered liminal in itself) and a kind of limbo state. Unlike Turner's liminal phase, this space indicates a change in the expected teleological progression leading to transformation as outlined by Turner. The multitude of optimistic possibilities and positive transformation suggested by Turner's liminal theory is not an obvious result of space constructed by Bowie. Rather, the result is pessimism and fear, and ultimately, the unknown. This unknown corresponds to the state of society upon the dawning of the twenty-first century, with the "transformative experience" being the actual turning of the clock on 31 December 1999. Ultimately, *1. Outside* is a reflection of societal anxiety toward the end of the millennium, through its construction of a sort of liminal space.

Mediation in Performance

In his exploration of the spectacle of wrestling, Roland Barthes observes, "bullfights and Greek theater: in all these places a light without shadow elaborates an emotion without secrets."[69] This is one way to illuminate the construction of the celebrity persona in performance. There are multiple threads that come into a discussion of performance: authenticity, mediation, enigma, presence, spaciality, and so forth. A rare film included with some packages of Bowie's 2003 album *Reality* feature a half-hour interview with the singer, which is interrupted by musical performances. In the video, Bowie is featured, at times, in almost complete darkness. How can one reconcile Barthes' observations of "light without shadow" generating emotions, with the darkness and shadows in which Bowie bathes in the "Never Get Old" video (a part of his celebrity persona), which is meant to elicit a fan response?

Bowie is not the only popular music performer who negotiates the mediated space. Canadian songstress Leslie Feist uses her mediation in live performance in order to cultivate a sense of enigma. While being *with* her audience (spacially), she is *more than herself*; she calls her persona—that which is mediated by the stage, and in fact by the discourse that surrounds her—a kind of "hologram." Bowie's "hologram" is, in the example of the video, a shadow.

By drawing primarily from Roland Barthes and David Pattie, this section explores the power of the mediated persona of the enigmatic celebrity. Bowie is mediated by the stage itself (whether that stage

1. The Beginning of the End

be a live concert stage or the set of a music video), and, in particular, by the lighting therein. Obfuscation happens for many reasons: Bowie creates enigma in order to elicit desire from his audience and to deflect the gaze of his audience. He may also be using Feist's strategies: her strategies allow her to cope with the mechanisms and machines of celebrity.

In his exploration of the spectacle of wrestling, Barthes suggests that it is the "dense vertical character of the flood of light" that creates this notion of "solar spectacles" and "an emotion without secrets."[70] Later, he writes, "Leaving nothing in shadow, the gesture severs every parasitical meaning and ceremonially presents the public with a pure and full signification, three-dimensional, like Nature. Such emphasis is nothing but the popular and ancestral image of the perfect intelligibility of reality." Thus, Barthes calls the spectacle of wrestling—that is, bathed in light—"an ideal intelligence [or understanding] of things" (the word "intelligence" is translated as "understanding" in an earlier translation of Barthes' text).[71]

The discussion here must turn to what is meant by Barthes' "ideal intelligence [or understanding] of things," what in this context might refer to what the televisual viewer, concert attendee or whomever is on the receiving side of the mediated experience, actually experiences in experiencing a performance. While one might attend (or watch) a performance for many reasons—to be in the same physical space as the performer (in the case of a live concert), to physically feel the music being performed, to see the performer with one's own eyes—there is a sense that one attends a performance to experience the "authenticity" of a band, to experience that band or musician *authentically*—that is, unmediated, not mediated through recording or any medium (other than amplification and whatever other sort of processing that might occur in live performance—the less the better, though, as made clear by the popularity of acoustic performances such as the *MTV Unplugged* series of concerts in the late 1990s). David Pattie suggests that authenticity is "derived from white music's idea of black music and its intimate relationship with the lived experience of its audience."[72] He suggests that at the centre of the discussion of authenticity is the determination of what is real and what is not. Pattie refers to Richard Dyer's essay "*A Star*

Is Born and the Construction of Authenticity" in order to quantify how authenticity is manifest, how it is played out in popular music: "sincere, immediate, spontaneous, real, direct, genuine."[73] Pattie continues with a startling revelation: "it is not enough that the star is real; he or she must 'act realness.' ... To be said to exist, they [the stars] have to be demonstrated; they have to become clearly visible to an audience." Repeatedly, Pattie uses the phrase "rock performance," as authentic communication between performer and audience; so, though performance, it is also, somehow, authentic. Pattie also uses the term "communion," as a kind of direct communication with the audience in performance. Finally, Pattie mentions intimacy, a kind of shared experience between an audience member and performer. All of these notions apply to authenticity in performance.

Directed by Steven Lippman, the accompanying film to the 2003 release, *Reality*, features Bowie as both interviewer and interviewee, speaking directly to the camera and answering questions that his own disembodied voice asks. This disembodied voice is shown to be coming from a recorded monochrome (*absent*) Bowie that appears on a television screen in front of an answering (*present*) Bowie. The televised Bowie is, thus, doubly mediated: the viewer sees Bowie through two mediations—the immediate *Reality* video, and the television within the video. The distance is compounded; who is this interviewer and who has generated these questions? There are moments when his *other* voice interrupts the answering Bowie and sometimes makes understanding what is being said quite difficult (such juxtapositions also collude the *present* Bowie with the *absent* one). The topics of the interview jump from occult gothic architecture in London, the effectiveness of infomercials and speculation as to whether buildings have personalities. Answers that Bowie gives earlier in the video are revealed to be answers to questions given later: it appears the interview is not only "cut up," but also layered on top of itself.

The first music video is for the single "Never Get Old." Bowie is shown in what appears to be a stylized studio space, or perhaps a performance venue. The camera stays quite close to Bowie, and thus the context of his performance remains outside of the frame of the film. He is wearing a dark-colored suit and a white shirt, but without a tie. He is

1. The Beginning of the End

singing into a single, old-style pill-shaped microphone. In some of the shots, Bowie's face is bathed in bright light. There are other moments, though, where Bowie's face is in complete darkness, with the light coming from behind, resulting in his face and upper body being revealed only in silhouette. In order to mark a transition back to the interview portion, Bowie's face in interview is interspersed with the performance toward the end of the song.

In the video for "The Loneliest Guy," Bowie sings his first few phrases bathed in dark blue light and out of focus. As the song progresses, Bowie face becomes in focus, though he remains lit by dark blue light. A mirrorball begins to reflect flickering, shimmering lights. At one point, the camera directs the viewer to the back of Bowie's head, while at another, Bowie covers his face with the back of his hand. Toward the end of the song, Bowie moves back into complete darkness, with only the shimmering reflections from the mirrorball as light.

In the third video, featuring "Bring me the Disco King," the camera searches through a darkened forest. Lights are flashing aimlessly, reflected on the trees and branches. For the duration of the first verse, Bowie is absent; the only images are those of the trees and reflections of light. At the first entrance of chorus material, a man's hands are shown, though at this point it is unclear whether they are Bowie's. As the chorus continues, it is revealed in fragmented shots that Bowie is digging in the dirt of the forest. It should be noted that Bowie's face is not clearly shown until late in the video. He is then shown standing over a body lying face-down on the forest floor. He is seemingly standing over his own dead body. Throughout this video, Bowie is not performing as one would conventionally expect. Instead, he seems *half present*, existing in the role of digging, and in the role of surveying his own dead body. At the end of this video, snippets of scenes from the previous videos as well as the interview portion show up again, demonstrating that the film needs to be taken as a whole.

The final video for "New Killer Star," the first single from the album, features trees passing at quick speed. As the bridge to the chorus begins, the scenery changes to quick and shaky shots of New York City, with only a couple of fleeting images of Bowie himself. The film ends with the city images and a short clip of Bowie speaking in passing. Just before the final video is shown, Bowie is heard saying, "That's what it sounds like when you're dead: doors opening."

An integral part of a popular music celebrity's presentation in performance is lighting. Throughout the *Reality* film, Bowie is ill-lit. That is, for the most part, he is featured in shadows, in a blurred and unfocused state, covering himself up with his hands or featured not at all. In many of the shots, Bowie's face and body are illuminated only in what might seem "secondary" light, that is, light reflected off of the mirrorball or in the light reflected off of the trees. There are moments when the light appears as it would if it were reflected off of a surface of water—it shimmers on his face, rather than illuminating it completely. This sort of lighting not only, in a way, *obscures* his face (the focal point for much of the viewing audience), but it also cultivates shadow. Being lit in these ways creates a silhouette, a kind of outline only of a shadow; he is sometimes revealed primarily through reflection, and sometime he is not illuminated at all. The medium of music video invites the viewer to look at Bowie, to explore aspects of his physical self and to desire him, and to do so repeatedly. But how then can one reconcile this with the fact that the lighting functionally "erases" him or, at least, obfuscates him? In a way, the lighting might be how Bowie effaces himself.

Useful in the present discussion of a mediated Bowie is Leslie Feist. Feist describes this mediation of celebrity, which occurs primarily on stage, but also through various popular music mediations like music video, album covers and promotional material, as "hologram." In 2007, Feist released a kind of documentary film *Look at What the Light Did Now*. The film outlines how light and art were utilized on tour in order to create the spectacle of her live show in support of the album *The Reminder*. In an interview from that film, Feist comments, "In trying to describe what is being made, a sort of sculpture, you know, it's like a puzzle sculpture that we're 'mosaicing' together through thinking about who were the people who projected this strange hologram with me." Thus, for Feist, her mediated persona, that which she shows on stage, that which is created by and through the discourse that surrounds her, is *realistic*, but not ultimately real. Rather, it

1. The Beginning of the End

is a trick of light, a mediated image, an interference pattern that, when illuminated in such a way, creates a three-dimensional object, Feist herself.

For Feist, live performance includes the singer being featured completely covered by a screen, but with her silhouette illuminated from behind. This can be a strange spectacle: the audience knows that Feist is physically, spacially, present, but she is not fully seen, and she is presented as a processed or heavily mediated version of her self. She is much bigger than she is in reality, much like her celebrity persona. In another portion of the concert, Feist is featured as only a small part of the performance (something usually expected at a live popular music performance—that the concert is not necessarily a showcase of the musician, but rather a scene of spectacle, of which the musician is only a part). Behind her is a projection of the manipulation of clay and jewels on a light table to create a scene as Feist performs. During this art performance, Feist is lit primarily from above, an angle which seems to favor the silhouette. She is also lit by lights around and below her. These serve to illuminate her not unlike reflections might; she is illuminated softly and warmly. Though shadows are perhaps more scarce in this presentation, the sense is that Feist is purposefully *not* bathed in light; instead, her position is indicated by the bit of light while the real spectacle goes on above and behind her head, where a kind of phantasmagoric display is occurring. Her personal light is minimal, while "Feist," the performer, is featured to the audience through the complete performance.

What can one say, then, of Feist's presentation, in which she is present but obscured in the context of live performance? Feist refers to herself (her *true* self?) as a "tiny little source" from which *she* (or "Feist") is created. Thus, for Feist, her true self is not a part of her celebrity self. This is not new; Dyer and Pattie state as much. But for Feist—and her handlers, in particular—this celebrity persona is like a dream. From *Look at What the Light Did Now*, Clea Minaker, the show designer for Feist's tour in support of *The Reminder*, gives some insight into the use of shadows. She states: "Every human being born on earth has a relationship to their shadow, notices their shadow. Shadow is a source of light. There's an object, or a silhouette, and then there's the projection of the silhouette. It's everything that is parallel to the real world. It's the dream world." Elsewhere in the film, Feist's photographer, Mary Rozzi, has this to say about the shadow of mediated celebrity in the context of Feist:

> While they were discussing the cover [of *The Reminder*], and photography, versus not having photography, or her being on the cover, versus her not being on the cover, I thought, you have to have a photo on the cover. And, since she didn't want to be actually recognizable, or on the cover, which I thought she should be. Hence the silhouette, so she's on the cover, but you don't see her. She's not recognizable.

It seems, then, that Feist is really only seen in silhouette. She appears to be "authentic"; that is, she possesses most of the characteristics that Pattie and Dyer identify as "authentic" (sincerity, immediacy, spontaneity, realness, directness, genuineness). What makes Feist a particularly compelling case is made quite evident in *Look at What the Light Did Now*; the documentary reveals the immense amount of emotional stress that Feist seemed to be under during the tour of that extremely successful album.

Thus, for Feist, the mediation that is provided her by her stage and its phantasmagoric show, allows her to expand her "hologram," the three-dimensional image which she provides to the rest of the world, to include those who participate in its creation, the artists who create and participate in the performance through illuminated visuals. It also allows her, though, to lose herself in the particularly large lighted backdrop; attendees are likely to pay attention to the beautiful sequences that appear on the screen rather than on her. The focus of the audience on the stage and all that happens on it (apart from the actual performer) allows that performer to diminish, to relieve some of the weight that is garnered from celebrity.

Bowie uses mediation in order to deflect the gaze of the audience, to obfuscate the truth of a performance, which is an unexpected grand gesture: the move against authenticity in the face of authenticity, in the name of enigma. Bowie uses mediation in order to deflect the gaze of the audience away, to see the greater construction of the celebrity, so as to relieve pressure on the "authentic" or "true" person. In both of these cases, mediation through lighting in particular, serves to work against

1. The Beginning of the End

"authenticity." In these examples, the light (or lack thereof) creates shade, and thus does not offer, as Barthes suggests, "a pure and full signification." Instead, the audience is given an image of the *imperfect* "intelligibility of reality."

A Dystopian Utopia in "Valentine's Day"

The video for David Bowie's song "Valentine's Day," from his 2013 release *The Next Day*, evokes utopian notions. This section takes a detailed look at the works by Paul Virilio and Roland Barthes in order to create a sort of field in which the video operates. The connections between Virilio, Barthes and "Valentine's Day" are tenuous: the video can be read from within this theoretical context. It seems *informed* by Virilio and Barthes, and the details of their works elucidate the video as a whole. Throughout the video, Bowie employs iconic rock gestures, such as playing an electric guitar, singing with extreme emotion and holding the guitar above his head defiantly. Also, the video's setting of a concrete structure might evoke what Paul Virilio calls the "Very High Building," an ideal urban form in which displaced people find community.

That very setting, though, is crumbling, one element which suggests to the viewer that a dystopia is just beneath the surface of the text. There are visual codes throughout that connote speed, madness and violence. In a way, this is similar to Virilio's notion of the "administration of fear." That state of fear coupled with the speed of the modern world equals what Virilio calls a *Blitzkrieg*: "a military and technological phenomenon that occupies you in the blink of an eye, leaving you dumbfounded, mesmerized."[74] Furthermore, both Virilio and the music video try to answer the same question: "Where is being-in-the-world in the era where speed is at the limit?" Bowie's answer is that "being-in-the-world" is a strange place: it is a place of disembodiment and madness. In a way, the video displays a sort of arrhythmia, that is, lack of rhythm. But it also displays a dysrhythmia or heterorhythmy. Roland Barthes introduces these terms in order to define what he calls idiorrhythmy, which is the recognition of different rhythms, a utopian sort of space. In order to properly define the term, Barthes clearly defines its opposites with the following image:

> From my window.... I see a mother pushing an empty stroller, holding her child by the hand. She walks at her own pace, imperturbably; the child, meanwhile, is being pulled, dragged along, is forced to keep running, like an animal.... She walks at her own pace, unaware of the fact that her son's rhythm is different. And she's his mother! Power ... is effected through disrhythmy, heterorhythmy.[75]

Thus, the video not only depicts iconic images of Rock music utopia, the Very High Building of Virilio's displaced populations in the twenty-first century, but also the strange juxtaposition of disembodiment and madness in the speed of the world and the dystopia of arrhythmy and disrhythmy or heterorhythmy.

The video contains many conventional images of rock music, but further images—dystopian in nature—are introduced as well. At the very opening of the video, the viewer is shown the height of the concrete structure. The viewer is also introduced to the immediate surroundings of the singer, and his defiant stance. The video also contains instances of obfuscation, during which Bowie's likeness is blurred, an image that is often associated with madness.

Bowie holding an electric guitar over his head evokes notions of rebellion and power, a gesture of defiance rather than a gesture imbued with what David Pattie suggests is phallic, masculine, power.[76] However, this sort of gendered power is tempered by his clothing—a fashionable, linen shirt—as well as by his age: he is a 66-year-old male who has been out of the celebrity spotlight for a decade. While he is still handsome, he is not conventionally so, a strange fact considering how much of the music video is focused on Bowie's face in close up. The guitar he is playing is also slight, headless and thus perhaps "less powerful." That is, the conventional portion of a guitar situated at the end of the fretboard in which the strings are attached to turning pegs, the "head," is not part of this particular guitar's design. In a couple of ways, then, Bowie himself provides the utopic impulses in this visual presentation. First, he presents himself as a rebellious musician (in a more conventional sense), harnessing the defiant power of the guitar against whatever established powers might be at play against him. Second, he provides an image

1. The Beginning of the End

decidedly different from the conventional masculine power in rock music. It is not only that he is older and fashionable, but also that he seems to express a sort of madness, a manic manifestation of a seemingly underlying psychosis. His immediate surroundings do nothing to bolster the initial emancipatory power of his gestures and presentation. His surroundings are wet, crumbling and full of "ghosts," blurred versions of himself or others, appearing and disappearing at various moments in the video.

There is a subtext of more obvious and less theoretical violence through the video: at one point, the shadow of what seems to be a rifle appears, and at another, a close-up shot seems to show a bullet flying past the strings of a guitar. It is possible that the song alludes to school shootings, and, as such, can be read as a sort of diatribe against the firearms lobby in the United States. While this is supported by certain readings of the video, this is not the approach that this present study takes. This study is taking into consideration the theoretical *space* of the video, and what might be happening therein. Such visual images— the shadow of a rifle, the movement of a bullet across the field of vision— move so quickly. The viewer has much more time to study the manic face (and facial expressions) of the singer, as well as his gestures, his apparent reactions to the ghosts in his surroundings, and the simply juxtaposition of the celebrity and the stark concrete of his surroundings.

Consider the notion of the building in which Bowie is featured. Besides its concrete structure, the fact that it is deserted and full of water, or in a state of disrepair, it is also somewhat tall. While it is obviously not a residential building, it nevertheless evokes Paul Virilio's notion of the "Very High Building." In his book *The Futurism of the Instant: Stop-Eject*, Virilio approaches the subject of future environmental migrants, those displaced by conflict as well as by development projects. He explores the problematized notions of citizenship and nationhood brought about by contemporary communications and transportation technologies (if earlier eras were about "sustainable staying-put," this new era will be one of "habitable circulation," which calls into question notions of citizenship and nationhood), calling the resulting upheavals the "portable revolution," which, along with revolutions in transportation and transmission technologies, will lead to what he calls an "interactive planisphere."[77] Throughout the work, Virilio moves from the smaller scale (for instance, discussing the loading dock or the train station) to the larger scale (the city as a whole, or the whole world in movement), suggesting that these spaces of movement are ultimately ungovernable, at least in terms of conventional legal governance.

In fact, translator Julie Rose's preface indicates the themes of this complex book: "mass population flows, displacement, exodus, exile, expatriation, exurbanism, extraplanetary exploration."[78] Virilio is exploring speed in the early twenty-first century and its effects or results: it seems that Virilio is fundamentally discouraged regarding the state of the world, its speed, the destruction of the suburban landscape, and the creation of the vertical "ultracity."

Virilio also sees some worth in some of these global transformations. The book is an uncompromising look at the power of what he calls *révolution de l'emport*, or what Rose has deemed the "portable revolution," a movement enacted because of the increases in the "payload capacity," or *capacité d'emport*, of the twenty-first century, in terms of transportation and communications technologies. While Virilio's tone seems to be negative, it is not without compassion. In the first part of the book, entitled "Stop-Eject," Virilio both seems to mourn the loss of suburbs (or the spread of cities, a movement brought about by the introduction and appropriation of the automobile in the 1950s), and mourn the movement of immigrant and displaced populations to urban centers.

In the section entitled "The Ultracity," Virilio remarks that, while there exists movement away from suburbia to the city, as well as movement of displaced people, there is also the movement up, into what he calls the VHB, that is, the "Very High Building." While the skyscraper seems the ideal urban architectural form (he even calls it a kind of "space craft" allowing humanity to leave the planet for more spacious surroundings), it also marks a sort of loss of pedigree or history. In other words, just as immigrant communities, those relegated to transportation by shipping container, constitute a diaspora, so then do skyscraper occupants. They are just as unrooted to a sense of attachment to the land. It

1. The Beginning of the End

is an interesting notion, and one applicable to many, especially in the urban West. Later, Virilio suggests that the Very High Building can be a site of community, for those displaced people to constitute a community of unrootedness.

If space is problematized in the twenty-first century, due to progress in terms of communications and transportation technologies, so is time, as Virilio argues in the third section, "The Futurism of the Instant." These changes ultimately lead to a loss of memory—a loss of the past, but also a loss of the future. Virilio argues, rather, that the result is the experience of a kind of perpetual instant. Such ideas are elegantly evoked in the moments of speed change in the video: there are moments when Bowie is displayed in blurred movement, as if speed has stopped for the viewer. The viewer sees Bowie himself stuck in a perpetual instant, with this loss of memory creating a sort of liminal state of loss, and ambivalence toward future possibilities (remember also Bowie's experience with his mirror self in "Thursday's Child").

Startlingly, what Virilio sees as a blight he also sees as a solution: in order to solve problems such as the erasure of space and time, and the chronic consumption of the Earth by its occupants, he suggests that humans become nomadic, to counteract the sedentary characteristics of the Ultracity. In its constant communication and transportation flows, one can find, in a way, *rootedness*. This is a rootedness in the notion of global citizenship, a community of all peoples, for the sake of the planet, not to mention a possibility made physically available in the context of the Very High Building. If Virilio's work seems too negative, he at least offers some glimmer of hope in a method of reversal of what, in other parts of his book, seem to be inevitable results of technological and spacial globalization. While the video does not highlight this possibility directly, there is a sense that the very presence of a quasi-"Very High Building" alludes to this notion of community. But if a community formed by rootlessness is a utopia in Virilio's dystopia, surely the dystopia appears in the video as well. This is manifest in the notion of the "administration of fear."

Virilio's *The Administration of Fear* is an intensely personal work. In his preface, Bertrand Richard defines the "fear" as a result of the postmodern condition: "If there is fear ... it is because the Earth is shrinking and space is dwindling, compressed by instantaneous time."[79]

This dense book is written as a dialogue, or more accurately, an interview of Virilio by Bertrand Richard (though Richard calls it a conversation). The interview format is curious; in a way, it makes the text easier to comprehend. Richard's questions serve to clarify Virilio's comments. The work should more properly be seen as a kind of collaboration, in which Richard has a direct role: his questions and comments serve not only to clarify but to guide the conversation. Virilio's thoughts are ultimately structured—and perhaps determined—by Richard's questions and comments.

For Virilio, the "administration of fear" refers to the fear that surrounds members of society, and it refers to the policies created by the State to manage fear, which ultimately threaten democracy. Virilio makes a (tenuous) connection between the occupation of France in the Second World War and the current state of fear: fear is the occupier today. In fact, Richard wonders if the comparison between the current state of fear and the Second World War is appropriate: "can't you [Virilio] be accused of being overly dramatic"? In response, Virilio states that "terror cuts to the quick: it is connected to life and quickness through technology."[80] That state of fear coupled with speed of the modern world equals what Virilio calls a *Blitzkrieg*: "It is a military and technological phenomenon that occupies you in the blink of an eye, leaving you dumbfounded, mesmerized."[81]

The two authors then suggest the relationship between occupation, resistance and collaboration. Virilio embarks on a discussion on the relationship between science and philosophy, from the Cuban Missile Crisis preceded by the development of the Doomsday Clock and the creation of the Atomic and Hydrogen bombs. Virilio concludes that "this is the domination of the military-industrial complex: it is all the more frightening for political philosophy today because this philosophy has not thought about speed or speed articulated in space."[82] The Cold War and the Arms Race were a period of a "balance of terror," but in the current age, there exists an "imbalance of terror." Virilio defines it as "the possibility for a single individual to cause as much damage as an absolute weapon," but also the "making of fear."[83]

1. The Beginning of the End

Furthermore, the atomic bomb has been replaced—or perhaps joined—by what Virilio calls the ecological bomb, referring to various catastrophic changes that will be brought about by climate change. He suggests also that the ecological bomb will result in a new genetically modified humanity, engineered to make less of an ecological footprint, to consume fewer resources.[84] Most powerful, though, is the informational bomb, brought about by the almost instantaneous communication of local catastrophic events to a global audience: "the same feeling of terror can be felt in all corners of the world at the same time." He suggests that this constant feeling of terror can be attributed to the loss of geographical space in contemporary society due to the proliferation of communications technologies, but this has also contributed to the loss of the body.[85]

Virilio makes it clear that he is not a technophobe: "Our societies have become arrhythmic. Or they only know one rhythm: constant acceleration. Until the crash and systemic failure."[86] He is fighting against what he calls the "propaganda of progress" rather than progress itself, which is related to the cult of speed.[87] The constant speed of postindustrial society has caused the demise of rhythm, be it seasonal, liturgical and so forth. Instead, society runs at all times and without any sort of break. Virilio is aware, though, that he sounds like a technophobe, something that he denies throughout this work. Though his denials are constant, the tension between his tone and his claims (like the environment of fear which he reveals) is omnipresent.

One of his most compelling ideas is the relationship between power and speed: those who control speed, or the communications technologies and "propaganda" that run on these networks of speed (and, of course, the arrhythmy mentioned above), have power. The "fear" of the title is one that is ultimately hidden by the "ideology of progress."[88]

Throughout this work, Virilio mentions the term "the futurism of the instant," which obviously refers to his previous work, *The Futurism of the Instant: Stop-Eject*, published in 2010. This work, then, can be thought of as an extension of the earlier book and its ideas. In that book, Virilio discusses the phenomena of transience and speed, but in this book, he seems to explore the result of these phenomena, the cultivation of fear. His earlier book is often negative, with little solutions to the problems presented therein. This book reads in a similar way, though solutions are presented; Virilio makes a grand global call for a renewed rediscovery of philosophy: "'Where is being-in-the-world in the era where speed is at the limit?' This is the question we should be asking and the question we must answer."[89] The format of the book itself, even with its problematic presentation of an interview, might illustrate Virilio's utopian solution. Ultimately, the book presents a dialog or conversation between active participants; they are asking questions precisely about "being-in-the-world." Their dialog introduces a rhythm into the book, something that Virilio claims is missing in the arrhythmy of the world. Also, it is in this work that Virilio revisits and expands the notion of rootedness: all humanity is now portable. Rootlessness defines the current way of being.

Virilio raises a particularly interesting question in terms of what he calls "tele-technologies" as prostheses, that is, those communications technologies that promise to give us emancipation. He suggests that their augmenting powers make them impossible to refuse (consider those in North America who are mocked because of their lack of cellphone). Thus, these technologies, prostheses of augmentation, are not emancipatory, but rather enslaving. It is impossible to be without them.

Ultimately, Virilio puts into practice the concepts which he outlines, making his reader pause with each of Richard's questions and comments, and with the format of the book as distinct chapters, each involved what is seemingly a single conversation. This physically unassuming book is, in a way, powerful in that it demonstrates the enactment of rhythm into a world that is overcome and obsessed by the cult of speed, and ultimately under the oppressive power of the various bombs mentioned above. In order to overthrow these oppressors, Virilio implores the reader to simply slow down, something which the reader must do in order to successfully navigate the text. And once the text is finished, the reader is afforded the opportunity not only to contemplate the ideas presented, but simply to rest.

Virilio's concerns regarding speed and rhythm are important to consider in terms of Bowie's video, especially Virilio's claims of the arrhythmy of society. The constant speed of postindustrial society has caused the demise of rhythm; society runs at all times and without any

1. The Beginning of the End

sort of break. Conversely, Roland Barthes explores how individuals—each with different rhythms—can co-exist and co-create at their own pace. Barthes uses the term "idiorrhythmy" to describe a form of living together in which both parties respect each other's individual rhythms.

Barthes' *The Preparation of the Novel* consists of lectures from his last course at the Collège de France, delivered from 1978 to 1980. In a way, these lectures are the last of a recently published trio of collections: they were delivered after *The Neutral* (published by Columbia University Press in 2005) and after *How to Live Together* (published in 2013). The publisher's decision to publish the three courses out of chronological order is a curious one; for some reason, the middle course was published first, followed by the final course (which is, of course, *The Preparation of the Novel*) and then the first course.

Like Virilio's later book, Barthes' work begins as something quite personal: he writes about his age, well past middle-aged at the time of writing. He ponders the days left to him before death, and suggests that the repetition of past days needs to change. He writes, "When this text, this lecture course is over, there'll be nothing else for it but to start over again, to begin another one?" He concludes, "I have no time left to try out several different lives: I have to choose my last life, my new life," which he calls "Vita Nova." For Barthes, this is manifest in a new writing practice.[90]

It should be noted that this is, if fact, a collection of lectures, and perhaps needs to be understood as a part of a larger project at this stage of his career (and life). The three courses are presented in lieu of writing; Barthes did not produce major written works during this time. His autobiography (of sorts), *Roland Barthes by Roland Barthes* was written in 1975, and *Camera Lucida* was published only in early 1980. In the first lecture of *The Preparation of the Novel*, Barthes mentions the importance of his not publishing the previous year's lectures (that is, those as part of his course on "The Neutral"). In fact, at the start of these lectures, he expresses his displeasure with the notion of publishing his lectures at all. He feels that some things should "be set aside for the Ephemeral," but he also points out his reluctance to "manage the past."[91] Even so, these lectures should be treasured for what they are; like photos, they are ephemera arrested in the form of the printed page. The reader is reminded in the preface that "those who attended the course recall the remarkable fluidity of his delivery, the deep and enveloping timbre of his voice, the warm phrasing that endowed his authority with infinite goodwill."[92] Some of these sentiments come through when reading the text but, as with all ephemera, any arresting cannot capture the full essence of being there in person.

The crux of the first lecture: "at a certain point in a life.... The Desire-to-Write (*scripturire*) can present itself as the obvious Recourse, the Practice whose fantasmic force would enable a new beginning, a *Vita Nuova*."[93] At the time of these lectures, Barthes was rumored to be writing a novel of his own, which he denies: "I'm at the Fantasy-of-the-novel stage, but I've decided to push that fantasy as far as it will go, to the point where: either the desire will fade away, or it will encounter the reality of writing and what gets written won't be the Fantasized Novel."[94]

Kate Briggs, the translator of the text, suggests that the text, while dealing with decisive shifts in one's life that allow for a new outlook on writing to emerge, is in itself a "break with previous intellectual practices." She states, "It's a novel experiment in how to integrate teaching and writing, a test to see whether it's possible to make those two activities into one and the same project."[95] If this was, in fact, a new kind of project for Barthes, it is unfortunate that he was not afforded the chance to embark on further studies, due to his demise just after the delivery of these lectures. Briggs suggests also that the allure of this new way of thinking, for Barthes (and, of course, those who enjoy Barthes' work), is the potential of a longer piece by the author, rather than the rather fragmentary (though novel) works that constitute his later *oeuvre*.

Barthes spends a large number of lectures on the haiku, a surprising move since the short and formal haiku seems antithetical to the long narrative of the novel, which, it is suggesting, its preparation is what he is mapping out. It seems that Barthes is trying to stress the importance of notation in the preparation of the novel, the transcribing of everyday occurrences that then mean something. These would be sprinkled throughout the text and then interweaved with the actual narrative (since they would be too emotionally powerful to make up the totality of the text for the novel). For Barthes, the haiku is the most efficient and effective example of this "notation."

1. The Beginning of the End

This collection serves as an excellent presentation of the last phase of Barthes' work. It is intrinsically a part of a trio of works, that is, one of the three courses delivered at the Collège de France. But it is important to note it as such: while the courses focus on different subjects, their methodologies are similar. Beginning with *Roland Barthes by Roland Barthes* in 1975, Barthes was trying to conceive of a novelistic work. These lectures are simply that—lectures (rather than a novel)—but they point to the creation of the novel. In other words, if one considers *Roland Barthes by Roland Barthes* as a beginning in 1975 and *Camera Lucida* as an ending in 1980, with the courses filling in the middle, *The Preparation of the Novel* is the focal point of his project. It is the clearest reflection of his later work, the ultimate insight into what was predominantly on his mind at this time. This is not to say that the text is not extremely complex; it would have been quite challenging to sit in on his lectures, without the ability to refer back in his presented text. But the reader does glimpse something of the person of Roland Barthes here. This is what makes Barthes' later works so valuable as well. The reader is afforded a genuine look behind the enigmatic curtain of Barthes' writings; here the physical, spacial, vocal Roland Barthes is arrested—captured—for all to experience.

Elsewhere in Barthes' work, he mentions the notion of *paideia*, another one of many Greek terms he uses as a kind of "terminological grid" to lay out his ideas. For Barthes, "paideia entails the idea of a journey without a fixed schedule." Maarten De Pourcq, in his exploration of Barthes' teaching methodology while at the *Collège de France*, states, "Barthes would like to submit himself and his audience, as subjects, to a *dressage*, literally: 'a cultivation,' a coming and going of the mostly unexpected forces of culture," or *paideia*.[96] Thus, the rhythm of the course, with Barthes contributing ideas at some points, and at others "coming and going," expecting responses from his students and listeners, echoes his ideas regarding idiorrhythmy.

Idiorrhythmy is an idea "most often associated with monks and which describes a method for people to live together but also to live apart—individual planets orbiting in a communal galaxy."[97] It occurs in "any community that respects each individual's own personal rhythm."[98]

It should be noted that Barthes lived this notion, not only in the dissemination of the lectures themselves, but in his own living conditions. Barthes did not live in solitude, but lived with his mother until her death in 1977. Richard Howard, Barthes' translator of many of his written works, states: "She [Barthes' mother] was a wonderful woman, just remarkable. Roland lived with her. He had a room where he worked in the attic that he sometimes slept in. He lived a perfectly satisfactory, not very happy life in the room upstairs."[99] Idiorrhythmy also "names any attempt to reconcile collective life with individual life, the independence of the subject with the sociability of the group."[100] Barthes calls it "something like solitude with regular interruptions."[101] For Barthes, there is "nothing contradictory about wanting to live alone and wanting to live together."[102]

This seems to be somewhat antithetical to Virilio's respect for the various seasons, the rhythm of time. In fact, what Barthes so wants to promote or protect—the idea that people can live alone and together, at differing rhythms—would, according to Virilio, be in the purview of those in power. One of Virilio's most compelling ideas is the relationship between power and speed: those who control speed, or the communications technologies and 'propaganda' that run on these networks of speed (and, of course, the arrhythmy mentioned above), have power. The 'fear' of the title, *The Administration of Fear*, is one that is ultimately hidden by the "ideology of progress."[103]

Consider Virilio's question again: "Where is being-in-the-world in the era where speed is at the limit?" Rootlessness defines the current way of being. While a community of rootlessness might be Virilio's solution to twenty-first century problems, it is also the problem. This is what, ultimately, the video suggests. First, Bowie is presented alone, without any other people present. There are moments when other bodies are featured, blurring in the space, but these are ghosts rather than supportive members of a transient community. Second, and in relation to the ghostly figures, Bowie seems somewhat mad. His grimace is one of insanity rather than of happiness. What might begin as emotive singing ends as an awkward display of strangeness. The space that Bowie both occupies and creates is one of darkness, madness and solitude. Ultimately, it is the conflation of utopic and dystopic dynamics in a single visual artifact. In answering Virilio's question, "Where is being-in-the-

1. The Beginning of the End

world in the era where speed is at the limit," the answer is that Bowie's answer is that "being-in-the-world" is a strange place: it is a place of disembodiment (ghosts and perpetual instants) and madness.

"Sue (Or in a Season of Crime)"

In November 2014, Bowie released a new single, "Sue (Or in a Season of Crime)," the first new single in over a year and a half. The single is a strange amalgamation of jazz and rock, ever so slightly seeming to remain firmly in the popular musical mainstream. The track is a collaboration between Bowie and German contemporary jazz composer Maria Scheider and features her 17-piece big band. About the song, Ivan Hewett, music critic for the *Telegraph*, writes, "Bowie has spent much of his life evading genre boundaries, and this song is the latest example of his genius for self-reinvention."[104] Sonically, it almost immediately evokes the sounds of *1. Outside*: Bowie's vocals sound as if they are tentative, that the melody line is being created at the spur of the moment, as the lyrics are read off of a page. What sets this piece apart is the power of Bowie's vocals, but not only in their physical power of delivery (that is, in terms of volume of voice) but rather in the depth of emotion that is conveyed through the vocals. There are portions of the vocals in which Bowie sings with such emotion—anger, actually—that the vocals are distorted. While, in this recording, Bowie's voice might not be as solid as it was in the past, his expression of anger is palpable.

The lyrics of the song suggest two personae, a narrator and antagonist, who might very well be the same person. In the first section of the song, the narrator conveys a sense of positive potential for the future: he tells Sue that he got the job, and that they will be able to purchase the house. He proclaims that they will "make it," that everything will turn out, even though Sue will have to convalesce. The next stanza suggests more of the story after some time has passed.

After some medical tests, Sue is deemed clear from disease and allowed to leave the hospital. The narrator brings Sue home, a classification of the house that pleases the narrator. In conversation with Sue, the narrator laughs at the suggestion that "Sue the Virgin" should be engraved on her (now unneeded) tombstone, since—he knows—she has a son. This is not proclaimed in anger, but rather with humor: it is ridiculous for Sue to have something like this engraved on her tombstone.

It is at this point that there seems to be a break in the narrative of the song, and an introduction to the antagonist of the piece. The antagonist is also speaking to Sue (or, more specifically, *of* Sue). He recollects touching and kissing her face, and pushing her down under water. In doing so, the antagonist says "good bye" to her: his vague descriptions of actions suggest murder. These lines are particularly poignant because of Bowie's forceful, emotion-filled singing. The singer expresses unmistakable anger here: his voice exhibits distortion, with the singer singing at the very top volume possible.

There follows another break, with a return to the voice of the narrator: he found a note written by Sue which suggests that she left with a mysterious "him," who might have been the antagonist of the middle section or someone else.

Notable is the track position of this difficult new song on a compilation of Bowie's last forty years, entitled *Nothing Has Changed*: it appears first, a position which seems to corroborate the central thesis that has been argued so far, that Bowie turns from his fans while requiring them. All of his seemingly loved hits follow, chronologically moving backward in time to the very beginning of his career. The single is accompanied by a second new song called "'Tis a Pity She's a Whore," a strange piece that uses samples of gunfire over a drumbeat that would not have been out of place on *Black Tie White Noise*, along with a vocal that sounds literally called in, as if it was recorded through an older telephone or a microphone with weak signal. Bowie is not flaunting accessibility with these new pieces.

2

The Descent of Anxiety

It is no surprise that David Bowie engages with themes of violence—particularly bodily violence—in *1. Outside* (the video for "Time Will Crawl" certainly testifies to this). As early as 1993, with the release of *Black Tie White Noise*, Bowie presents the listener with word images that bring attention to the modification of the body, violence and nihilism. In a cover of singer-songwriter Scott Walker's "Nite Flights," Bowie sings of coldness, of dogs digging into dark spaces (which, of course, connotes suspicious proceedings and criminal activity), of torn stitches and bloody and raw flesh marked by violence.

The lyrics of "Nite Flights" are suggestive of the physical and the violent, and although the song was not originally written by Bowie, his choice of this particular song shows that he was interested in conveying this subject matter at this time. Perhaps Bowie was not willing to have such subject matter directly attributed to him, choosing instead a respected, though somewhat eccentric, British singer-songwriter's work. Although the song does not directly refer to the behavior of body modification, it can be argued that it does foreshadow the grotesque details of "murder as art" in *1. Outside*. The *1. Outside* album's themes of nihilism and violence are foreshadowed here by sung phrases that refer to torn and broken stitches and choking. These lyrics are suggestive of violence as well as of destruction. This is reinforced with the image of stitches: stitches and sutures serve to close a wound, a site of destruction in itself, but those stitches are then destroyed, suggesting further damage to the wound. These lyrics are further suggestive of death with a reference to raw meat, and choking, a state of lack that leads the subject toward death. Making reference to raw meat, to fists and to choking all seem to contribute to the sense of the visceral in the song: meat is, by its very nature, connotative of substance, and it being raw conveys notions of messiness as well as contamination. The reference to fists so close to choking might suggest both strangulation and the brutal violation of the mouth or throat by a fist. The gag reflex is palpable simply by hearing the words being sung; it is a visceral experience in the "grain" of the words, not unlike literary theorist Roland Barthes' notion of the "grain of the voice."

Barthes explores what he calls the "grain of the voice," the way that he articulates the pleasure, or "individual thrill," that he feels when listening to the singing voice in particular. The "grain," for Barthes, exists in a liminal space between two communicators of meaning: music and language. The "grain" refers to the physicality or materiality of the voice, and its direct referencing of the body that produces that voice. In this case, the voice directly references the visceral body under duress. As well, the "grain" refers to a process that Barthes suggests is manifest in the relationship between the listener and the singer: Barthes listens to the *literal* inner workings of the body of the man or woman who is performing. For Barthes, this is an "erotic relationship," carrying with it the workings of desire.[1] Barthes provides some guidance for this current discussion of Bowie's lyrics: "we rarely listen to a voice *en soi*, in itself, we listen to what it says … we must in the same way learn to listen to the voice's text, its meaning, everything in the voice which overflows meaning."[2]

It is curious, then, to consider what is happening in the lyrics of Bowie's (and Walker's) "Nite Flights." The "grain of the voice" occurs here, both in Bowie's singing voice and in the words—the text—that he sings. The meaning, then, is twofold, in both the singing of the text and the medium through which the text is sung; everything in the voice that "overflows" initial meaning can only be considered a second order of meaning. The body, whether it be Bowie's, Walker's or some Other, is in the words. In displaying the "grain" so explicitly here, Bowie works to destabilize the listener, who becomes lost in the singing voice to which he or she is listening: "What is listened to … is not the advent of a signified, object of a recognition or of a deciphering, but the very dispersion, the *shimmering* of signifiers, ceaselessly restored to a listening which ceaselessly produces new ones without ever arresting their meaning."[3]

2. The Descent of Anxiety

Bowie works against the strategy of the listener to arrest the meaning of the voice: the "grain" points to this "shimmering of signifiers," and Bowie's direct appropriation of Walker's words that so substantively refer to the body, doubly *engrains* the voice. Furthermore, the words transport the listener, "lost" in the act of listening to the singing voice, to a world or context of violence and bodily harm.

Later that same year, Bowie released *The Buddha of Suburbia*, a soundtrack for the BBC2 miniseries of the same name. In an essay which appears in the liner notes of the recording, Bowie suggests that music (and one must assume he is referring to popular musical forms here) has been stifled by narrative form, something he must have realized as early as his album *Low* in 1977, with his embracing of William Burroughs' cut-up technique of lyric writing. In the cut-up technique, a set of lyrics is written, literally cut up and reassembled to create much more "difficult" sets of lyrics, destroying any sense of intended narrative or flow. The results are often surprising and lead to an interesting "shimmering of signifiers," to borrow Barthes' language. But Bowie is ultimately not satisfied with its opposite, what he himself deems violence and chaos. He continues in the liner notes essay: "modern circumstances having had a dysfunctioning capacity upon pure chronological perspective, my writing has often relied too arbitrarily on violence and chaos as a soft option to acknowledging spiritual and emotional starvation." Buried in the context of a critique of British music (which is basically how this essay functions), Bowie is admitting his own shortcomings in his commentary of society. Even so, Bowie turns to this "soft option" of violence and chaos two years later with *1. Outside*. This short passage reveals that Bowie is already thinking about the chaos of late twentieth century society at this point. He is making a direct link between violence and chaos and spiritual and emotional lack well before embarking on his strangest journey of the 1990s, the *1. Outside* album. It should be noted that Bowie returns to Burroughs' cut-up technique for *1. Outside* lyrics, after a long hiatus in the "narrative" compositional world, acknowledging how difficult the chronological perspective is in contemporary society, while being a slave to it in terms of the musical medium: organized sound through time.

Black Tie White Noise and *The Buddha of Suburbia* both feature notable musical players, who also mark something of Bowie's evolution at this point. Guitarist Reeves Gabrels is also featured in *Black Tie White Noise*, as guitarist and cowriter of the track "You've Been Around" originally written for Bowie and Gabrels' band Tin Machine. Multi-instrumentalist Erdal Kizilcay and pianist Mike Garson both appear heavily on *The Buddha of Suburbia*, and then both appear on *1. Outside*; Kizilcay is credited with co-writing the earlier album. David Richards, a producer known for his work with the British rock band Queen, and also known for producing Bowie's 1987 album *Never Let Me Down*, produced and mixed *The Buddha of Suburbia* with Bowie, and went on to co-produce *1. Outside* with Brian Eno. Eno is credited as the source for most of the unorthodox composition methods which Bowie utilizes in *The Buddha of Suburbia*. Bowie mentions Eno in the liner notes essay; he writes, "Brian's perceptions on form or purpose within culture leave most critics tap-dancing on the edge of the abyss spouting virtually nothing but fashionable blathering." It is curious that Bowie dedicates four—albeit short—paragraphs to Eno, who does not appear on the album at all. The notes demonstrate how important Eno's philosophies are for Bowie's compositions.

With this in mind, *Black Tie White Noise* can be thought of as a first attempt at new musical directions, using daring musicians sparingly (thus the call for Gabrels to contribute a single track, and, for that matter, to play so low in the mix), though much of the music on that album is quite removed from the Industrial and chaotic leanings of *1. Outside*, exploring instead jazz and polished pop styles. *The Buddha of Suburbia*, then, becomes the next step toward something new, trying new compositional strategies with new collaborators; while Garson worked with Bowie on the song "Aladdin Sane (1913–1938–197?)" in 1973, he is invited as a more substantial collaborator on *The Buddha of Suburbia*, featured on two tracks. Bowie calls Erdal Kizilcay a "longterm friend," and "more than inventive." Kizilcay had worked with Bowie from as far back as *Let's Dance*, when he helped construct the demos at the start of those sessions. Their relationship, though, seemed to sour at some time during the *1. Outside* sessions. In 2013, Kizilcay stated, "[Bowie] changed his way of being with me at the end of the recording of Outside. I don't even know why, for what reason."[4] Nevertheless, it is nearly impossible not

2. The Descent of Anxiety

to read these accolades in the liner notes without thinking that Bowie is working to secure relationships for further—and more daring—collaborations. Of course, Brian Eno also worked closely with Bowie on what has been called the Berlin trilogy in the late 1970s, which includes the albums *Low*, *"Heroes"* and *Lodger*, all produced by Bowie and Tony Visconti.

It seems, though, that the evolution of Bowie's music that occurs in the early 1990s might have its roots even further back than the Berlin trilogy. Christopher Sandford, in his book *Bowie: Loving the Alien*, suggests that the road that leads to *1. Outside* begins with Bowie's 1974 album *Diamond Dogs*. Sanford suggests that that album marks the start of Bowie's "postmodern" period, "in which life [is] not a coherent story of biography, but merely a succession of moments, each unconnected to the last or the next."[5] What marks *Diamond Dogs* as important as well is its subject matter, similar to *1. Outside*, at least in theme. First suggested as a musical based on George Orwell's novel *1984*, the album presents a dystopian future within which society lives in a state of limbo, without hope for the future. According to O'Leary, the concept for the album barely exists: "Its story is told only in abstracts: the back cover and the inner sleeve of the LP, and the record's first two songs." Rather, the album supports this extremely loose narrative through what O'Leary calls an "aural montage," not unlike the opening of Lou Reed's 1973 album *Berlin*.[6] The cover of *Diamond Dogs* features the last appearance of Bowie's Ziggy Stardust persona as a combination of human and canine, painted by the Belgian artist Guy Peellaert. Christopher Breward suggests that this presentation—both visual and aural—anticipates the darkness of the Berlin trilogy. For Breward, the cover art reflects the dystopian vision of the album, more accurately expressed by O'Leary's "aural montage." What is particularly striking is Breward's suggestion that the cover art (and the album's nihilistic themes) reflect "the deteriorating state of Bowie's mental equilibrium." The album also marked the beginning of a self-imposed exile for the singer, first to New York and Los Angeles, and ultimately to Berlin in 1976. Breward also suggests that, while it has been proposed that the material from which *Diamond Dogs* was created—and then contributed to—were firmly entrenched in the Punk movement that developed in the second half of the 1970s, "its visual codes and nihilistic nastiness did seem to herald the coming of the end of glam aesthetics for something far more disturbing."[7]

Nick Stevenson suggests that Bowie's move to Berlin allowed him to cultivate a more intentional "low profile," and to effectively destroy the Ziggy Stardust persona that had been so successful for him in the recent past: Stevenson quotes Bowie as saying, "I wanted to move out of the area of narrative and character."[8] Furthermore, Berlin seemed to provide what Bowie was desiring at the time, what Lorne Murdoch calls "its cultural reputation and interdisciplinary possibilities." Bowie was attempting to return to some of his earliest artistic roots, trying to conceive of artistic expression that was not solely musical, something particularly unusual for an artist initially recognized as a singer and musician rather than what he became later, an actor, painter and even a deft businessman.[9]

As for the Berlin trilogy, its conception came about because Bowie had run out of creative ideas, and, as a full collaborator, Eno was able to provide for him new approaches to the compositional process, "beyond the limits of rock," as Eric Tamm suggests.[10] But Eno was not the only player to contribute to the new creative expressions being unleashed in Berlin: Eno brought with him guitarist Robert Fripp, who would become an extensive collaborator with Bowie. Eno and Fripp worked together on Eno's solo material in the early 1970s. It was for the second album in the trilogy, *"Heroes,"* that Eno employed his *Oblique Strategies*, a game consisting of choosing a card from a deck and following its somewhat strange and appropriately *oblique* instructions as a creative inspiration in the composition process. Tamm recounts a humorous anecdote in which Bowie and Eno chose separate cards without revealing the instructions to each other; the instructions were completely opposed to each other, but resulted in the instrumental piece "Sense of Doubt." Of that difficult track, O'Leary writes, "it's providing background music that's also a series of disturbing sounds, making it hard to serve as aural wallpaper yet having no real sense of progression." O'Leary suggests that this track evokes Eno's original ideas for his own "Ambient" music aesthetic: its purpose is to maintain "all *sense of doubt* and uncertainty (and thus all genuine interest)."[11] Thus, Bowie and Eno work to destabilize in

2. The Descent of Anxiety

their new compositional strategies as well as in their aural interaction with their listeners.

If there was a strategy of self-imposed exile in New York, Los Angeles or Berlin, or the notion of "killing off" Bowie's earlier personae with every new project, it was made obvious with the cover of *Lodger* in 1979. The cover features Bowie, observed from above, with arms and legs splayed as if he has fallen, complete with a broken nose and a bandaged hand. The cover visible to the buyer only features his legs, presented at odd angles, connoting a terrible accident: something is not right with them. As pointed out by Stevenson, the cover is meant to be a postcard to his record company, pointing to an obvious sort of (artistic as well as literal) self-destruction. Bowie is also a plaything, a puppet for many different puppeteers. Stevenson explains, "The dangling man [on the cover] is also a performer to be worked by the industry, his fans and of course Bowie himself ... but the effect of this process can be catastrophic."[12]

There is a progression apparent in the covers of the Berlin trilogy. *Low*, the first album of the three, features a still photograph of Bowie as the narrator alien from Nicolas Roeg's 1976 film, *The Man Who Fell to Earth*, with Bowie's red hair matching the background color of the scene almost exactly. In a way, this cover looks back in time and at artifice, to the character in the film and not to Bowie—the singer—at all. The next album, *"Heroes,"* features the clearest (and cleanest) image of the three, featuring a somewhat robotic, monochrome Bowie posing, with his gaze downward and to his left. This is an iconic cover, memorable and easily reproduced (by fans and others wishing to pay tribute). It is so iconic, in fact, that Bowie himself used it for his 2013 album *The Next Day*, except that the title was simply crossed out and a large white block was placed over the younger Bowie's face, and the text "The Next Day" placed in the box in black lettering. Bowie might have suggested that the notion of narrative was problematic even at this stage of his career (that is, during the conception of the Berlin trilogy), but the covers suggest that a narrative framework is at play. The final cover, for *Lodger*, is washed out and unfocused; if *Low* looks back in time, and if *"Heroes"* evokes a certain timeless iconography, then *Lodger* points to a more chaotic future (and artifice as well: the viewer knows that Bowie is not dead or injured, as the cover purports to show). In a way, the narrative of the covers suggests that the future is not particularly bright. Even if one reads the *Lodger* cover as humorous (as Stevenson does), it is humor in the face of violence and injury, a theme that returns in Bowie's later career.

While preparing to tour in support of *1. Outside* in 1995, the singer looked back to the Berlin trilogy as a source for live music. O'Leary notes that the songs performed on the tour were mainly from the late 1970s and the Berlin trilogy, suggesting that Bowie's glam-era singles were no longer interesting for the singer.[13] Strikingly coupled with the "Berlin"-era repertoire for this tour was Bowie's choice of Industrial band Nine Inch Nails for the American leg of the tour. This was in direct response to what O'Leary claims was a brutal assessment of Bowie's brand image at this point. It was through a survey in the summer of 1995 that Bowie's management team discovered that teenagers had little sense of history or legacy, especially with regard to Bowie and his career. The survey revealed that the terms most closely associated with Bowie in the minds of the teens sampled were "gay" and "Let's Dance," not necessarily those desired by Bowie and his team. David Buckley makes the point, then, that it was the marketing division that wished to reconnect with this younger demographic, suggesting that Bowie record an album of cover songs, or rework his own songs as "new-blood hip-hop and rave." The choice of Nine Inch Nails seems less of an artistic move, then, but rather a move with a more commercial slant. Buckley does add, though, that the association with Nine Inch Nails and its leading figure Trent Reznor caused Bowie to be added to the "list of influential rock icons in the States."[14]

In 2013, the relationship between Reznor and Bowie continued to be fruitful, in that Reznor chose Bowie's album *The Next Day* as one of the better albums of the year. In an article in *Rolling Stone*, Reznor remarks, "I'm still getting new meanings out of the lyrics. What I thought was conservative production now feels forward-thinking. Like any great album, it's revealing itself to be something that wasn't what I initially thought."[15] This is not to say that Bowie's 2013 release is a commercial triumph; Reznor considers the album a "riddle" that he is still working through. It is crucial to recognize Bowie's link,

2. The Descent of Anxiety

though, through his work with Eno and the Berlin trilogy, Reznor and Bowie's later experimentation and engagement with the genre of Industrial music.

Industrial Music

In 1990, Bowie embarked on a tour call *Sound+Vision*, during which he claimed he would perform, then put to rest, the hits from his back catalogue. In anticipation of the tour, all of his albums up to that point were re-released, along with a compilation box set of singles, demos and rarities. Once it was over, *Sound+Vision* became an example of what Bowie *did not want to do next*, which may have contributed to his selection of Reznor and Nine Inch Tails as co-headliners—not to mention market and commercial considerations. More than this, though, Bowie's work with *1. Outside*, both musically and visually, on video and in live performance, indicates a radical and intentional reaction *against* his traditional fan base. If *Sound+Vision* was about appealing to the fans (which might not even be the case, but is a sympathetic stance due to the performance of established hit songs from the Bowie canon, albeit for the "last time"), the *Outside* tour was about alienating them. Bowie seems to acknowledge as much: "I slip onstage after a set by the most aggressive band ever to conquer the Top 40.... I do not do hits, I perform lots of songs from an album that hasn't been released, and the older songs I perform are probably obscure even to my oldest fans."[16] The context of Industrial music had a particular role to play in contributing to this alienation.

Jason Hanley provides a concise, if a somewhat simplistic, definition of what Industrial music is, primarily for an academic musicological audience. He writes of Industrial music as a "loud, powerful and often shocking style of avant-garde popular music" having as its musical characteristics "mechanical rhythms, harsh and distorted timbres, and dark minor key or modal harmonies." Important in his description of the musical style is the notion that all of these elements "contribute to the creation of a dystopian soundscape." It is within this context, though, that the bands are able to work against "the evils of disguised fascism and totalitarianism in general." Ministry, a band originally formed within the Chicago independent industrial scene, creates music "based around pounding drums, distorted guitars, cold synthesizer tones, and sampled voices taken from violent popular films." In addition to such distortion and noise is the addition of lead singer Al Jourgensen highly processed and highly distorted vocals; in a way, the aural "wall of sound" disorients the listener, effectively creating a sonic "wall" which taunts the listener to *dare* to continue listening. Hanley suggests that a large part of Ministry's project is to use analogy "to compare the evils of the Nazi party to what they perceive as the control of the American government." He continues to outline how the political message of Ministry can be easily misunderstood (not necessarily by any fault of Jourgensen or the band itself) and can be construed as *hate politics*. Thus, it is not a stretch to read into much Industrial music (in the 1990s) at least an implicit sense of nihilism and the alienating effects of technology. The latter theme is almost inherent in the sound of the music, with its sheer noise both in voice and instrumentation, and in its use of sampling and harsh rhythmic noises.[17]

In 1992, Ministry released the album *Psalm 69: The Way to Succeed and The Way to Suck Eggs* (the spine of the CD indicates that the actual title is Greek word for "head" and the Roman numerals for "69"). The cover itself does not refer to the band's name nor indicate the title of the album. It features an etched drawing or photo of an angelic figure seen from behind, framed by various items including an eyeball, razor blade, glove and various mechanical parts. The image is monochrome, primarily dark grey and without detail. The two most obvious characteristics of the music on this album are its extremely harsh and artificial sound, and the blatantly critical lyrics employed in the songs, often aimed at organized religion in America and Christianity in particular. The song "N.W.O.," for instance, features a sample of the 41st president of the United States, Republican George H. W. Bush (president from 1989 to 1993), saying, "A new world order." This is an explicit reference to the new state of the world as conceived by Bush after the end of the Cold War between the United States and the former Soviet Union in the second half of the twentieth century. It can also be a reference, by extension, to Republican foreign policy, the American Christian Conservative polit-

2. The Descent of Anxiety

ical lobby and power base and, if one keeps Hanley's reading in mind, it hints at the dangers inherent therein.

Musically, Ministry employs drum machines to produce very rapid rhythms, often stressing all four beats with the emphatic bass drum beat. This beat is then combined with extremely distorted guitars that are placed at the front of the mix, and also highly processed and aggressive vocals, treated with distortion effects until they are hardly recognizable as human. This results in an extremely confrontational and aggressive musical expression. Lyrically, songs like "Scare Crow" and "Psalm 69" seem to mock traditional Western spirituality. Certainly, songs like "N.W.O." make a link between conspiracy theories, oppressive, controlling and aggressive governments, and the Republican government in the United States.

"Scare Crow" invokes an image of Christ: the narrator in the song describes a state of loneliness, being in a place of vulnerability and on display. The lyrics mention crucifixion and death, damnation and rotting. On the one hand, these lyrics might be suggestive of a criticism of worldliness and a recognition of the tragedy of Christ. On the other hand, it seems that Ministry labels Jesus, upon his crucifixion, simply as a "scarecrow," hanging to scare the birds away.

The track "Psalm 69" is much more blatant in its attack against traditional Christianity. The song begins with the voice of a recognizably stereotypical minister in a high-class British accent encouraging his congregation to be seated and open their booklets to the biblical passage mentioned in the title of the song. The music begins with a choir of voices—not unlike a traditional church or "gospel" choir—acting as an accompaniment to aurally impressive guitar power chords, with various audio samples which include a man's voice expressing his praise to Jesus, before the guitars begin with even fuller force. The voluminous guitars, upon their entry to the sonic landscape of the song, establish a faster pace. The vocals enter, and are gutteral, rough and highly processed; they sound almost demonic, certainly within the "religious" context into which they enter. The lyrics are violent while evoking images of ritual, with its direct reference to the Christian ritual of Eucharist. Rather than suggesting the normal characteristics of the ritual from Christian contexts such as forgiveness and grace, the songs suggests cannibalism, vampirism and the pursuit of prey.

The band Marilyn Manson—and its eponymous lead singer—released *Antichrist Superstar* in 1996. The first single from this release was entitled "The Beautiful People," and features many of the same musical characteristics of Ministry's earlier release. Lyrically, Manson deals with violence, the nature of beauty and its links to power, and the notion of infection. The lyrics seem to encourage unconditional hatred and are critical of both organized religion (again, Christianity seems to be the target, with Manson suggesting that beauty is relative to the size of the church building for those who control it, assumedly) and capitalism. Shockingly, Manson suggests that capitalism can be—or will be—usurped by fascism. Coupled with this is Manson's apparently dim outlook on life: the narrator states that all people are infected, and that all are being consumed from within. There is no escape from this demise, but some will be more quickly and more completely consumed than others. The music is confrontational, although it does not rely on electronics as heavily as is the case with Ministry. Because of the more "organic" nature of Manson's music, it could be perceived as more human. For instance, the vocal distortion is not produced electronically, but rather by perceived rage on the part of the vocalist. The result is not music produced by an emotionless machine, but rather by an extremely expressive human.

Humanity is also expressed in Nine Inch Nails' album, *The Downward Spiral*, released in 1994. The album is very technologically-themed, with songs such as "The Becoming" describing the alienation of technology and its dehumanizing effects. The lyrics are generally nihilistic throughout the album, dealing with violence, sexuality and suffering, referencing punctures, bleeding and death from drowning. *The Downward Spiral* liner notes feature close-up photos of what appear to be paintings or some other form of sculpture art, which consist of an assembly of dirt or sand, bits of string and twigs, bird feathers and a red liquid which resembles blood. These photos, which are placed throughout the lyrics booklet, contribute to a sense of destruction and decay. The humanness is manifested in decay and destruction rather than in life and vitality: life is constantly in a state of decay and life is full of pain and points constantly toward its end.

2. The Descent of Anxiety

Bowie on Stage

Bowie seemed to make a particularly strong link with the genre of Industrial music—and its associations—in the mid–1990s, not only by asking Nine Inch Nails to tour with him, but by asking them to *co-headline* with him. The concert experience would proceed with Nine Inch Nails performing, and then Bowie joining them in a joint performance. Nine Inch Nails would then leave the stage and make way for the rest of Bowie's own band. There was no strict end to one act and beginning of the next; the transition was fluid.

British singer Morrissey opened for Bowie for a brief period, during the English leg of the *Outside* tour. He was invited to take part in this musical transition as well; in an interview as part of the Channel 4 documentary *The Importance of Being Morrissey* (aired in 2003), Morrissey mentions that he felt that the transition meant that he would "fade away." Morrissey felt that this deprived the audience of the chance to say good bye, which he suggested was somewhat "cagey."

The transition sequence is an elaborate affair in itself. The transition begins with an atmospheric and moody rendition of "Subterraneans," the instrumental from *Low* (played by Nine Inch Nails), as Bowie slowly walks out on stage. He emerges from the side and rear of the stage, and without a spotlight indicating his presence until he reaches the microphone toward the front of the stage. Bowie then begins to sing over the originally instrumental piece, using lyrics from "Scary Monsters (and Super Creeps)," the next song on the set list, which are reinterpreted as delivered from the perspective of a character from the narrative presented in *1. Outside*. The full band (that is, members of Nine Inch Nails and at least Bowie's guitarist Carlos Alomar) joins Bowie in a somewhat updated arrangement of "Scary Monsters (and Super Creeps)," sounding more like a Nine Inch Nails single than the early 1980s Bowie composition that it originally was. The band then continues with Nine Inch Nails' "Reptile," with Reznor and Bowie singing alternating lines. At one point, Bowie moves to the back of the stage, and seems to slink around, giving the spotlight almost completely to Reznor, including what amounts to performing background vocals to Reznor's emotional and aggressive vocal improvisations toward the end of the song. Appropriately enough, the bands switch to another Bowie track, the very aggressive "Hallo Spaceboy," perhaps the most blatantly "Industrial" song on the *1. Outside* album. At this point, it is clear that Reeves Gabrels, Bowie's lead guitarist, and bassist Gail Anne Dorsey, are on the stage. Gabrels is then fully featured playing the guitar introduction of Nine Inch Nails' "Hurt," to which Bowie's rich vocal performance adds a certain sense of gravity. Bowie's open and rich voice contrasts Reznor's somewhat aggressive and tight vocal presentation; the two vocalists share the front of the stage during the performance of this song, alternating the singing of phrases in the verses, and singing the chorus together. Reznor is dressed in black, while Bowie is dressed in grey, with what appears to be a light grey or beige overcoat over light colored pants; his outfit, though, is not stylish, resembling painter's rags. At the end of "Hurt," Reznor waves to the crowd and walks off of the stage, while Bowie's band begins "The Heart's Filthy Lesson," and all traces of Nine Inch Nails vanish from the stage—if not musically, then physically. The transition consists, then, of five songs, and less than 30 minutes in total duration.

Though it might appear that this performance is devoid of explicitly theatricality, in fact, Bowie is theatrical right from the start: he is not performing as "David Bowie," as the audience might expect. Of course, the audience is present in order to experience the singer in performance. Rather, they encounter Bowie instead as some sort of character from the narrative of the *1. Outside* album. This happens from the start of the transition: he is not Bowie right from his first words, but rather "Baby Grace," or whichever character he is embodying in his lyrics for "Subterraneans" and the reinterpreted "Scary Monsters (and Super Creeps)." Bowie arrives on the stage in shadows and as an addition to the already present band. On the one hand, this is a particularly respectful thing to do: it shows Bowie's respect for Reznor. On the other hand, it is shocking for the older, more established and successful artist not to demand the full spotlight upon his introduction. It was Bowie's tour after all. Perhaps Morrissey's statement regarding Bowie's "cageyness" is uncalled for; why should the less prolific artist demand the opportunity to "say good bye" to the fans? In this case, notably, the more prolific artist denies his own opportunity to "say hello." Bowie's introduction is in shadows, both in

2. The Descent of Anxiety

terms of stage lighting and in terms of the focal point of the performance. Bowie begins his portion of the concept in transition, away from the primary focus that remains on Reznor. It is unclear if the English portion of the tour followed the same transitional pattern that the American tour did. For at least one performance in London in 1995, Morrissey ended his set with his band producing feedback noise from their instruments as he walked off. Each member of the band subsequently left the stage, as the stage became engulfed by fog produced from dry ice fog machines. It seems the transition, at least on this occasion, did not include a set of duets between Morrissey and Bowie. In fact, Morrissey did not remain with the European tour for very long, claiming "illness" after a couple of weeks. As he mentions in *The Importance of Being Morrissey* documentary, "You have to worship at the temple of David when you become involved."

1. Outside and Being "Outside"

1. Outside could be considered as coming from or being a part of broader musical *milieu* of Industrial music, drawing from this atmosphere of nihilism, the alienation of humanity through technology and the criticism of traditional Western spirituality, issues which also present themselves with Bowie's *1. Outside*. In his comments to Ian Penman of *Esquire* magazine in 1995, Bowie suggests that the acts of body modification that were so prevalent at the end of the twentieth century—and continue to be common among many members of Western society through the second decade of the twenty-first century—constitute a sort of "ritual art," acting as "quasi-sacrificial." He even goes so far in suggesting that there is an increase in cults revolving around the acts of piercing, tattooing and scarification. It is unclear whether he looks at simple prevalence of the action in American society in particular, or whether he is referring to an actual cultic practice or a formalized and ritualized expression that involves body modification. Nevertheless, Bowie feels this is symptomatic of a spiritual lack in society, and suggests that the "great spiritual starving" has not been satisfied by the Judaeo-Christian ethic, that is, the prominent religious tradition of the Western world: "the Judaeo-Christian ethic doesn't seem to embrace all the things that people actually need to have dealt with in that way—and it's sort of been left to popular culture to soak up the leftover bits like violence and sex."[18] Bowie also directly engages with various manifestations of body modification in the written narrative which accompanies the album, such as the "body play" or performance art of Ron Athey and Chris Burden, and the physical transformation of the fictional "Ramona A. Stone," all while describing the investigation into the murder of a young girl, whose mutilated body is found on "artistic" display at the entrance to a museum. For many, the act of body modification in its various forms, including piercing and tattooing, is an act of transformation not only of the body, but also of the spirit. In other words, for some (and for Bowie himself, it seems), the act of body modification is a transformative ritual, replacing the traditional role of Judaeo-Christianity in Western society.

There is a sense that what Bowie was doing with *1. Outside* was not going to be accepted by records companies for fear that it would be a compelling commercial venture. Gabrels claims, though, that this was not the case: "I just thought the decision was made that the double CD *Outside* operatic set would have been insane to put out from a commercial point of view, which for me is always a questionable criterion, and that we needed to rerecord some more songs." There were not only some 35 hours of additional preliminary material recorded for the album, but also an operatic portion entitled *Inside*, as well as visual footage of the whole sessions.[19]

But there seems to be some disagreement around the idea of commercial feasibility of the material from the *1. Outside* sessions in any case: in an article for the year in review (presumably from 1995) in the online fashion magazine *Groove Culture*, the author writes, "So what's commercial about all this nasty business on *Outside*, anyway? The splattered image of Bowie on the CD cover, the cheap photo-shop Impressionism—Virgin [Bowie's record company at the time] must have loved that move."[20] Buckley suggests that the very title of the album meant to convey something else, for Bowie to be thought of as "being outside of the pop mainstream."[21]

The title *Outside* can convey many different meanings: it can simply be a title, possibly descriptive, suggesting that the object is apart from

2. The Descent of Anxiety

something, or that the object refers to something apart from it. In his unfinished essay "On Being an Artist," Brian Eno suggests two kinds of artists: an "inside" artist and an "outside" artist. Eno explains that the "inside" artist deals with what Eno calls the "internal conditions of the work," that is, the conventional elements of a musical work: its melody, harmony, rhythm, lyrics and so forth. The "outside" artist deals with the "world surrounding the work—the thoughts, assumptions, expectations, legends, histories, economic structures, critical responses, legal issues and so on and on." Eno calls all of these elements "the frame of the work," which, in turn, creates a "little world" around it. Eno continues by addressing the critics of Madonna, who suggested that she was committing too much of her attention to her fashion and lifestyle considerations compared to her music. He counters the critics with the question, "Who said music should be at the centre, and then these other things should be seen as packaging, the wrapper?" Eno questions whether music needs to be at the centre of the experience, and why it is not acceptable to consider an artist who controls other aspects of his or her project, of which only one element is the music. He ends, "Why not, further, accept the idea that the music could itself become the package?"[22] Eno's suggestions here are imperative in considering the role of the various extra-musical elements of *1. Outside* as contributors to a creation of a framing world, and a surrounding fictional context.

Ian Penman, in the *Esquire* article, suggests that Bowie himself is "outside." He explains, "Perhaps it is worth pointing out that the person he is today (Outsider: calm, collected, sane) is not the person he was ten years ago (Insider: a dancing fop making a fool of himself for the parched Good of Live Aid; treasured ... but no longer truly idolized)." Penman's terminology appears vague though, causing one to question what is so pejorative about being "inside" (or, perhaps better, what is so positive about being "outside"). Bowie was not "truly idolized" in 1995 either. In fact, Bowie suffered from an apparent lack of commercial popularity (at least by the radio-listening public); it may be more appropriate to label him "outside" because of his inaccessibility to the mainstream rather than for his repentance from Penman's suggested "inauthenticity." The first single from *1. Outside* was "The Heart's Filthy Lesson," which went to #35 and #92 in the UK and U.S., respectively. "Strangers When

We Meet" peaked only in the high 30s, and did not make the U.S. chart. The third single, "Hallo Spaceboy," remixed by UK band Pet Shop Boys, peaked at #12 on the UK chart, making it the most successful of all three singles. Nonetheless, even if only on the account of Bowie's lack of commercial airplay, the label of "outside" in reference to Bowie may be appropriate.

3
Mugging Demons for Wisdom

After Bowie's stint with Tin Machine, he reconnected with collaborator and producer Brian Eno. The essay from *The Buddha of Suburbia* makes it clear that Bowie was considering Eno's processes and philosophies in the creation of music in the 1990s. It should be noted that, of all of the solo albums in Bowie's later career, *1. Outside* is the only album produced by Eno. The two late 1990s albums, *Earthling* and *'hours...,'* are produced by Reeves Gabrels (with Mark Plati, in the case of *Earthling*), and Bowie's last three albums, *Heathen*, *Reality* and *The Next Day*, are produced by Tony Visconti, as is Bowie's most recent single, "Sue (or in a Season of Crime)," released in November 2014.

Bowie is listed as co-producer for all of these releases. It is easy to think of the 1980s output as a sort of anomaly: the late 1970s Berlin trilogy—the collaborations between Bowie and Eno, produced by Visconti—could lead directly into the early 1990s albums. The most obvious example of Bowie's strategies for negotiating his celebrity in his later career is *1. Outside*. In order to understand *1. Outside*, it is important to consider Brian Eno: his philosophies and compositional methods heavily inform this later material.

David Toop, in his book *Ocean of Sound*, talks about Ambient music and its creators, and suggests that Ambient music is often considered as escapist, an avenue for the listener to escape from the pressures of the everyday, both internal and external, psychological and political. But if this is the only role that Ambient music plays, then its creators are simply what Toop calls "mere functionaries," who only serve to placate "overheated urban info-warriors." Instead, for Toop, these creators are "shamans" who "mug demons for wisdom." The strong suggestion that sound should be escapist is anathema to the potential that music holds. In its very evolution as a recorded popular music medium, Toop concludes: "Music—fluid, quick, ethereal, outreaching, time-based, erotic and mathematical, immersive and intangible, rational and unconscious, ambient and solid—has anticipated the aether talk of the information ocean."[1] It reflects the possibilities afforded the world with the advent of these new communications technologies.

Brian Eno is considered one of the pioneers (some would say the single originator) of the genre of Ambient music; Eno has been involved with the creation and production of Ambient music since 1975 when he produced his album, *Another Green World*. From this musical background he has emerged to produce albums by David Bowie and U2, bringing to those projects his unique methods and processes, to garner the most from the artists involved and to produce imaginative and, ultimately, progressive material. This chapter examines Brian Eno as a musician and as a producer, to gain some understanding of his creative process, a process that informs the work that he produces.

First, it is important to consider biographical details of Eno's life, as well as the musical and artistic influences that inform his own musical expression and aesthetic. The notion of "contextlessness," the music of Eno's youth, *avant garde* Art music (particularly that of Cage, Satie and the Minimalists) and his education in visual arts, are of utmost importance to Eno, and thus serve to help one understand the music that is then produced by Eno. His musical philosophy and ideas, the "vertical vs. horizontal" nature of music; Eno as "non-musician"; the studio as compositional tool; musical emotion and function; and cybernetics, all come into play in Bowie's music in particular, and, of course, the music of U2 and others. Eno employs five specific methods of composition (useful in the discussion of Bowie's own works); this chapter explores some of Eno's own works, specifically *My Life in the Bush of Ghosts* (1981) and the notion of "fictitious ethnicity," *Apollo: Atmospheres and Soundtracks* (1983), *Thursday Afternoon* (1985), *Here Come the Warm Jets* (1973) and *Another Green World* (1975).

Eno's *Oblique Strategies* are also introduced with a look at Eno's involvement with David Bowie's monumental album *1. Outside*. Brian Eno was also heavily involved with David Bowie's Berlin trilogy: *Low* (1977); *"Heroes"* (1977); and *Lodger* (1979). Also, in the 1980s and early

3. Mugging Demons for Wisdom

1990s (and then in the 2000s), Eno has had much exposure in the media due to his involvement with the Irish band U2, acting as album producer beginning with *The Unforgettable Fire* (1984) and then with *The Joshua Tree* (1987), *Achtung Baby* (1991) and *Zooropa* (1993). Eno was also heavily involved with the creation of U2's *Zoo TV* tour and became a full collaborator with the band on the album *Passengers: Original Soundtracks 1* (1995).

Brian Peter George St. John le Baptiste de la Salle Eno was born on 15 May 1948, in Woodbridge, Suffolk, England. From 1953 to 1964, he was educated by the nuns and brothers of the de la Salle order in Ipswich, and later attended the Winchester Art School, where he completed his diploma in fine art in 1969.[2] It was around this period that Eno wrote a theoretical handbook entitled *Music for Non Musicians*, and established the *avant-garde* performing ensemble Merchant Taylor's Simultaneous Cabinet and then The Maxwell Demon. These ensembles performed works by Cornelius Cardew, George Brecht, Christian Wolff and La Monte Young as well as other contemporary composers. He later moved to London to live in an art commune and played with Cardew's Scratch Orchestra and the Portsmouth Sinfonia.[3] Eric Tamm comments that the Portmouth Sinfonia was "committed to high-camp satire and consisting of non-musicians and musicians playing instruments they didn't know how to play, stumbling through deliberately butchered versions of the classical repertoire."[4]

In 1971 while in London, Eno was invited to join the band Roxy Music, from which he departed in 1973, due to conflict with band leader Brian Ferry. After meeting with guitarist Robert Fripp, Eno released the collaboration entitled *No Pussyfooting* in November of 1973. Three months later, *Here Come the Warm Jets* was released. After recording and releasing three albums, Eno collaborated with painter Peter Schmidt to create the *Oblique Strategies* (1975), a series of cards designed to spur creativity and new thinking. In 1977, Eno began a very important collaboration with David Bowie, producing *Low*, *"Heroes"* and *Lodger* in Berlin. Between 1975 and 1980, Eno continued the development he began with *Discreet Music* and *Another Green World* (both from 1975) with many albums employing the concept of "ambient" music. In 1980, Eno began working with Canadian producer and engineer Daniel Lanois.

This association culminated in the production of four highly successful and critically praised albums by the Irish band U2 (he and Lanois continued to produce U2's albums in the 2000s). After a fallow span of nearly 15 years, Eno released *Nerve Net* in 1992, a solo album that fused "electronically-treated dance music, eccentric English pop, cranky funk, space jazz, and a myriad of other, often dazzling sounds."[5] He returned to Ambient music with *The Shutov Assemby* (1992) and *Neroli* (1993), and caused an anxious stir in the media when he worked with David Bowie on *1. Outside* in 1995. Many hoped that the output would be equal in scope to what was produced in the Berlin trilogy; although critically accepted, it was only a modest commercial success. Becoming a full collaborator with U2 in 1995, Eno released *Passengers: Original Soundtracks 1*. In 1997, Eno released *The Drop* to almost no notice, which may be due to the possibility that his solo work had been overshadowed by the impact he has made with his recent collaborations with both U2 and David Bowie. It is worthwhile nonetheless to explore the nature of Eno's music and thinking about music, and it is through the music and thought that influenced him that one can begin to discover where this nature originated.

When discussing influences on the music of Brian Eno, one may be tempted to ask simply *how* influential a certain context or composer was. Tamm states, "Eno's favorite adjective is 'interested.' The word denotes to him more than a merely intellectual flirtation with a passing idea; when he is interested in something, it has awakened that sense of wonder, and he is palpably engaged in it, fully, existentially, and personally."[6] This insight would certainly set the doubter's mind at ease, placing much importance on any elements that have been labeled as influences. Tamm expounds on the following: the notion of "contextlessness"; the rock music of Eno's youth; *avant-garde* art music (specifically that of John Cage and Erik Satie as well as the composers of the Minimalist movement) and his education in the visual arts.

Growing up in the small town of Woodbridge, England, Eno's first musical influences came from two U.S. air bases located close by. Because of the town's proximity to the military bases, many local cafés had a jukebox well stocked with American popular music. This music was quite different from the British music of the time (consisting of Cliff

3. Mugging Demons for Wisdom

Richard and Tommy Steele, described by Eno as "very poor imitations of the larger American stars").[7] For Eno, the American music was alien; it was an Other to the British music that was around him.

> It plopped from outer space, in a sense. Now, in later life I realized that this removal of context was an important point in the magic of music. One of the things I've been concerned with quite a lot is to deliberately dismantle or shift contexts around so that something comes from an area where you didn't expect it, or something appears and it has a certain mysteriousness to it.[8]

It is this mystery resulting from "contextlessness" that Tamm suggests Eno has tried to capture in most of his music.

Of the popular music of the 1960s, Eno has specifically mentioned the New York band The Velvet Underground and the British band The Who as musical influences. Tamm explains that context had become more important to the teenaged Eno who had grown up amid the "contextlessness" of the British countryside:

> the Velvet Underground ... were directly associated with the pop art movement of Andy Warhol—who in 1965 used them to provide the music for his moveable multimedia show, the Exploding Plastic Inevitable. Context was also important to the Who, who began as heroes of the Mod scene in England and were among the first to create concept albums—a development that culminated in their rock opera of 1969, *Tommy*.[9]

In addition to the popular music of the time, art music also had an influence on the young composer, especially the ideas of John Cage (that "everything we do is music"), Erik Satie and the Minimalists.[10] In the 1960s, Eno read Cage's *Silence* (a collection of lectures and writings dating from 1939 to 1961). The effect of this book on Eno's compositional style and thought processes regarding music was sufficiently profound to warrant a closer look at Cage.

One of Cage's series of lectures is entitled "Composition as Process," a concept that would be cemented in Eno's mind by his art school experience. In a lecture given at Darmstadt in September 1958, Cage discusses the processes occurring in his *Music of Changes*. For Cage, "structure" is the formal division of a musical piece into sections, while "method" is what he calls the "note-to-note procedure." These two elements of a piece, along with "material," or the actual sounds and lack thereof of a composition, are the concerns of the mind rather than the heart: "one's idea of order as opposed to one's spontaneous actions." He also suggests that method and material, together with form, are equally concerns of the heart. For Cage, composition is an activity of integrating these opposites, of the heart and mind, the irrational and rational, "bringing about, ideally, a freely moving continuity within a strict division of parts, the sounds, their combination and succession being either logically related or arbitrarily chosen."

In Cage's earlier work, *Construction in Metal*, structure, method and materials were subject to organization, while the form was free. Later, with *Sonatas and Interludes*, only the structure was organized, based on rhythm rather than the frequency of sound (tonality) so as to allow for the absence of materials as well as their presence (in other words, silence is accounted for). Cage concludes, "the deduction may be that there is a tendency in my composition means away from ideas of order towards no ideas of order." This move away from order culminated in *Music of Changes*, where chance operations are introduced into the body of the structure, so that the very structure becomes indeterminate. Being indeterminate but still present, the structure is no longer necessary but can be useful in the determination of density, the materials potentially active in the continuity, and also in the determination of the beginning and ending of the compositional process. So structure is no longer a part of the compositional means nor is it a way of integrating the mind and heart, but rather a view of activity characterized by process and essentially purposelessness. Thus, the mind is present in the process, yet no longer allowed to control the outcome. Cage asks, "What does it do, having nothing to do? And what happens to a piece of music when it is purposelessly made?" He then asks how silence is perceived by this now freed mind. Formerly, for Cage, silence functioned only as a space between sounds, useful for the composer in creating a tasteful piece, in separating sound and allowing one to perceive the relationships between those sounds. Furthermore, silence allowed for expression, where silence worked like punctuation in a sentence. Silence also worked to define a structure, by its introduction or an act of interruption. If silence no longer has any of these goals, it is, for Cage, not silence at all, but *ambient* sound. If the mind is no longer allowed to control, it is free instead to

3. Mugging Demons for Wisdom

listen to sounds a they exist.¹¹ This concept of "ambient sound" is very important in understanding Eno's concept of "ambient music." The "problem" of purposeless music is solved by Cage's reassignment of the mind, now freed by purposeless music, to listening to silence.

Erik Satie has another view of music: he assigns a purpose to it, although certainly not in the traditional sense, but rather music "like furniture." Where Cage wanted the listener to be engaged in the background sound as "ambient sound," so Satie moves the whole of music into the background. In *Silence*, Cage also has an imaginary conversation with Satie, with Satie's comments being taken from his writings. It is here that Cage quotes Satie speaking about "music as furniture," with music existing as part of the environment, the noises that make up the mundane surroundings of the running of a common household. This "music as furniture" does not impose or dominate, but nevertheless fills the space between those who might be in its presence (working in the same ways as silence). For Satie, this sort of music would be functional inasmuch as it would neutralize awkward silences between diners in conversation, or eliminate outside, unwanted noises: "To make such music would respond to a need."¹²

In the conversations with Cage, Satie makes a claim that is later made by Eno, that of "non-musicianship": "Take the *Fils des Etoiles* or the *Morceaux en forme de poire* ... it is clear no musical idea presided at the creation of these works."¹³ Eno himself had much praise for the French composer: "He was a systems composer, you know, planning chord changes by numerical techniques. In the midst of extraordinary chromatic experimentalism, with everyone doing bizarre things, he just wrote these lovely little pieces of music."¹⁴ For Eno, the discovery of Cage's *Silence* and the music of Satie was a step on the road to appreciating the Minimalist music of Terry Riley and Steve Reich. About Reich's phase tape pieces, Eno suggests that something happens when one listens to them: the listener ceases to hear information which is repeated several times. Instead, the brain only recognizes portions of information that changes. He concludes, "The amount of material there is extremely limited, but the amount of activity it triggers in you is very rich and complex."¹⁵

Later, the music of La Monte Young taught Eno an important lesson in the potency of repetition in music. In a 1974 lecture, Eno recounts his own performance of Young's piece *X for Henry Flynt* from around 1967, in which the performer is instructed to produce a single sound over and over for an unspecified amount of time. Eno met the requirements by playing large clusters of notes on the piano with his forearms, once each second, for an hour. He suggests that listeners, once they got used to hearing the massive wall of sound produced by the 50-note cluster, would become bored. But those who remained listening to the performance would become increasingly absorbed in it. Once their attention was captured, they would notice any small changes as drastic. All slight changes are noticed as major compositional elements, contributing to the overall form of the piece, its emerging melodies and rhythms. For Eno, then, error is welcome in his work. Further, he holds to a law that has informed much of his work since, that "repetition is a form of change."[16]

Between 1964 and 1966, Eno attended the Ipswich Art School, where much of his philosophy regarding art and creativity was established. The Cage idea of "composition as process" was presented to Eno as "process over product," and it was under these conditions that the creator thrived. Tamm recounts Eno's first recorded piece created on Ipswich's taping equipment, created by recording the sounds of a metal lampshade being struck, and then altering the speed of the tape, resulting in a pronounced rhythm of beats.[17] In his painting projects, he was continually fascinated by the processes, each painting becoming a performance piece in itself. Ultimately, this led him to music, which he felt had always been a "performance art" involving real-time processes. Tamm explains that Eno was most interested not in the performance aspect of the music but rather the potential of its tools. Using a tape recorder made the process of composer similar to the process of painting, allowing the composer to manipulate time directly, transforming music into a "plastic art."[18]

Eno has been an interesting subject for interview over the years because of his fascination with process and his ability to explain his own compositional processes in a clear and articulate manner. Although his art school education did influence him, with its emphasis on "process over product," Eno felt that the input (that is, the musical material of

3. Mugging Demons for Wisdom

the composition) was important. Eno suggests that the various sorts of "systems music" are particularly boring, which points to a failure of the legacy of Cage and others. Eno concludes that it is not the fault of the systems (in that some are less elegant than others) but the fault of the content itself.[19] Even with Eno's affinity for "contextlessness," music as "ambient" sound and "process over product," the content of the music is of utmost significance.

To describe the music of Brian Eno in simple terms is difficult, due to the complexity of influences on the composer and the variety of styles in which he has worked and to which he has contributed. Tamm has outlined various elements in Eno's music and, while the list may not be exhaustive, it may be a good place to begin an exploration. Following in the footsteps of the Minimalists, Eno is trying to change the way that his audience listens to music. The conventional method of listening to music is similar to reading a book: in English, the reader generally begins at the top left of a written page and reads, following the words to the right until the end of the line. The reader then moves down a line and begins reading at the left and moves right. There is a starting point and ending point to the text. There is a teleological progression in reading, as there is in conventional music. Thus, music can be thought of "horizontal": one listens in the same way as one reads, across the page and through time. Eno, though, wants the listener to consider "vertical music," music that should be considered all at once rather than over time. "Vertical music" allows a listener to enter or exit the act of listening at any time. Ultimately, the "logical" progression of music is of no importance. Narrative might exist, but it exists in the absence of teleology (Bowie's *1. Outside* as a non-linear narrative comes to mind here).[20] In the essay "Generating and Organizing Variety in the Arts," Eno writes about the "fade" ending that occurs at the end of a piece of recorded music. According to Eno, such an ending implies that the piece continues, but out of the hearing range of the listener. The music which the listener hears is only a portion of a piece of music which is hypothetically continuing, and thus the piece is not necessarily directional: its progress does not end with a resolution as the piece continues out of the range of the listener's hearing. There is no way for the listener to know whether the piece is resolving or not.[21]

David Bowie in Darkness

When Eno used the term "non-musician" in reference to himself, he was not placing himself in the category of one who could not perform or compose music. Rather, the term refers to his rejection of certain traditional artistic conventions and ideas regarding musicianship. Eno explains that it was the notion of virtuosity in music that was problematic, in that there was no other way of being a serious creator of music without being virtuosic. Eno, while emerging from the visual art world, also spent time in the Rock music world (as a member of Roxy Music and with his early albums firmly entrenched in that context). He would not refer to himself as a musician, though he is a keyboard player. Instead, he considers himself *ingenious* rather than manually skilled in an instrument. He is able to manipulate sound, whereas the conventional musician has what Eno calls "digital skill"; in the context of keyboard playing, this refers to skill in the fingers. Eno would consider himself skilled in terms of imagination instead.[22]

The lack of conventional musical technique forces Eno to be creative. Rather than relying on technique, he relies on ingenuity and skill, particularly in the area of the recording studio: the recording studio is Eno's primary instrument. Eno has singled out artists whom he feels have realized the potential of the recording studio: Glenn Gould, Jimi Hendrix, Phil Spector, The Beach Boys, The Beatles and others.[23] The studio has allowed Eno to take a "sculptural" approach to recording: the studio composer takes pieces around him or her, combines them in novel ways and sees what results from such combinations. If something does not work, it is erased and the process begins again. This is not much different from how a painter works.[24] Eno also places a philosophical importance on the studio and recorded music. Before the advent of the recording studio, the musical work disappeared when its performance was finished, and so it existed only in time (this remains the case in the live performance of music). Recording removes music from the passage of time and fixes it in space. Music is reified in the process of recording. As soon as the abstract music, present in one moment and absent in the next, is reified, the listener is able to become familiar with details of the music only obvious with repeated exposure to the exact same recorded music. The listener might enjoy details of the recording not intended by the composer or musicians: mistakes, ambient noise

3. Mugging Demons for Wisdom

and so forth. What recording affords the composer is the inclusion of sonic material that would not be obvious to the listener on the first (and only) exposure to a piece, but made evident upon subsequent listens.[25]

Eno's attention to detail can be accounted for by the advantages that a recording studio can provide for an artist. It is in such an environment that the artist can combine the roles of composer, lyricist, arranger, producer, engineer, and performer. Tamm concludes,

> Eno's music—his progressive rock to some degree, and his ambient music to a very great extent—is a music in which timbre and sound texture are accorded an extremely high level of importance. Much of the meaning of Eno's music hinges on very subtle factors having to do with the vertical spectrum of tone color; the exact hues of a sound, down to almost imperceptible shifts in overtone structure, are for Eno the substance of the music itself.[26]

It is not only in his own music that Eno uses the resources of the recording studio to the greatest extent, but also in the projects on which he has collaborated or produced. Eno speaks about the recording of his first solo album, *Here Come the Warm Jets* (1973), and the coordination that went on during recording:

> I assembled musicians who normally wouldn't work together in any real-life situation. And I got them together merely because I wanted to see what happens when you combine different identities like that and you allow them to compete. My role is to coordinate them, synthesize them, furnish the central issue which they all will revolve around, producing a hybrid ... [The situation] is organized with the knowledge that there might be accidents, accidents which will be more interesting than what I had intended.[27]

This is a process that Eno has used on other projects like Bowie's *1. Outside* with great success, and it is only in the environment of the recording studio that such a luxury is afforded. But Eno's reliance on the recording studio and its environment apparently has limits. Upon the opportunity to spend three days working with one of the world's most advanced recording console (costing $2,000 a day in studio fees in 1999), Eno seemed to discover the negative aspects of technology. Eno realized the potential of the recording studio to become an instrument in itself, in its ability to transform sound into a malleable material, allowing the composer to create new worlds of sound. The studio offered the creator of music possibilities that did not exist previously. But Eno seemed to have some reservations with the movement of musical creation from the purview of "digital skill" to an intellectual pursuit. For some reason, Eno recognized that much creativity is "stored" in the muscles: musicians spend years practicing and developing these "digital skills." If this muscular activity is removed from the process of creation, Eno suggests that audiences will not respond to the creation, and the very act of creation will be stunted. Thus, even such "intellectual," recording studio-based musicians invest in older electronics with various knobs and buttons, in order to reengage with the physical or "muscle" aspects of musical creation. This tendency is what Eno refers to as the "revenge of the intuitive." The weaknesses and limits of the traditional tools have become their cherished qualities. As much of one's experience in the world is mediated, one becomes increasingly sensitive to the characteristics inherent in these media: "In the end, the characteristic forms of a tool's or medium's distortion, of its weakness and limitations, become sources of emotional meaning and intimacy."[28]

Interestingly, emotion and intimacy are not usually associated with the music of Brian Eno. Tamm states,

> If the emotional component is strong, however, it is usually present as a kind of deep undercurrent: it does not burst from the surface of the music or confront the listener with unambiguous, expressionistic intent. This is, by and large, as true of his progressive rock as of his ambient music, and it may be construed as reflecting a "classical"—as opposed to "romantic"— strain in Eno's temperament.[29]

This sentiment is reflected in the music that Eno enjoys, particularly a music devoid of emotional surprises and which "presented an emotional situation that held steady for quite a long time ... a 'steady-state' kind of music."[30] Whether these views have changed in recent years is uncertain, although the projects of which he acted as a producer (especially those of U2) would suggest that they have.

Eno's philosophy of the function of music is similar to the views put forward by Satie and Cage, with music as "furniture," freeing the mind to perform other tasks. Whereas certain genres of music seem to predestine their place in the mind of the listener (for instance, many aggressive popular music's wish to be at the forefront of the listener's mind, while so-called "elevator music" wishes to take a background place), Eno wishes to create music which could be moved into and out

3. Mugging Demons for Wisdom

of by the listener: the listener is free to engage in other "mindful" activities *while* listening. The listener need not be totally invested in the process of listening, but can accomplish other tasks, employing his or her attention onto other activities.[31] Douglas Rushkoff, in his book, *Cyberia*, discusses Eno's music in terms of being a form of "anti–Muzak." For Rushkoff, it was Eno who inspired the whole genre of "cyber music" by taking the emphasis away from structure and placing it on texture.[32] Eno was inspired by Muzak to the extent of using similar techniques but for different purposes. In the liner notes to Eno's 1979 album *Ambient I: Music for Airports*, Eno writes:

> Whereas the extant canned music companies proceed from the basis of regularizing environments by blanketing their acoustic and atmospheric idiosyncrasies, Ambient Music is intended to enhance these. Whereas conventional background music is produced by stripping away all sense of doubt and uncertainty (and thus all genuine interest) from the music, Ambient Music retains these qualities. And whereas their intention is to "brighten" the environment by adding stimulus to it (thus supposedly alleviating the tedium of routine tasks and leveling out the natural ups and downs of the body rhythms) Ambient Music is intended to induce calm and space to think. Ambient Music must be able to accommodate many levels of listening attention without enforcing one in particular; it must be as ignorable as it is interesting.

Eno's cybernetic approach to music is fleshed out in his essay "Generating and Organizing Variety in the Arts." It is here that Eno defines the term "variety" by using cybernetics (or the science of organization) as originated by W.R. Ashby in his book *An Introduction to Cybernetics* from 1956. For Eno (and the cyberneticists), "variety" in a system refers to "the total range of its outputs, its total range of behavior."[33] Eno suggests that most *avant-garde* pieces begin with an "algorithm," or "system," a set of instructions in order to achieve a particular goal. In Eno's book *A Year with Swollen Appendices*, he adds:

> Since reading this essay, Stewart Brand has pointed out a different sense of the word "algorithm." This may be the result of a gradual change of usage over the 25 years since [Stafford] Beer used it in his original text [*Brain of the Firm: The Managerial Cybernetics of Organization*]. Stewart says, "I think that 'algorithm' does not require a goal, as Beer stated. It is much more like the instruction or instruction set that made the pieces you describe come to life ('hold a chord till you can't hear it'). My American

Heritage Dictionary defines 'algorithm' as 'A mechanical or recursive computational procedure.'"[34]

While the original definition of "algorithm" limits the amount of choices available to the performer, as they must reach a certain goal, Eno suggests that pieces begin with a kind of instruction called a "heuristic," which is a set of instructions that lead to an *unknown* goal (rather than a *certain* goal), and do so through exploration. In order for this process to be successful, there must be a system of response in place, which continually evaluates the progress made on the journey toward an unknown goal. As the process continues, any anomalies or irregularities must result in adjustments in the piece: the environment informs the structure of the piece itself. If the anomalies or irregularities make the continuing of the process untenable, then the system of response must find another way to organize the piece, for instance, on change rather than immovability.[35]

Compositional Techniques

It is only through Eno's actual music, and the processes accompanying it, that these ideas are made clear. In an interview with Glenn O'Brien in 1978, Eno talks about his specific methods of composing, which includes: the piecing together of compatible musical ideas; sonic texture creation in the studio; setting deliberate practical constraints on music making; creating music by assembling a certain group of musicians together; and using mathematical and structural means. One very interesting and influential method of composition for Eno is to use a deck of cards he created entitled *Oblique Strategies*.

Eno explains his first method of composition, what he calls the "traditional category." Eno carries with him a recording device (at the time of O'Brien's interview, in 1978, this was a microcassette recorder). Whenever Eno thinks of a lyric idea, or a rhythm or melody, he would put it on record, accumulating thousands or aural "notes" in this way. From this library of ideas, Eno would go on to see if they could fit together in some way, and thus move the more developed pieces of sound to the "demo" stage, where they will hopefully become the seeds for

3. Mugging Demons for Wisdom

future pieces. These demos are then filed away for future reference. Through these processes and work flows, Eno orders sound.[36]

My Life in the Bush of Ghosts (1981) was a collaboration between Eno and David Byrne (from the band Talking Heads). The idea of the album was developed through a conversation between Byrne, Eno and Jon Hassel. Hassel had been working on a concept called "Fourth World" music, a new kind of "classical music of the future." For this new genre, Hassel proposed a new kind of structure and a new musical vocabulary with which to talk about this structure, in the face of what Hassel calls the "Eurocentric tradition." The goal would be to break the hold that conventional Western Art Music has over serious artistic expression.[37] It was through Hassel that Eno and Byrne were introduced to non–Western music, which became a substantial element of the sound of the album. The idea of creating a fictitious ethnicity (which the music of *My Life in the Bush of Ghosts* suggests to the listener) was also a concept discussed by the three artists, and one which was made more "authentic" by Eno and Byrne's use of samples of both exotic and carefully chosen domestic sounds. *My Life in the Bush of Ghosts* succeeds in ordering sounds and ideas to create a new aural world.

Eno also works intentionally to create "vertical music," in which the listener devotes his or her attention "along the timbral rather than the temporal dimension" of the music.[38] Eno recounts an interesting experiment which revealed to him the nature of the ordering of sound: he had taken a portable digital tape recorder to Hyde Park in London, where he recorded a duration of ambient noise. He decided to take a three-and-a-half minute portion of the recording and learn it by listening to it repeatedly. Whenever he had the opportunity he would listen to the recording and was able, after time and repeated listenings, to predict when certain sound events would occur: he began to remember the order of sounds and their duration. He concluded, "Something that is as completely arbitrary and disconnected as that, with sufficient listenings, becomes highly connected." Eno felt that the listener could imagine without much difficulty that such a recording was constructed once he or she has discovered the pattern, even though the listener is hearing a recording of random ambient sound. This exercise changed Eno's method of listening.[39] Like the Hyde Park recording, one can begin to appreciate such a piece only after spending time with it: the minute changes are what are important.

It is both the expansive and the minute that are important in Eno's music. Ambient music is fundamentally textural, and Eno uses the studio as his sketchpad in developing the sound surfaces. While Eno employs "field recording" as a catalyst for creativity, he will also spend time in the studio using instruments or technologies with which he has not extensively engaged. Playing with these various elements, Eno will create a sound surface or texture that suggests a mood that will, in turn, suggest a lyric of some sort.[40]

In 1983, Eno (with Daniel Lanois and Roger Eno) released *Apollo: Atmospheres and Soundtracks*, an album of music that accompanied a documentary of the Apollo missions to the moon. The music itself consists of sustained pedal points, ghost-like sliding figures in the higher range and very low rumbling frequencies below. In the liner notes of the album, Eno comments that the work "afforded an opportunity to explore the feelings of space travel: being weightless, seeing the night-time campfires of Saharan nomads from high above the earth, looking back to a little blue planet drifting alone in space, looking out into the endless darkness beyond, and finally, stepping onto another planet." Eno hoped that the music would provide a mood that would suggest an absolutely new experience for those listening.

Eno suggests a third method of composition to O'Brien, in which he sets deliberate constraints on the creative process; the constraints can involve the length of the piece, the formal outline or the timing of musical events. Eno suggests that a piece can be mapped on a piece of graph paper beforehand, a reified graph before its somewhat abstract interpretation.[41]

Thursday Afternoon was a work commissioned by Sony Japan in 1984, consisting of a video and accompanying soundtrack created specifically for release on compact disc. The piece consists of 61 minutes of uninterrupted music (comprising a single track on the recording). To arrive at the results that Eno desired, he needed to slow the recorded sounds down by fifty percent or more, and, in doing so, caused initially short, somewhat insignificant, events to take on a much larger proportion of the work. The music is built up like some of Eno's other sound

3. Mugging Demons for Wisdom

textures, but with a number of "sound-events" occurring for a certain period of time, and then vanishing. Eno presents all the sound-events of the piece within the first fifteen minutes, and the piece maintains a static tonality throughout. Non-musical constraints are inherent in the composition since it was commissioned for release on compact disc, which, on one hand, freed the composition from the trappings of two sides of around twenty minutes (as on a conventional vinyl record), but, on the other, constrained it to a single track of sixty minutes (a capacity which was expanded to seventy-four to eighty minutes as the compact disc specifications evolved, well after the timing of Eno's project). Furthermore, the music was required to function as an accompaniment to visual images.

Another of Eno's processes is to work with a group of musicians who would not normally work together.[42] This process was most evident on *Here Come the Warm Jets* (1973), but a similar process occurred on *Another Green World* (1975). The musicians were encouraged to enter the studio with no preconceptions or preparation. Without knowledge of how the musicians worked together, the methods would be impossible to predict. The resultant music from the coming together of these disparate players would be ultimately surprising and unable to be predetermined. The only goal would be that of experimentation: "And if something failed, we tried again."[43]

Although Eno often uses improvisation as a creative tool in the studio, he does not think of it as an end in itself. Rather, he always wants to control and constrict chaos. Ultimately, Eno enjoys simple structures and stable rhythm tracks because they can act as a "container" for important information (like the grid on a piece of graph paper acts as a "container" for the graph line itself).[44]

Finally, Eno has made attempts to use mathematical systems—and structural systems—as bases for his work, but he claims that these attempts have not been successful (his criticisms of "systems" music suggest his ambivalence toward this compositional technique).[45] To provide an example of a work using or suggesting this process is difficult, although one might argue that *Thursday Afternoon*'s constraints might have made the work suited to this kind of compositional process. Eno's own confession of a lack of success in works constructed by this method might explain the difficulty in finding an instance of its use.

The *Oblique Strategies* were written in 1975, and were subsequently published multiple times with revisions and additions. The function of these so-called "dilemmas" (the set of cards has the subtitle "Over One Hundred Worthwhile Dilemmas") was "simply to bring the consciousness one has as a listener to one's consciousness as a composer—to deal with things in a more *studied* way." The *Strategies* come in a deck of cards, each card having an axiom written on it. The cards were often uncovered in times of extreme pressure during the creative process. In many cases, the cards seemed uncanny in their ability to supply the instructions that were needed in order to inspire creativity: "Even on occasions when the card [that is, the card's meaning] would have been open, in other circumstances, to a number of interpretations, it seemed that everybody reached the same conclusion about it."[46]

Recently, rather than resorting to the *Oblique Strategies* as a compositional aid, Eno has used similar but new methods for the encouragement of creativity. Bowie's *1. Outside* was a project that required Eno (as producer) to create certain personae for each person involved in its creation. It was by such a process that Eno wanted to create a new way of thinking about recording: "Instead of facing an amorphous mass of time defined only by a release date, most of it spent in a roomful of electronics, we think in particular times, places and people. We think in terms of constructing original events that have recordings as their output. We build recording situations around events." The "event" information was printed and distributed to each person to interpret as they choose (as with the *Oblique Strategies*). Reeves Gabrels, for instance, was placed into the role of a musician in a new "Neo-Science" band playing in an underground club in the Afro-Chinese ghetto in Osaka, Japan. The characterization continues, but does not dictate to the musician exactly what must be played. Rather, vague and quite visual descriptions of the music are conveyed: "You are in no particular key—making random bursts of data which you beam into the performance."[47] The process of designing new games, and then playing those games, is Eno's strength, showcasing ingenuity rather than "digital skill." It is through such processes that creativity is sparked and Eno's creative vision is realized.

3. Mugging Demons for Wisdom

The relationship between Eno and Bowie has produced much interesting and original music. Eno received much critical acclaim for his collaborations with Bowie on the Berlin trilogy of albums. *Low* (1977), *"Heroes"* (1977) and *Lodger* (1979) were the fruits of the collaboration, which came as a result of Bowie hearing *Another Green World*; like his 1990s work, the Berlin trilogy was spawned because of Bowie's need for creative rejuvenation.

Like *Another Green World*, *Low* is organized with its more uptempo songs on the first side of the vinyl record release, followed by the more sombre and ambient music on the second side. Of the eleven tracks on the album, only one, "Warszawa," is listed as being co-written by Eno. Eno's musical character is certainly evident in the music of the second side, but Bowie also makes his presence known. Interestingly, Bowie's composition style is quite different from that of Eno. In some ways, Bowie compositional style is diametrically opposed to Eno's philosophies, which make their successful collaborations curious. For instance, Tamm suggests that Eno almost always constrains his melodic material to the diatonic scale, whereas Bowie enjoys less conventional melodic material and harmonic settings. Furthermore, Bowie's compositions are teleological and conventionally "active," whereas Eno's are not. In terms of sonic material, Bowie's compositions are generally busier and denser than Eno's. As for "Warszawa," Eno created the instrumental tracks in the studio before Bowie added the vocals. Tamm suggests that this piece is slow and brooding, featuring various tones and drones stacked into harmonies in ways that would not be expected in Eno's solo work. Such uncharacteristic compositional elements demonstrate Bowie's compositional influence on Eno. The producer recounts his saving of a piece entitled "Art Decade," which has been attributed solely to Bowie (which may not have been the case): "Art Decade" began as a tune played simultaneously by Eno and Bowie on piano, which, when recorded, Bowie found particularly unsatisfying, and the recording was thus discarded. During one of Bowie's absences, Eno retrieved the recording and began to layer instruments on top of what they had originally recorded, and Bowie approved of the result. They then began to work on the track, adding even more instrumentation, resulting in the version of "Art Decade" that is included on the album.[48]

David Bowie in Darkness

The second album that came from further sessions in Berlin was "*Heroes*." As on *Low*, the first side contains more upbeat music, and the second side, though it is opened and closed by conventional rock songs, consists of three instrumental tracks that meld into one another. "Sense of Doubt" is one of the instrumental tracks on the second side of the album. Eno used the *Oblique Strategies* to create this haunting piece: the musicians took turns recording overdubs on the piece, approaching the task as if it was a game. The *Oblique Strategies* were meant to be followed as closely as possible, even if they were opposed to each other, which happened to be the case. Referring to the *Oblique Strategies* cards that were drawn, Eno states, "Effectively mine said, 'Try to make everything as similar as possible,' ... and his [Bowie's] said, 'Emphasize differences.'"[49] When interviewed about *1. Outside*, Eno reminisces about some of Robert Fripp's guitar playing on *"Heroes."* What was most appealing to Eno was the simplicity in some of the musical material the guitarist produced (which would fit into Eno's own musical character): Eno suggests that such playing is the result of either a very skilled player or a rudimentary player, but not one in between. Eno believes that the results are, in fact, only possible coming from good players: it is their restraint that Eno finds most attractive. A less than ideal player would want to impress and thus never produce simple musical material.[50]

Lodger, from 1979, is of a different sort than the previous two albums. Eno seems to suggest that the project was not as successful as it started out to be, and the results were not as satisfying. Tamm suggests that Eno and Bowie argued about many of the tracks resulting in many compromises that were detrimental to the results.[51]

The chapter began with comments from Toop regarding Ambient music as escapist and as an avenue for the listener to escape from the pressures of the everyday. And if this is the only role that Ambient music plays, then its creators are "mere functionaries," who only serve to placate "overheated urban info-warriors." For Toop, these Ambient musicians are "shamans who travel to gruesome corpselands in order to mug demons for wisdom."[52] Taking into account Eno's appreciation of Cage and Satie, with their notions of ambient sound, and Eno's obvious progression from those initial concepts, Eno's music may be a kind of reflection of the existing, actual "ambient world," as Cage would call it, and

3. Mugging Demons for Wisdom

not escapist at all. It is possible that Toop's "gruesome corpselands" may be the world itself. As a travelling shaman, Eno would probably be happy; to assault demons, he would be discontent. Eno is too subversive for a frontal assault, and would probably consider that there would be no wisdom to be gained from such unsightly victims. To clarify this point, the *Oblique Strategies* were conceived not as a head-on approach to problem-solving in the studio, but rather as a series of prompts. It is the self, through some inventive suggestions from a deck of cards, that ultimately solves the problem, and it is the self that ultimately holds wisdom (no demons needed for consultation).

4
The Culture of Body Modification

In "The Diary of Nathan Adler," a narrative printed as part of the liner notes to *1. Outside*, David Bowie writes about the blood-rituals of the Viennese castrationists in the 1970s and the performance art, or "body play," of Chris Burden and Ron Athey. As he makes clear in his comments to Ian Penman in the *Esquire* article from October 1995, Bowie suggests that the increase of piercing and tattooing that took place in the 1990s, from the common piercing of ears ranging to the more macabre forms of "body art," such as public displays of bloody self-mutilation, are an indicator of a new spirituality. Bowie is referring to the behavior of self-mutilation as a substitute for the Judeo-Christian ethic in satisfying a deep spiritual longing in society. By also discussing the "ritual art" of Burden and Athey, Bowie is asking if there is a discernable line between pathological self-mutilation and culturally sanctioned body modification and public "artistic" displays. Bowie is also exploring the ritual nature of these activities and how they define and contribute to the spirituality of those who take part in them. Because "ritual" is thought of as actions particularly removed from everyday activities, the "ritual" of body modification can be considered an act which connects a participant to something other than the everyday, something that transcends the mundane.

In the narrative, Bowie presents a fictional story of the investigation of a gruesome murder. The body is that of a young girl, her dismembered parts put on "artistic" display at the entrance to a museum. The investigator's primary task is to determine whether this murder could be considered art. Bowie, in the guise of narrator and investigator Nathan Adler, suggests that a precedent for this display of "murder as art" could be found in the violent and bloody performance art of Ron Athey and

4. The Culture of Body Modification

Chris Burden, as well as in the art of Damien Hirst, in which dead and preserved animals are put on display. In his comments to Ian Penman in *Esquire*, Bowie suggests that these somewhat macabre and "quasi-sacrificial blood-obsessed" art forms could be an embodiment of "neo-paganism," a return to non–Western, non–Abrahamic religious traditions, associated with the culture of body modification. Specifically, Bowie says that body modification as a form of neo-paganism has helped people to deal with certain issues in their lives that have not been appropriately addressed by the "Judaeo-Christian ethic," that is, the prominent Western religious establishment and its rituals. The behavior of body modification is often considered transformative not only in the physical sense (obviously), but also spiritually. Body modification can be considered a statement against the Judeo-Christian ethic, and also against the notion of the split between the mind and the body.

Bowie, while engaging with the notion of body modification as a replacement for an ineffective Western religious system, seems to suggest that an atmosphere of fear and limbo in regards to the future has emerged with the popularity of various manifestations of body modification in the 1990s. Along with this sense of the impotence of modern Western religious systems to satisfy spiritual longing, Bowie suggests that an atmosphere of fear regarding the future emerged at the end of the twentieth century. While he does not explicitly link these two elements, his comments seem to conflate in *1. Outside* at the mid-point of the last decade of the twentieth century. Bowie does not propose that this pessimistic atmosphere is directly linked to the activities of body modification, but rather that fear in society is a manifestation of the unknown state of the world after the change of the calendar to the year 2000: in short, millennial angst. In turn, this angst manifests itself in the activities of body modification. In an interview in *Musician* magazine, Bowie states, "There is almost an unconscious, collective paranoia about hitting a brick wall at the end of every hundred years.... An intoxicating swirl of paranoia! It was hard enough ending a hundred years—how do you end a millennium?"[1] Through his album, Bowie creates a *liminoid* space (Victor Turner's "liminal" in industrial societies), a space that denies known outcomes, as a metaphor for societal anxiety at the end of the twentieth century. This chapter explores body modification and its possible meanings, in order to elucidate the veracity of Bowie's claim regarding the ritual nature of body modification as a return to spirituality.

Various writers on the subject of cultural body modification use differing terms to describe it. For this discussion, the term "modification" will be primarily used, as per Kim Hewitt's discussion of terminology in the introduction to her book, *Mutilating the Body: Identity in Blood and Ink*. She comments that some might object to her use of the term "mutilation" rather than "adornment," because of the somewhat pejorative connotations of the former, often used to refer to violent destruction so as to render an object imperfect.[2] Here, "modification" will refer to the action of the removal or alteration of a body part. This discussion will begin with the comments of social anthropologist Ted Polhemus in his book *The Customized Body*, which he explores the general motivations for the behavior of body modification.

Polhemus suggests that humans are the only creatures who choose to manipulate their appearance, and whose appearance has never been dictated only by genetics, a claim that is difficult to prove, and Polhemus makes no attempt to do so. He suggests that a most likely reason for such modification is self-expression, but that it also marks group membership. Polhemus suggests that body modification, as a semiotic act, expresses deeper meanings. Thus, the modified body can express complex ideologies and belief systems: the body becomes a medium for the cultural expression of a group or tribe. Polhemus suggests that, in the Western world, a person has a choice regarding with which tribe they would like to be associated at any given time, resulting in a "perpetual motion machine of different, constantly changing ways of altering the appearance of the human form."[3] Polhemus is ignoring the fact that the ability to choose one's associations can be limited by socio-economic factors, such as race, class, religion, and so forth. Nevertheless, against this notion of constant change are the forms of permanent body modification such as piercing and tattooing, offering a kind of stability and continuity to the physical self. Without this stability and continuity, a person can feel absolutely powerless and lost in an environment of continual change. By gaining control over the body, one can take ownership of the self: he or she has control over what happens to the self, not allow-

4. The Culture of Body Modification

ing anything that is not sanctioned by the self. While control can never be absolutely attained, a person is no longer completely at the whim of constant changes in society; rather, a person is now able to control his or her own appearance in the face of these changes.

In discussing the culture of body modification in his book *Customizing the Body: The Art and Culture of Tattooing*, Clinton Sanders presents another possible underlying motivation for the behavior:

> Deviation from and conformity to the societal norms surrounding attractiveness are ... at the core of discussions of appearance and alterations of the physical self. Those who choose to modify their bodies in ways that violate appearance norms—or who reject culturally prescribed alterations—risk being defined as socially or morally inferior. Choosing to be a physical deviant symbolically demonstrates one's disregard for the prevailing norms.[4]

According to Sanders, some of the examples of the modification of the body serve as a rebellion against the *appearance* norms of society. By rejecting these norms, the act of body modification becomes an act of individuality, through which one gains power to determine one's identity. But where do the roots of body modification lie? Examples of body modification through mutilation have been located in various aspects of both Western and non–Western cultures. By exploring these origins of body modification, as well as through a discussion of the various types and their motivations, one may move closer to an understanding of the behavior. With this understanding, a critique of Bowie's comments regarding the spiritual nature of body modification is possible.

Mutilation in Religion and Society

In *Bodies Under Siege: Self-Mutilation in Culture and Psychiatry*, Armando Favazza explores both the clinical behavior of self-mutilation—for example, "cutting," or the pathological behavior of slashing the skin—as well as the more culturally accepted (rather than pathological) forms of the practice, such as tattooing, piercing and scarification. "Cutting" is often engaged in as a means of remedying the sensation of "depersonalization." A "cutter" will slash the skin, often on her or his arms or legs, with a razor blade or another sharp object. This activity will continue until blood appears, which gives the "cutter" a renewed sense of self. Scarification—the deliberate cutting of the skin for the formation of scar tissue—is a widely accepted practice in non-Western cultures, but is becoming increasingly popular in Western culture. Favazza outlines mutilative images in both Western and non-Western religions and in sacred art and secular literature, and then continues to outline specific forms of mutilation or modification in which people engage.

Laying a foundation for the practice of body modification, Favazza explores the role of blood and mutilation in religion, beginning with Tibetan Tantrism. The *Tibetan Book of the Dead* outlines a series of meditations on death and birth experienced in various psychological states. Throughout these various states, the meditator experiences the visitation of various peaceful deities, but these make way for terrifying deities of violence and mutilation. For the meditator, enlightenment occurs when he or she realizes that these images are being projected from within him- or herself (Favazza does not describe the appearance of the "deities of mutilation" beyond their identification as "wrathful" and "terrifying").

In North American indigenous religion, and particularly in the Sun Dance of the buffalo hunting tribes found in the Plains region, the mutilation is not limited to a psychological experience, as in the case of Tibetan meditation. The Sun Dance is an eight-day ritual and culminates in the Gazing-at-the-Sun dance, a dance which portrays the dangers of warrior life, capture, torture and release. In the ritual, the dancers are "captured" and incisions are made in their backs and chests. Pieces of wood are attached to leather thongs that are then inserted under the cut muscles, and the thongs are attached to a tall pole. The participants dance trying to break free from their bonds, some struggling so violently that the wooden pieces rip through their flesh. The "pure in heart" should be able to withstand the pain of the ritual and are expected to receive a vision that would make clear the meaning and course of their lives.

Throughout its history, Christianity has included mutilation at its very core, namely in the passion of Christ. Favazza comments that the

4. The Culture of Body Modification

most powerful images of Christ and his suffering were developed in paintings between the fourteenth and seventeenth centuries. Art historians have categorized the various images, which find their origins in the biblical account of Jesus' crucifixion. These image categories include the flagellation of Christ, the wounded Christ displayed (*Ecco Homo*, or "Behold the Man"), Christ nailed to the cross and crucified, Christ mourned, Mary's grief (*Pietà*), Christ's sufferings exemplified (Jesus as Man of Sorrows), and *Arma Christi* focusing on Christ's suffering—*Arma* referring to the tools of suffering, such as the spear, nails, the crown of thorns, and so forth. Christian art has also associated instruments of torture with biblical figures (the inverted crucifixion of Peter, for instance), and devotional books often vividly depict the gruesome fate of martyrs in both words and drawings. Favazza also mentions apocryphal images such as the pierced sacred heart, surrounded by a crown of thorns below a cross.

Other examples of sacred art that refer to acts of mutilation include Hieronymus Bosch's triptychs of the *Garden of Earthly Delights* and *The Last Judgement* (from the sixteenth century). Bosch's paintings exhibit various punishments for sin, including being gnawed by animals and having limbs removed. References to mutilation in a religious context also appear in secular literature. In Flannery O'Conner's book *Wise Blood*, the author, informed by a deeply held Roman Catholic sensibility, presents Hazel Motes, a character who, late in the story, puts rocks into his shoes before placing them on his feet and wears strands of barbed wire under his shirt, because he is not "clean" without Christ. By identifying in such a material way with Christ's suffering, Motes endeavors to cleanse himself of his iniquities. Through pain—something that can be felt—he is able to empathize with and thus come closer to Christ. The lack of tangible or physical evidence of salvation is resolved in this case by a definite feeling of pain and a resulting permanent mark—proof of an event of seeking and perhaps attaining salvation. O'Conner thus presents the character of Motes who strives to reach Christ through his own ritualistic self-mutilation and not through any other religious means.[5]

As a particularly potent example of sacred art which focuses on Christ, Richard Leppert explores Annibale Carracci's painting, *Salma di Cristo*, or, as Leppert calls it, *The Dead Christ* (c.1583–1585), through which the observer is invited to survey the mutilated body of Christ. The painting features the dead body positioned with the viewer at its feet: the brown-hued scene features a body set upon a broad, flat, covered surface. The light from the foreground of the painting reveals the body, naked but for a bloodied cloth draped over the loin and lower waist. The viewer observes a pair of open wounds, one through each bare foot; both wounds are flowing with bright red blood. To the left of the feet are two bent and misshapen spikes, as well as a set of pliers, those used presumably to remove the spikes from the feet. To the right of the feet is a circle of thorny branches, also bloodied (in the biblical story of Christ's crucifixion, the wreath of thorns was placed as a painful laurel or crown around the man's head, as a mockery of his alleged "kingship" as the son of God). As the eye moves along the body, and toward the middle of the painting, the observer comes across another open wound on the side of the body. The man's torso is shifted toward the right, and his head, almost in the complete darkness at the back of the painting, is hanging with mouth open. The man's face is covered in stubble. The man's head is also bloodied: there appears to be a flowing wound on the man's head as well. The details of the body add to the realism of the scene: the man has red hair on his chest, and the wrinkles of his underarms are clearly portrayed. The hands are also marked by substantial, flowing wounds. This is the aftermath of a terrible death. Leppert writes:

> The angle of view gives us access to the multiple penetrations of Christ's body and the principle means by which his body was wounded: the crown of thorns and, especially stiletto-like nails, their irregularly flattened heads visually reverberating with the force of the invisible hammer strikes used to drive them home…. Christ's hand is grotesquely misshapen in stiffened reaction to the iron nail; and its greenish cast, the shade even more evident on the ghastly profiled face, indicates the onset of decomposition.[6]

The painting draws attention to various physical mutilations, and brings to light some of the more gruesome aspects of the execution, such as the force necessary to drive nails through a body part. In so doing, the painting makes the event more real; the Crucifixion is no longer a romanticized event or fable. The grotesque details, such as the stiffness of the hand or

4. The Culture of Body Modification

the onset of decomposition, serve to emphasize the terrible experience of Christ's sacrificial death.

The notion of sacrifice as the only means by which to achieve salvation underlies much of Western thought due to the vast influence of the Christian Church. Generally from the perspective of evangelical Protestant Christianity, the idea of salvation through personal suffering would be discouraged, because in such an action salvation is arrived at through the self or self-action rather than through faith or belief in Christ. Therefore, the examples of attaining salvation through some physical action, whether by empathizing with Christ or by some analogous sacrifice to that of Christ, represent alternative methods of salvation. Through the cultural saturation of Christian images of mutilation, spilling also into secular literature in the case of O'Connor, the idea of salvation through physical means may be a motivation for the act of body modification as a transformative action.

Images of mutilation are also present in various myths of creation—in particular, in the *Rigueda* (India), *Greater Bundahisn* (Iran) and *Prose Edda* (Scandinavia) religions—where creation is the result of the sacrifice and mutilation of the primordial hermaphroditic being. Favazza explains that this sacrifice and mutilation resulted in the establishment of the ordered world. With the repeated reenactment of religious rituals of sacrifice and mutilation, the world and its social order are recreated. In such rituals, the suffering that accompanies sacrifice and mutilation is replace by well-being and order.

Finally, Favazza discusses examples from disparate traditions which suggest that bodily mutilation is a method of attaining wisdom, healing and a transcendent sense of self. He goes on to explain the importance of sacrifice and suffering in the context of religion, suggesting that there is a link between sacrifice and prayer. For example, a person offers a valuable sacrificial gift, in the form of an animal, to a deity anticipating a favorable response in return; the blood and flesh of sacrificial victims serve to rejuvenate the deities themselves. Also, there is a communion that is established between a people and their deity as a result of their partaking of the sacrificial animal. Furthermore, a sacrifice is an act in which, through the consecration of a victim, the moral state of the one who offers the sacrifice is changed; the act establishes a communion between the sacred world and the present one. As with O'Connor's character, a relationship with the divine is facilitated through physical sacrifice.

Some may view the behavior of self-mutilation or body modification in a religious context as pathological. To differentiate between clinical self-mutilators and those involved in activities mentioned above (for instance, self-flagellating monks in ascetic orders), Favazza comments that the acts of clinical self-mutilators have no transcendency: their activities affect themselves only, and are enacted outside of the larger community.[7]

The obvious question is whether the activities of culturally sanctioned body modifiers have meaning for the community at large as well. The "community at large," or the "mainstream," is defined in opposition to the marginalized segments within society. The culture of body modification as ritual is marginal, or outside of what is dominant in society. Those who are involved in body modification are simply a segment of a greater population in Western society. The larger group does not perform body modification as ritual. Extreme forms of body modification are often seen by mainstream culture as deviant, and thus the actions of body modifiers only affect themselves and their relatively small social network, in relation to the mainstream. While mainstream culture has increasingly accepted lesser forms of body modification like tattooing and piercing, there are still limits to so-called "acceptable" practice. This is not to say that the practices of subcultures are unimportant. Rather, the larger community does not recognize the meanings of their actions. Some of the lesser practices of body modification, such as various ear, facial and navel piercings, have seeped into mainstream culture, and in so doing have lost much of their association with ritual and transformation. Although, in one sense, the actions of body modifiers are aimed directly at the community at large as an act of rebellion against the mainstream aesthetic, in another sense, the belief of the transformative nature of the action to which some body modifiers subscribe, is lost to mainstream culture. In the mainstream, the modifications have become adornments which serve an aesthetic purpose or as a means by which an individual follows a particular trend. Therefore, Favazza's means of differentiating between clinical self-mutilators and those involved in

4. The Culture of Body Modification

culturally sanctioned body modification is not successful, since both groups' actions are misunderstood by the larger community, and in some cases, completely acceptable. The line between pathological self-mutilation and culturally sanctioned body modification remains difficult to determine.

Body Modification as Art

Polhemus mentions Orlan, as examples of those pushing the envelope of "body art," displaying extreme plastic surgery modifications and other changes, such as muscle restriction (to produce a bulge above and below the restricting band) and penis stretching.[8] Some may even implant foreign matter beneath the skin, creating a distinctive contour on the surface.[9] More recently, musician Lady Gaga appeared in promotional material (such as on the cover and promotional video for the single "Born This Way") with pronounced, angular cheekbones and horn-like protrusions from her forehead and shoulders. These all appeared as genuine subcutaneous implants. These artists (perhaps including those who are doing so only temporarily, like Lady Gaga) are pushing the boundary of the definition of art, asking what is appropriate to be considered as such. Similarly, in the accompanying narrative to *1. Outside*, Bowie presents the case of a murder in which the investigator must establish whether the resulting mutilation should be considered as a work of art. It could be extrapolated that Bowie is asking the same question regarding the more common manifestations of body modification prevalent in present society.

Miller uses the term "body art" rather than body modification when discussing the various manifestations of modifying the body. She also discusses non-permanent adornments such as *Mehndi* and body paint. *Mehndi* comes from the Indian tradition of decorating a woman's hands and feet with complex patterns with henna dye (originally done to celebrate her wedding). The dye lasts from ten days to six weeks, and body paint is immediately removable using water.[10] Polhemus suggests that the temporary nature of body paint can serve to underline the significance of certain rituals or events, setting the events apart from the everyday. Also, body paint can function as a marker of personal development (defining age groups among the *Nuba* of Sudan, for instance) or as a transforming agent in the form of war paint.[11] Camphausen comments that henna is regarded as magical, making the wearer "more receptive to the invisible yet omnipresent fields of energy in which we live."[12] Sanders considers clothing and hair styling as important physical alterations as well; Polhemus suggests that clothing tends to focus attention to body parts that remain uncovered.[13] He also suggests that hairstyle works in similar ways as the more permanent modifications discussed previously, citing the hairstyles of the males of the *Nuba* tribes of Sudan and young *Masai* warriors.[14] Various acts of hygiene, including shaving, along with wearing wigs and manicuring nails, as well as clothing accessories (such as shoes and masks) and, as a less common phenomenon, gender modification, come under the rubric of body modification.

In many of the cases listed above, the boundary between body modification as "art" or as aesthetic adornment and as ritual is being blurred. This blurring of the boundaries can perhaps be attributed to the place that ritual inhabits in these non–Western societies, as suggested by Victor Turner. Through his discussions of the notion of "liminality," Turner suggests that the idea of everyday life, or the banal, as separate from ritual is a Western postindustrial one. In these non–Western tribal societies, Turner suggests that the everyday is permeated with ritual.[15] The idea that a Western subculture may exhibit this same blurring of boundaries could be an example of the movement of these cultures towards non–Western worldviews. Camphausen calls this a "return to the tribal," embodied in those that refer to themselves as "Modern Primitives."

Piercing is a rapidly increasing phenomenon in Western culture, with "Modern Primitives" creating new piercing possibilities. The term "Modern Primitive" is attributed to Fakir Musafar, who was one of the first Americans to publicly practice body modification as ritual and is considered a pioneer in the teaching of proper piercing and ritual techniques. Musafar, born Roland Loomis in 1930, states, "We used the term to describe a non-tribal person who responds to primal urges and does something with the body."[16] He suggests that the "primitive urge" works by someone performing a modification spontaneously, not necessarily being connected with any group. Vale and Juno point out that the term

4. The Culture of Body Modification

"primitive" in this context is used to connote "original" and "primary" rather than "less advanced" or "less civilized." They state, "Obviously, it is impossible to return to an authentic 'primitive' society.... What is implied by the revival of 'modern primitive' activities is the desire for, and the dream of, a *more ideal society*."[17]

This desire for a better society finds its most powerful recent expression in the countercultural movement of the 1960s. Youth culture's dissatisfaction with Western ideology resulted in their appropriation of non–Western practices and ways of thinking as an alternative. With the advent of the 1970s, the counterculture fragmented in various directions. John Clark, Stuart Hall, Tony Jefferson and Brian Roberts, in their overview of subcultural theory, suggest that from among this fragmentation emerged two distinctive strands: "one way, via drugs, mysticism, the 'revolution in life-style' into a Utopian alternative culture; or, the other way, via community action, protest action and libertarian goals, into a more activist politics."[18] Although these authors are primarily speaking of British subcultural movements, their comments shed light on the origins of the "revolution in life-style" to which many Modern Primitives hold. Rather than being overly activist in their desire for a better culture, the Modern Primitives look to other means to achieve their goals. The subversion of society in an effort toward its transformation occurs through the transformation of individuals within that society, achieved through body modification rituals.

Recognizing the increase of "Modern Primitive" behavior in late twentieth century society, Polhemus suggests that body piercing has become very popular because of the lack of ritual and rites of passage in industrial societies. He explains that the rediscovery of body modification amounts to a rediscovery of ritual, and a renewed acceptance of "body arts" once though uncivilized and unacceptable. Furthermore, these rituals place the physical body at the centre of what it means to be a human being. Body modification allows people to control their body during a time in which things seem to be out of control.[19]

Polhemus shares these views with Favazza, Camphausen, and other writers on the subject of body modification, that body modification allows control in the midst of a society out of control. Furthermore, they would seem to blame societal control for the repression of this behavior.

Also, Polhemus' comments suggest the privileging of the body over the mind. The desire to reclaim control over the body comes about as a result of the split between the domains of the mind and the body, which has been prevalent in Western philosophy and culture since seventeenth century philosopher René Descartes' well-known statement, "I think, therefore I am." From this statement, his followers deduced that the human mind should be privileged above the human body and even God. With the increasingly fast pace of late twentieth century society, the tangible control over the body is often seen as a viable option for a sense of stability, rather than the traditional emphasis on the mind.

Body Play

Among the most extreme forms of body modification is the notion of "body play." Although the term often refers to acts of body modification, the emphasis is on the *event* of being modified. The act of modification is focused upon as a ritual and as a transformative experience. An example of this is found in the Sun Dance ritual as described earlier in this chapter. Jean-Chris Miller explains:

> Body play takes many forms. It can be temporary piercings or cuttings that are done for a specific event and then removed. It can be more intense, like body suspensions, where piercings are made in key points in your body, chains are attached to the jewellery, and you are then lifted off the ground, suspended by your piercings.... People who partake in these extreme forms of body play usually do so for their own spiritual or sexual reasons.[20]

Camphausen also talks about the popularity of "body play," in that there have been recent rediscoveries of what he calls "old and new uses of pain." He recounts "ball dances" in which the more daring participants hook weighted balls into their flesh and dance until their flesh rips from the weight. He concludes that many participants "enthusiastically report on the liberating and transforming effects of the pain thus created and transcended."[21]

Marilee Strong discusses "blood play" or "blood sport" (yet more terms for "body play"), which grew out of sadomasochism, in which

4. The Culture of Body Modification

partners slash and pierce each other, resulting in sexual excitement. Strong recounts the comments of a young participant in such activities, discovering her motivations as "overcoming the fear and shame she has been conditioned to feel about the blood in her body, marveling at the sight and touch of it." Raelyn Gallina, a piercer from the San Francisco area, suggests that when one gets pierced or scarred, a sacrifice is made with blood and pain, opening a door for transformation or healing to take place.[22] This is yet another instance of the line between ritual and art being blurred, where the ritual nature of body modification is seeping into the act of body adornment. This blurring of lines is also evident in Strong's account of the life and performances of Bob Flanagan, a performance artist and self-proclaimed "super-masochist." Flanagan was born with cystic fibrosis and grew up with the inevitable approach of death at the forefront of his thinking; he maintained that he wanted to experience as much sensation as he possibly could before his death. Strong suggests that Flanagan's fascination with bondage stemmed from his status as "prisoner" of a disease over which he did not have any control. Flanagan proceeded to sexualize this bondage rather than be controlled by it, determining to which authority he would surrender: ultimately, he would be in control of his bondage, life and death. Flanagan subscribed to the belief that "little deaths," in the form of his various performances, would prepare him for ultimate death. Strong recounts Flanagan's experiences with these planned activities that were *like* dying, but limited to short periods. Flanagan felt that, after the period of pain (or "dying") ended, he felt empowered to live his life calmly and in peace.[23]

Bowie appropriates the notion of "body play" in the accompanying narrative to *1. Outside*, in the form of graphic descriptions of the work of artists such as Damien Hirst, Ron Athey and others. In a particular performance described by Nathan Adler, the writer of the narrative, American performance artist Ron Athey repeatedly pokes what appears to be a knitting needle into his forehead until his own HIV-positive blood appears; later in the performance, he cuts a fellow performer's back and blots the wounds with the paper towels, creating "inkblot" patterns with the blood. Like the actions of Flanagan and others, Bowie suggests (implicitly) that Athey's performance acts as a means of therapy or transformation. The question also asked (implicitly) is, if this sort of bloody and injurious activity can be considered art, why not something more extreme, like murder?

Toward an Understanding of Body Modification

It is very difficult to come to a single conclusion regarding the motivations behind the behaviors being explored here. As is evident in the following discussion, there are many, often disparate, reasons for body modification. Favazza suggests that culturally sanctioned body modification in non–Western cultures are traditional and reflect and reinforce societal ideologies, affecting both the individual as well as the community. All types of body modification, whether they be culturally sanctioned or deviant, serve to attempt to correct a "destabilizing condition" that is a threat to the individual as well as the community. These practices often require the participation of a group of persons, acting in a social way as well, thus fostering group solidarity. They prevent social disorder by clearly, and often permanently, defining statuses and differences between sexes and generations.[24] Body modification seems also to act as a relief of tension and aggression, offering a sense of control to the participant in a chaotic environment.

Specific modifications often serve specific purposes. Regarding scarification, Favazza suggests that the cutter performs a "sort of self-surgery" from which he or she ultimately heals, and that such wounding can mark an emotionally hurtful event in one's life. Such acts can also serve as an alternative to suicide (a substitution of the destruction of the whole with the destruction of a part), an indication of desperation, a manipulative ploy for attention, a remedy for perceived internal or external flaws, and as an act of creation: a wound is produced, and is then cared for and nurtured to health.[25]

Jean-Chris Miller suggests that body manipulation is a form of self-expression. Miller explains:

> These permanent marks are what define us as human beings. They are a means of self-expression and a vehicle of self-awareness, two qualities that separate us from other living things on this planet.... Tattooing, piercing

4. The Culture of Body Modification

and other adornments have been used for centuries in rites of passage, in religious rituals, or as a form of tribal identification—in *all* cultures.... [they are] a permanent souvenir of a life-changing moment.[26]

Miller suggests that body art is used by some to reclaim an ancestral custom, or to symbolize an important event or transition in their lives. She comments that the various forms of body art are important for two reasons: "They give us control over our bodies and they express things about our inner selves that words alone often cannot articulate."[27] Miller gives a different reason than Favazza for engaging in such corporeal modification, in that the act of body modification becomes a personal ritual in a society made up of members who hold to few rites and rituals. Her comments mirror Bowie's: the rituals of body modification fill a voice, a basic human need. Some might argue that Western institutionalized religion, primarily Christianity, provides rites and rituals, and affords the opportunity for a participant to be devoted to a particular group. With Western society's move away from institutionalized religion, body art *does* fill that void. Also, Miller suggests that body art serves as a way to recognize and celebrate the physical body, often increasing sexual stimulation (in the case of certain nipple and genital piercings).[28] What is most interesting to Camphausen is the fact that the invisible self is becoming more visible; many choose to have genital piercings and even tattoos done in semipublic settings. Camphausen explains that it is not only people's nude bodies that are being exposed, but also their experiences of intense sensation: "what we see in essence is a new member joining the tribe in a bond that is beyond family or nation or race or gender."[29]

Building on Musafar's definition, Miller also uses the term "Modern Primitives" to describe some of those who modify their bodies, people who not only rediscover and utilize rituals from traditional "primitive" cultures, but also embrace new technologies, using the latest advances from robotics, cybernetics, surgical and chemical technologies to *recreate* their own physical selves. Miller agrees with Favazza, and others, that there is a political element involved in body modification, where one is asserting control over their own physical being.[30]

Sanders argues that group membership is the underlying reasoning behind all types of physical modification, in that the body becomes aesthetically pleasing to the relevant group, no matter what other reasoning might also be in play. Sanders also suggests that less frequent forms of piercing (of the nose, cheeks, nipples, genitals and so forth) are commonly viewed with disfavor, therefore "eminently suited for symbolizing disaffection from mainstream values."[31] Many of these forms of body modification have, in fact, become increasingly favorable. In apparent contradiction to Sanders, Camphausen suggests that many types of body adornment and modification have little to do with attaining a "look" or conforming to a social vision of beauty. Rather, many of these techniques are aimed at awakening potentials of consciousness that are fully human and natural, rather than extrasensory or paranormal, but that need to be trained and activated in order to function at their very best.[32] Interestingly, in this instance Camphausen is suggesting a rather non-spiritual role of body modification, as a facilitator of revealing human potential. Elsewhere, he provides a more spiritual motivation for body adornment, and tattooing in particular:

> It becomes clear that the contemporary return to the tribal represents a swing of the pendulum of history, another loop in the continuous flow of time. Humanity, on reaching the end of one cycle and entering a new one, is more open to change at such crucial moments and seems to become sensitive yet again.... What we currently witness is a reemergence of the tribal spirit from within the human psyche: genetic memory manifesting itself. Amid the concrete and silicon with which we've fashioned our world, the mythical serpent of the dreamtime is once again arising, reminding and recalling us to roots almost forgotten.[33]

According to Camphausen, the "return to the tribal" is caused by the reemergence of instinctual behavior, due to a "genetic memory." His evoking of the idea of genetic memory being "awakened" at the end of one cycle and at the beginning of another is interesting, and corresponds with Bowie's idea of the increase of the behavior of body modification (and a new spirituality) at the end of the millennium. He continues by suggesting that this popularity of body modification is also accompanied by a return to tribal activities and ways of looking at the world. He supports this by pointing to the increasing number of youth and adults experimenting with altered states of consciousness, which Camphausen associates with tribal shamanism. The profile of tribalism is also raised through the ecological movement and herbal rediscovery. Camphausen suggests that the expression of the tribal impulse is evident in forms of dance music that

4. The Culture of Body Modification

come close to being trance inducing. In fact, the phenomenon of "Rave" culture revolves around the notion of a formation of community and a communal experience of spiritual transcendence. He suggests that within the subgenre of "Trance," a kind of dance music, the participants in "rave" parties experience not only styles of dance that evoke conceptions of tribalism, but also a communal rather than individual experience. In other words, a community is formed for the short time in which the gathering takes place. The dance becomes a release for the community gathered, rather than just for the individual. Elsewhere, Camphausen suggests that the increase of sexual freedom in the 1990s, which finds its roots in the 1960s Counterculture, is a move toward the tribal.[34] Such a comment is difficult to support because, although the author mentions the resurgence of Tantra workshops (during which, it is assumed, the fundamentals of Tantric sexual activity are explored) and events occurring in dark corners of nightclubs, there are also many people, particularly teenagers, moving in the opposite direction, choosing sexual abstinence. The evidence for this lies in youth campaigns such as "True Love Waits" (which claims to have over one million adherents) and other primarily Christian youth sexual abstinence movements. Whether this move to a more strict sexual conduct is a response to the supposed tribal tendencies of society is hard to determine; the abstinence movements, fueled by the support of public figures such as Alison Gertz, a heterosexual woman who contracted AIDS after a one-time sexual encounter, also stress a move towards "safest sex" as a response to the threat of the AIDS virus.[35]

Camphausen suggests that body modification redeems what he calls "wet" and "dirty" characteristics of human life, including pain and experimentation. These things have been effectively erased from everyday discourse; body modification works to reestablish these "truths" in the common discourse.[36]

Marilee Strong suggests that young people began to desire a break from normative discourse in the 1960s, and thus chose to reject normative standards of dress and ways of carrying themselves. In doing so, youth culture in the West also strove to break the bonds of normative Western spirituality, turning to more ancient (and non–Christian) mystical rites. Like Camphausen, Strong also traces the popularity of body piercing in Western society through the 1960s and the exploration of Eastern mysticism during that time. Strong mentions Fakir Musafar's views toward body manipulation as a transformative experience hearkening back to primitive ritual. Musafar feels that the physical body is under no other authority than the self, and thus should not be under the control of any institution, be it religion, science, the state or the family. Body modification not only acts as a wresting of control from hegemonic forces but also a striving for a new—better—state of being. Like Favazza, Strong is attempting to provide a clinical view of the behavior, which she makes clear throughout her chapter, and suggests that many people who engage in piercing or scarring, although not all, are motivated by some of the same reasons as those with pathological problems—for instance, reclaiming their body from abuse. She suggests that even if a behavior has a ritual or rationale, it is not necessarily healthy: it can be a sign of attempting to connect to the primal, primitive and physical, but can also be a sign of extreme need. Psychologist Mark Schwartz adds that piercing the body is a way to indicate to one's self that one is alive: the overstimulation that exists in Western society can result in numbness. It is only through physical pain that one experiences renewed vitality.[37] Schwartz's comments echo those expressed by Nine Inch Nails' Trent Reznor in the song "Hurt": the singer must hurt himself in order to feel pain, the only part of life that he feels is authentic and not fabricated. In the case of "Body Play," pain is often used to find relief from guilt, or to atone for some debt. Pain can also be a means to transcendence of ordinary consciousness, and as a sign of strength, discipline and endurance.[38]

As Polhemus and others have suggested, the act of modification is also an act of rejecting the notion of the split between the body and mind. The body becomes the focus of attention and the subject of adornment, mutilation and modification. In Flanagan's case, the fear of death was encompassed in his physical body, and thus by addressing it through its modification, he was able to transcend fear. The mind is relieved of fear through a change of the body; the split between mind and body is transcended through modification. In the other examples of body modification, there is a constant emphasis on the body and a return to the awareness of the body and its sensations, including pain and pleasure.

4. The Culture of Body Modification

The culture of modification does not only act as a replacement for the Judeo-Christian Church, as per Bowie's suggestion, but also as a rejection of the split between the mind and the physical body.

Body Modification as Alternative Spirituality

The idea of the various manifestations of ritualistic body modification as rebellion against the Judeo-Christian ethic is but one possible motivation for the behavior. As mentioned previously in this discussion, the narrative that accompanies *1. Outside* refers to artists such as Chris Burden and Ron Athey, who are known for their forays into the more macabre realms of performance art. Dominic Wells, in an interview for *Time Out* magazine, asked Bowie about his apparent morbid fascination regarding body modification, wondering if it was an expression of the old myth that art could only result from suffering. Bowie responded, "Also it has something to do with the fact that the complexity of modern systems is so intense that a lot of artists are going back literally into themselves in a physical way, and it has produced a dialogue between the flesh and the mind."[39] The increase of tattooing and piercing—and the extremes of such behavior often manifesting themselves in works of art—might be read as a sign of society turning to a new form of spirituality as an alternative to the institutionalized Christian Church, and that in an increasingly chaotic world, the body is the last bastion of control for the individual.

From within the Christian institution, there have also been criticisms that suggest the return of ritual in those factions of Christianity which have laid them aside. In a study of the state of Christian liturgy in postmodern culture, Frank C. Senn supplies an explanation for the downfall of traditional liturgical forms of Christian praxis from the viewpoint of someone inside the Church. He suggests that Western culture at the end of the twentieth century has no coherent sense of history:

> Their sense of living [is] only for the moment with no meaningful tradition on which to build and no destiny of promise toward which to move.... This puts historical Christianity in an untenable cultural situation because

it proclaims a salvation event that happened in history. There is a minimum historical awareness that is required to tell the story of salvation and to proclaim the promised destiny of the people of God. The church's mission is to tell the biblical story to the world and to enact it before God in worship. How does the church pursue this mission in a world that lacks narrative coherence? If, in the past, the church could correlate its mission with the culture's general quest for certainty, or its use of reason to construct a worldview, or its romantic yearning for an ideal society, or its liberal agenda for social reform, how does the church correlate its mission to proclaim a historical gospel with the nihilism of the postmodern world or the gnosticism of the "American Religion"?[40]

The reference to the "American Religion" is drawn from the writing of critic Harold Bloom, who suggests that it refers to a religion whose most basic tenets stress the need for individual salvation from a personal Jesus, shown to humanity in an inerrant Bible, not affected by any sort of ambiguity.[41] Senn suggests that the introduction of the lament in liturgy may provide a balance to an escapist church experience. The author suggests that the lament provides a more realistic representation of the human experience, and allows parishioners to request help from God. If society is marked by decay, destruction and various forms of limitations, Senn suggests that the Christian Church could provide a liturgical counter.[42] Senn is suggesting a greater emphasis on the sacraments and ritual of the Christian Church to better serve postmodern society. With all of this suggested, could it be possible that some of the more macabre elements residing in the realm of performance art are functioning in a similar way? Bowie seems to suggest this; perhaps the blood and violence is a type of sacrament for a culture without (a) God.

In "The Diary of Nathan Adler," the narrative of *1. Outside*, Bowie writes that art-murder probably had its beginnings with the Viennese castrationists and the blood-rituals of artist Hermann Nitsche. Through his own non–Christian blood-rituals, in which cattle are slaughtered and displayed, Hermann Nitsche provides another critique of traditional Christianity from outside of the Church: in Christianity, life is understood to take place in the physical world for a span of time, but then to continue for eternity in the presence of God, without the physical limitations of earthly life. According to Nitsche, such a division, between earthly life and eternity, has ultimately suppressed the dionystic.[43]

4. The Culture of Body Modification

Nitsche's complaint is that the Church has destroyed the instinctual and festive element of human nature. His purpose is to try to recapture a sense of the dionystic through non–Christian ritual and pagan-like sacrifice. Certainly, the actions of Nitsche and others would seem to be positioned on the "outside" of society (as is made clear by the protest that occurs around such events). Interestingly, an article in the *Ottawa Citizen* from 19 July 1998 suggested that David Bowie and Yoko Ono were patrons for one of Nitsche's events (which was being protested against by many animal rights groups). This claim was quickly denied by a statement from Bowie's publicity company stating that the singer was, in no way, supporting this "theatre of blood."

It is possible that the increase of body modification in Western society points to the failure of the institutionalized religious establishment. The Christian Church has long been the legislator of moral laws and the regulator of cultural behavior to a certain point; Western society has often had a subculture that has rebelled against what they perceived as the Church's repression. With the propensity of piercing and other forms of body modification, there has been a reclaiming of the body, which could be read also as a move against the adage that the body is untouchable because it is formed in the image of God. Bowie suggests that the Church has not dealt with sex or violence in an adequate manner; this has resulted in culture taking the initiative in creating new rituals and transformative experiences. As has been suggested by this discussion, many of these cultural "concerns" have been addressed by Eastern mystical and tribal religions (or some piecemeal appropriation of them by Western culture). Remembering Camphausen's comment regarding the banning of "wet" and "dirty" truths from the everyday, it is probable that he is also blaming the Church for the ban. It is irresponsible to blame a single (albeit extremely powerful) institution for society's ills, or for the difficulty some have in living in such a society. Nevertheless, there is a move away from the Christian Church by a segment of Western society, as is clear by the discussions in this chapter. Of course, there are those who genuinely ascribe to Christianity who also have tattoos and piercings. The appropriation of the *ritual* nature of these non–Western forms of body modification is generally undertaken by those not ascribing to Western Christianity, or by those who would not consider themselves conventional followers of Christ. The next chapter will argue that Bowie perceives a segment of society as caught in a kind of rite of passage before the "transformation" of the twenty-first century: the 1990s constitute a sort of *liminal* phase at the end of the twentieth century. Camphausen suggests that this "return of the tribal" is a historical phenomenon—the time is right—while others have concluded that the behavior is a response against the seemingly chaotic aspects of late twentieth century society. The only possibility for consistency and control lies in the control achieved on or over one's own body. Perhaps it is only through pain that one can truly *feel* in a society out of control and it is through this pain that a better state of being is attained.

5

An Analysis of *1. Outside*

In Douglas Coupland's 1995 novel *Microserfs*, he writes that "narratives (stories) traditionally come to a definite end (unlike life); that's why we like movies and literature—for that sense of *closure*—because they *end*."[1] The narrative of *1. Outside* is much like the story of living, an ongoing sequence of events, without definite closure. *1. Outside* is an important album in Bowie's late career: it acts as an anchor for his more recent material, and is a manifestation of his late career strategy of obfuscation to negotiate his celebrity. It has also been discussed in relation to Bowie's statement concerning its engagement with the culture of body modification and its critique of the Judeo-Christian ethic. Because the act of body modification has often been viewed as a transformative experience, one possibility is that it has moved in to replace what is not being supplied by institutional Christianity; as an element of non–Western culture, body modification, while also serving other purposes, can act as an alternative to the Western belief system.

1. Outside can also be thought of as a reflection of an element of society at the end of the millennium, particularly those involved in the "new cults of tattooing and scarification and piercings," as Bowie says. This reflection is created by the various elements that make up the album. These include the lyrics, and a narrative in the liner notes which presents a strange world of the absurd and violent. The lyrics are generally pessimistic, addressing themes of hopelessness and the alienation of technology, while much of the music sounds improvised, without traditional teleological tonal movement and closure. Reprinted in the liner notes, the lyrics are practically illegible, transformed and blurred into masses of letters and shadows. The album art contains digitally manipulated photos of Bowie as the various characters in the narrative, including Nathan Adler, Baby Grace Blue and Ramona A. Stone. This chapter will explore the *1. Outside* album and its accompanying narrative, with a discussion of the album art, lyrics and music, with the view that these various elements contribute to the formation of a space that is in between two states. The first state, or "preliminal" state, is one of incompletion, in anticipation of some form of transformation. The final state, or "postliminal" state, is an unknown, analogous to the state of society following the arrival of the new millennium. In Victor Turner's notion of the "liminal," this resulting state consists of the reintegration of a participant of a rite of passage into society as a complete or new element. Bowie constructs a space that is "liminoid" (the liminal in postindustrial society), before a transformative event, or the turning of time to a new millennium, in which the participants are unaware of a positive outcome after the transformative event. To begin, the diary will be examined to determine how it contributes to the formation of this theoretical space.

The Diary of Nathan Adler

The liner notes included with the compact disc edition of *1. Outside* open with the title "The Diary of Nathan Adler; or The Art-Ritual Murder of Baby Grace Blue." The narrative is additionally titled "A non-linear Gothic Drama Hyper-cycle," and it recounts the investigation of the murder of a 14-year-old girl named Baby Grace Blue. Assigned to the investigation is Detective Professor Nathan Adler, an officer of the Arts Protectorate of London, who works in its art crime division. His job is not to find the murderer, as one would expect, but rather to determine whether the act of murder constitutes art.

The first section of text acts as an introduction to the crime scene and the investigators. What is first graphically described is the rather grotesque appearance of the victim, found in the fictitious Oxford Town Museum of Modern Parts, New Jersey. The location is a curious one: while there exists an Oxford, New Jersey, it is a census-designated place with a population of just over a thousand, located around 90 kilometers west of New York City. The very name of the place is a juxtaposition of two actual locations: one represents the pinnacle of intellect and history,

5. An Analysis of 1. Outside

Oxford (in the United Kingdom), while the other is New Jersey, the popular antithesis of New York City. Of course, New York City is a major hub in the circulating system of the arts and global culture, whereas New Jersey is not.

In the context of the murder at the Oxford Town Museum of Modern Parts, it is asked not whether the murder constitutes a crime, but whether it constitutes a work of art. The art crime division, for which Professor Adler works, is described as a corporation funded by the Arts Protectorate of London, as it was believed that the investigation of "art-crimes" itself was an art form and thus worthy of financial support. As part of that support, Adler then notes that the art crime people were given the opportunity to exhibit three rooms of evidence and comparative study work at the 1994 Biennale in Venice. The object of study for the exhibition was Mark Tansey's painting *The Innocent Eye Test*. Tansey's painting features within it Paulus Potter's *The Young Bull* from 1647.

Potter's *The Young Bull* features a pastoral scene complete with cattle, some sheep and what appears to be a farmer, the keeper of these animals. Axel Rüger emphasizes Potter's "remarkably accomplished rendering of space and radiant natural light," while Michiel C. Plomp states, "Potter's close observation of deer and other animals could only be the outcome of long and sympathetic study from life."[2] The subject of the painting is the aforementioned young bull, an animal that is set before the viewer who has full view of its body from the side. The bull looks over its left shoulder toward the viewer. The right of the frame features a lone bird flying in the background. Potter's compositional style here is not unique in his catalogue of works: the composition of his later painting, *The Watchdog* (1653–1654), is similar, "with its dense right section and, on the left, a view leading off into the distance."[3] The left of the frame features the farmer in the background leaning against a tree. In front of the farmer is a ram, an ewe and a small lamb. Beside them sits an adult bull, also addressing the viewer with its gaze. The focus in the centre of the frame is, clearly, the young bull (perhaps progeny of the reclining bull). The painting is life-sized (as made clear by Mark Tansey's later depiction of the work in *The Innocent Eye Test*), and is full of realistic details: there are insects flying above the back of the young bull, there are other cattle in the distant field in the right-hand portion of the painting and even a small frog appears on the soil among the fallen leaves in the foreground of the work. The striking feature of this painting is not only that the bull is looking back directly at the viewer, but that it is featured as anatomically accurate: its genitalia are clearly displayed. This is perhaps too strong a point: it would be completely expected to notice such anatomical features in an actual example of a bull, whether through photography or in real-life encounters. But this is an important point when considering the work that Bowie's Nathan Adler discusses next: Mark Tansey's *The Innocent Eye Test* from 1981.

Arthur C. Danto, in his book *Mark Tansey: Visions and Revisions*, comments:

> The painting is a comical masterpiece: a cow has been led into a picture gallery in which two paintings are hung—Paulus Potter's *The Young Bull* of 1647, ... and one of Monet's grainstack paintings of the 1880s or '90s, ... and the question is whether the artist has attained a degree of realism in depicting one of them—a young bull—that would dupe an innocent animal into responding as if it were confronting reality rather than representation—bull rather than a painting of one.[4]

Tansey's monochromatic painting features a cow much in the same orientation as the young bull in Potter's work, but with the animal obviously facing Potter's painting. To the right of the scene, a couple of male observers (one in a lab coat) are taking notes; two other men are holding Potter's large canvas in front of the cow. To the left, a man holds the cloth which had covered the painting and which has now come down to reveal the image to the cow, accompanied by another man curiously holding a mop. The image is realistic, evoking a representation of an actual event, if not being indistinguishable from an actual photo upon quick glance. On the one hand, the painting is realistic; it is also absurd.

What is truly remarkable about Tansey's painting is its ability to convince the observer that the event actually occurred in history. Danto suggests that the painting is presented in "serviceable realism, flatly illustrational, that vouches through the absence of artifice to the veracity of what is shown," similar to the illustrations in a children's science encyclopedia of some sort depicting various moments in science history. Danto continues:

5. An Analysis of 1. Outside

> Potter may fool an animal, but Tansey may fool you or me, if we believe that he is recording an actual event.... The realism of Tansey, ... belongs to our age by not belonging to it except as an archaism, but not so archaic that it falls outside remembered experiences of living personas.... *The Innocent Eye Test* is not itself, really, an experiment, but rather a demonstration of the truth that painting, even when realistic, is about more than what meets the eye, and hence the "test" for whether we understand a painting has less to do with our spontaneous, so to speak, "animal" responses, than our ability to reconstruct the meaning of the painting, construed as a kind of visual text.[5]

This reference to a reproduction of apparent reality evokes the notion of "hyperreality," a term coined by French theorist Jean Baudrillard. Hyperreality refers to the idea that one cannot differentiate between the "real" and reproductions of the real. Hyperrealism occurs when reproductions of something seem more authentic or powerful than the thing being reproduced. The study of *The Innocent Eye Test* as the depiction of reality is an example of hyperreality. Baudrillard would suggest that this participation in new "orders of simulation" leads to the disappearance of meaning. With the study of Tansey's painting in Bowie's narrative, the art crime people have decided that their spontaneous, or "animal," responses are most important; in other words, art crime has made no attempt to truly understand the meaning of the painting. Adler goes on to explain in the liner notes that the three rooms of evidence and comparative study work "proved that the cow in Mark Tansey's 'The Innocent Eye Test' could not differentiate between Paulus Potter's 'The Young Bull' of 1647 ... and one of Monet's grain stack paintings of the 1890s." Not only is this a conclusion arising out of a presumed event—the extrapolated end of a fictional event—but it could also serve as a rather strict judgment of the skill of an artist. Are the "daubers" (as the art crime people call themselves later in the text) simply supplying an educated guess as to the result of the test, or are they suggesting that Potter's cow was ultimately not convincing? Or perhaps they are suggesting that the cow does not have the intellect to tell the difference between simple paintings, which are not actually real (although realistic). What kind of corporation, then, does Adler work for? It serves to ask questions and answer queries that would seem absurd in the real world. It is probable that few would want to know the result of "The Innocent Eye Test," except perhaps as a fleeting curiosity certainly not worthy of a grand investigation. The idea that such a preposterous notion, the recognition between Potter's and Tansey's cows, would be explored sheds light on Adler's present investigation. It is also seemingly absurd that he would be in charge of determining whether the murder of Baby Grace Blue is art.

The subculture of body modification, of which body play and performance art are a part, is certainly visible in Western society. If some of the performances of Bob Flanagan, which he referred to as "little deaths," can be called art, then why not a more extreme case of violence resulting in actual death? While presenting Adler as a detective trying to sort out this particular case, Bowie asks larger questions of present day society regarding the definition and nature of art, and where and whether limits should be placed.

Bowie's text can be compared to Thomas De Quincey's "On Murder Considered as One of the Fine Arts" from 1839, in which De Quincey describes a club in which one murder is compared to another "in point of good taste."[6] In his darkly comic description of the club's dealings, De Quincey notes their discussions in detail concerning the weapon and method that biblical Cain used to kill Abel (not unlike the art crime discussions in which they try to determine the reaction of the cow in Tansey's painting). Later in the essay, De Quincey recounts the discussions in which a doctor and an undertaker collude to make a living. The beauty of the case, as determined by the club, is the elegance of it: because the undertaker was the doctor's *friend*, the doctor killed his patients. The undertaker is paid for his services, but the doctor is not. The generosity of the doctor is beautiful, thus making the act of murder beautiful.[7]

Adler claims that the precedent for art-murder (worked up through to "concept muggings" of 1998–1999, that is, petty theft as art) was set by the Viennese castrationists and Hermann Nitsche in the 1970s, among whom one performer, Schwarzkogler, is believed to have died mutilating his own penis in performance in 1969. The next precedent comes in the form of Chris Burden, who actually crucified himself on the top of a Volkswagen. The piece was entitled *Trans-Fixed* from 1974, and featured the artist on top of the Volkswagen, arms outstretched and palms nailed to the roof of the car. Burden was on display only for two minutes, with

5. An Analysis of 1. Outside

the car emerging from a closed garage and then returning to it. After a reference by Adler to Bowie himself (how "Bowie the singer" remarked about bar frequenters fully robed in surgery regalia in 1970s Berlin), Damien Hirst is mentioned, with his "Shark-Cow-Sheep thing." Hirst's claim to fame in the realm of the macabre included his response to Jeff Koons' parody of the art world consisting of a basketball suspended in a fish tank. Hirst suspended a dead sheep in a tank of formaldehyde (entitled *Away From the Flock*); the sheep was joined by a group of works that included a 14-foot tiger shark also in formaldehyde as well as cow and calf combinations, dead and preserved for all to see. Bowie is no longer referring to the fictional events described previously, but is now recounting actual events as precedents to the fictional. Perhaps it is here that Bowie is sincerely showing his concern regarding which direction the behavior of body modification, or more specifically performance art, could go. From the presentation of dead animals preserved in formaldehyde, perhaps the next possibility could be the display of a mutilated human much like the one Adler finds at the entrance to the museum.

The narrative jumps to Thursday, October 27, 1994, and Manhattan, to a performance by Ron Athey entitled "Four Scenes in a Harsh Life." In the performance, Athey continuously pokes a knitting needle into his forehead until he begins to bleed. Bowie writes, "Athey says he is dealing with issues of self-loathing, suffering, healing and redemption." The narrative returns to the "present," 31 December 1999, with Adler returning to his office that used to be artist Mark Rothko's studio, where the painter also committed suicide. By searching a "Databank," Adler links Baby Grace with three others: Ramona A. Stone, Leon Blank and Algeria Touchshriek. He feeds their combined vital information into a computer program designed to output a randomized melange of text: "[it] re-strings real life facts as im-probable [*sic*] virtual-fact" (evoking Bowie's own cut-up compositional techniques).

Here Bowie is hinting at the hypothetical link between performance art, body modification and ritual. Athey's comments serve to fuel Bowie's suggestion that, through these activities, the participants deal with issues such as healing and redemption, which would traditionally be dealt with through Western institutionalized religion. Athey's act of repeatedly poking a needle into his forehead constitutes a spiritual experience as well as a public spectacle. Mark Rothko may have been an artist who did not deal with his issues properly, or perhaps felt that the ultimate sacrifice of his own life would be his only redemption. Bowie gives an account of one who was not able to find what he desperately needed from this world, and who resorted to death rather than to continue the search.

From the swirl of random phrases, the narrative jumps yet again to Berlin, 15 June 1977. Bowie provides some context for one of the characters, Ramona A. Stone: she is a "no-future priestess ... vomiting her doctrine of death-as-eternal-party into the empty vessel of Berlin youth." The tongue-in-cheek tone of the diary is most apparent in this section, in which death and suicide are treated as simply ways to "check-out" with Ramona as some master manipulator rather than a murderer. Bowie is portraying Adler as one who has "seen too much," who must resort to humor to carry on in his line of work, much like a seasoned television detective. In another sense, Nathan Adler is as his name suggests; he is literally *addled*, or confused. By presenting the macabre topic of the diary text in this tone, Bowie softens the emotional blow of the event—the murder of a young girl. But he also brings a kind of order to a chaotic situation. It is a detective's role to provide a neutral perspective to a crime scene, detached from the horror of the event. By using humor and the absurd, Bowie is able to provide a narrative that is marked off from the real, making the reader able to reflect on the events. In his essay "Toward a Poetics of Performance," Richard Schechner suggests that this "theatrical frame" is necessary in contemplating events, the "gap between 'here and now' and 'there and then' allows an audience to contemplate the action, and to entertain alternatives."[8] The gap between these two chronological times ("here-and-now" and "there-and-then") allows the viewer or reader to reflect on the action taking place. It should be noted that Schechner condemns the actions of violent performance artists as a stimulant to more violence. Through the creation of a fictional account that, through the study of cows and so forth, contains elements of humor and the absurd, Bowie is able to cope with the horror of murder. He is dealing with the possibility of the real events by distancing himself from them in this way.

5. An Analysis of 1. Outside

This type of presentation also allows those who read it to contemplate the events that take place.

From within this fictional account, Bowie again directly references the real world. He refers to an issue of *The New Yorker* magazine, featuring fashion photos by French photographer Guy Bourdin. Bourdin was known for a photo spread in which he placed flies on pale-faced models, giving the appearance that the models were dead, and in another shoot gave models flesh "hats" made of flanks of cows. Adler says, "We're mystified by blood. It's our enemy now. We don't understand it. Can't live with it." The article from *The New Yorker* describes Bourdin's photography as morbid but fascinating.

> Masochism and narcissism pervade the fashion world, and from them Guy Bourdin, toting his own psychological burdens, distilled images of unsettling beauty. "What Guy did," Serge Lutens says, "was conduct his own psychoanalysis in *Vogue*."[9]

Bourdin is an example of one who needed to search for other means to deal with issues within himself, and he does so in a very different way than would be expected in Western society. Bourdin is somehow dealing with his "psychological burdens" through death and blood.

The final section of the narrative is back in the "present," rather humorously recounting Ramona's business endeavors including a body-parts jewelry store in London, Canada. Some of the customers were known to disappear and one rather recognizable celebrity did so after a visit to purchase a gift to celebrate her pregnancy. The text ends with a grand revelation: the child of that pregnancy would now be the same age as Baby Grace. The final words are "To be continued...," suggesting the lack of closure to the narrative. From the beginning, though, the Diary was not constructed as a complete narrative, with a firm beginning and end. Reeves Gabrels elaborates on the details of its conception. In an email with the author on 25 January 2000, Gabrels suggests that Bowie had a sort of general outline of ideas, or subject matter, but that "the whole plot outline unfolded out of a spontaneous free form improv that happened on the last day of full band recording in March 1994." The order and plot of the overall "narrative" was imposed by Bowie after that day. Gabrels indicates that the most faithful examples of the work that day are the spoken "segues" that are on the album, in which Bowie speaks in the voices of the various characters in the narrative.

Bowie suggests that the story of *1. Outside* is much like life, "an ongoing saga with no beginning and no end."[10] As with the theme of the narrative of murder as art, the style of the narrative as disjunctive stream-of-consciousness also points to the notion of boundary. Where is the division between improvised narrative and formal narrative? These questions also apply to the music of the album, much of which was created through improvisation. Through these many elements that make up the album, Bowie is questioning the idea of boundary and the crossing of lines. In addition to this, Bowie is constructing a space between these lines. This idea of space evokes Victor Turner's concept of liminality.

Victor Turner and Liminality

The questioning of boundaries is a thread that runs through the entire album, including the music, lyrics and narrative. For instance, the text is written without closure of any kind. Also, both the narrative and the music were conceived from improvisation (the boundary between improvised music and formally structured music comes into question). One example, entitled "The Motel," suggests a move across the boundary from improvisational to formal in terms of harmony, which will be explored in more detail later. The video for "The Heart's Filthy Lesson" also contains many images of juxtaposition that contribute to a sense of blurred boundaries. For instance, in the video, images of a plaster mannequin being sawed in half are juxtaposed with images of a real person actually being pierced. In the one case, an inanimate object is adorned and modified as a work of art. In the case of the actual person, the suggestion that he is being adorned and modified as a work of art is a more difficult claim to make. What is the difference between sawing a mannequin in two and doing the same to a person in the name of art. Implicitly, Bowie is asking what the difference is between piercing as art and the more extensive forms of body modification. These issues are not easily resolved, and Bowie does not concern himself with

5. An Analysis of 1. Outside

any sort of resolution. His refusal to give a sense of concrete resolution to these issues may stem from his own confusion regarding the culture of body modification. His refusal, though, is also a symptom of his stance at this point in his career, a strategy of obfuscation, a moving away from the spotlight and firmly into this liminal space.

Juxtapositions abound in the other elements of the album. The narrative structure consists of references to reality—the performances of Chris Burden, Ron Athey and others—with the description of a brutal murder and an absurd investigation. Through this juxtaposition, the narrative plays with the idea of the boundary between murder and art. Stylistically, the narrative is written in what appears to be a stream of consciousness, and much of the music was conceived initially from improvisation. What is the boundary between form and non-form, both in written narrative and in musical structure? The question of liminality is at the core of this discussion: this album plays with the liminal—or the "in between"—jumping in and out of it, from one side to the other.

Victor Turner addresses social and structural conflicts as motivations for ritual rather than psychological motivations from within individuals. Thus, he focuses on an individual as an entity controlled by group processes. Catherine Bell suggests that Turner's work has been used as a starting point for other scholars to explore the relationship between the individual psyche and society, and has been expanded upon to be applied to ritual not only in the social arena but also within each person. Bell comments that those drawing on Turner are concerned with how ritual integrates the social and the individual, both externally and internally.[11]

In his article entitled "Are there Universals of Performance in Myth, Ritual, and Drama?" Turner introduces the concept of the liminal stage in rites of passage, "a no-man's-land betwixt-and-between the structural past and the structural future as anticipated by the society's normative control of biological development." Turner is suggesting a stage that leads to a postliminal, transformed state of being. His liminal is like a cocoon for a caterpillar, resulting in a butterfly—a new form of life at the end of the experience. Turner refers to many forms of expression drawn from preindustrial rituals, among them ancient theatre and body marking and modification, as "liminal configuration[s]." Turner echoes

Bowie's views on society, stating, "there are today signs that the amputated specialized genres [such as ancient theatre, body art, and so forth] are seeking to rejoin and to recover something of the luminosity lost in their ... dismemberment." He refers to theatre, body art and so forth, as "amputated" and "dismembered" because these genres have been removed from the centre of society and confined to leisure time. Turner explains:

> Rapid advances in the scale and complexity of society, particularly after industrialization, have passed this unified liminal configuration through the analytical prism of the division of labor, with its specialization and professionalization, reducing each of these sensory domains to a set of entertainment genres flourishing in the leisure time of society, no longer in a central, driving place. The pronounced numinous supernatural character of archaic ritual has been greatly attenuated.... One source of this excessive "meta-" power is, clearly, the liberated and disciplined body itself, with its many untapped resources for pleasure, pain, and expression.[12]

This comment echoes Bowie's suggestion that body modification is a marker of a search for a new spirituality, different from Western Judeo-Christianity. Here, Turner is suggesting that industrialization is to blame, not the Judeo-Christian ethic. It is because of industrialization that societal ritual, possibly in the context of Western institutionalized religion, has been lost (consider also Virilio's opinion regarding the arrhythmy of contemporary society due to new communications technologies, a sort of advanced state of industrialization). Turner suggests that the body, as a source of pleasure and pain, is also a source of the numinous through rituals involving the body. These rituals contribute to Turner's "liminal configuration," which lead to a transformed state of being for the participants.

He further expands his explanation of the liminal (and what he calls the liminoid) in his essay "Liminal to Liminoid, in Play, Flow, and Ritual." In this article, Turner draws from Arnold van Gennep's book *Rites of Passage* (1908), in which van Gennep distinguishes three phases in a rite of passage: separation, transition and incorporation. Regarding the middle phase, he explains:

> During the intervening phase of *transition*, called by van Gennep "margin" or "limen." ... The ritual subjects pass through a period and area of ambi-

5. An Analysis of 1. Outside

guity, a sort of social limbo which has few ... of the attributes of either the preceding or subsequent profane social statuses or cultural states.[13]

He then discusses what he calls the "ritual symbols" of this phase, which fall into two categories: "those of effacement and those of ambiguity or paradox." Turner suggests that in this phase, the participants are moved towards "uniformity, structural invisibility, and anonymity."[14] This lack of individuality, while weakening the participants by removing them from cultural activities, also liberates them from cultural obligations. It is in the liminal stage that

> profane social relations may be discontinued, former rights and obligations are suspended, the social order may seem to have been turned upside down, but by way of compensation cosmological systems ... may become of central importance for the novices, who are confronted by the elders, in rite, myth-song, instruction in a secret language, and various non-verbal symbolic genres, such as dancing, painting, clay-molding, wood-carving, masking, etc., with symbolic patterns and structures which amount to teaching about the structure of the cosmos and their culture as a part of and product of it, in so far as these are defined and comprehended, whether implicitly or explicitly.[15]

Turner continues by discussing the concepts of work, play and leisure, and their roles in tribal and agrarian cultures versus their roles in this postindustrial culture. Turner then distinguishes between the notion of the liminal and the liminoid. He suggests that often in the liminal phases of tribal cultures—in rites of passage, for example—work and play are inseparable.[16] But in the postindustrial world, work has been completely separated from play, as well as leisure. Turner explains:

> Work is now organized by industry so as to be separated from "free time," which includes, in addition to leisure, attendance to such personal needs as eating, sleeping, and caring for one's health and appearance, as well as familial, social, civic, political, and religious obligations (which would have fallen within the domain of the work-play continuum in tribal society).[17]

Turner continues: "Leisure can be conceived of as a betwixt-and-between, a neither-this-nor-that domain between two spells of work or between occupational and familial and civic activity."[18] Leisure has become the new liminal phase, a place where popular culture is allowed to play with the *status quo*.

It is here that Turner's comparison of the tribal liminal phase and the postindustrial liminal phase (the liminoid, as he calls it) becomes problematic, at least in terms of the postmodern Western world. Where in the rite of passage, the initiand loses his or her individuality while also being set apart as enlightened—being instructed by the elders in "secret" arts, for instance—a postmodern member of society does not experience the same demarcation or privileging in times of leisure. No one recognizes a fellow member of society as any more privileged, or somehow enlightened, for being in a state of play. Some would rightfully argue that one who has received a certain level of success, who may be able to spend time in leisure activity rather than in the midst of work, may be recognized as fortunate by other members of society without this ability. The notion of leisure in this present argument refers to the worker in society who, for example, takes some time to relax in the evening or on a weekend. The worker is still destined to return to work at the beginning of the next week, or the following morning. This worker is no more fortunate in her or his state of leisure than anyone else in the same situation. If Turner were exploring a subculture of postmodern society, such as that of body play, then perhaps his comparison would be valid. Although those engaged in the activity of body modification are not stripped of their individuality, they are at least occasionally recognized as experiencing some form of spiritual enlightenment, and are treated accordingly. The notion that the body modifiers are experiencing some new spiritual knowledge through their activities supports the idea that their rituals inhabit a new liminal phase, more akin to Turner's tribal liminal phase than to the leisure time of postindustrial society.

Turner does make the distinction between the liminal in tribal culture and what he calls the "liminoid" of this culture: "In the so-called 'high culture' of complex societies, liminoid is not only removed from a *rite of passage* context, it is also 'individualized.'"[19] These phenomena are not collective, cyclical, or attached to any calendrical, biological, or social structure. They are "continuously generated ... in the times and places apart from work settings assigned to 'leisure' activities."[20] Further, Turner suggests,

> Liminal phenomena tend to be ultimately eufunctional [helpfully functional, as opposed to dysfunctional] even when seemingly "inversive" for the working of the social structure, ways of making it work without too

5. An Analysis of 1. Outside

much friction. Liminoid phenomena, on the other hand, are often parts of social critiques or even revolutionary manifestos—books, plays, paintings, films, etc., exposing the injustices, inefficiencies, and immoralities of the mainstream economic and political structures and organizations.[21]

Turner is talking about the theatrical in this case, and his comments can be applied most easily to performance art as social critique. But how can the modern liminal (which Turner refers to as liminoid) be applied to the less public behavior of body modification? Perhaps the connection can be made between the liminal in ritual and the behavior of body modification as a liminal phase and ultimately a transformative event—a notion that has been suggested by Musafar and others cited in the previous chapter. Bowie seems to support such a connection through his comments regarding the "neo-paganism" of body modification and its reestablishment of the numinous. With *1. Outside*, Bowie presents a space that does not fully match the characteristics of a liminal phase: Bowie's *liminoid* is not really a social critique at all, but rather symptomatic of what society is at a particular point in time. One way that Bowie achieves this is through themes presented in the lyrics of the album. Through the lyrics, Bowie is suggesting an environment that calls for the transformative result of a liminal phase, but the environment does not fully achieve this. He presents a world which cries for the endless opportunities of new life offered by the liminal, but the lyrics, through their themes of nihilism and the inhumanity of technology, contribute to this kind of liminoid phase: a place where one loses one's individuality, as in the liminal phase, but doomed to remain "betwixt-and-between." The hope of transformation is clouded by a fear of the unknown, perpetuated by the liminoid state's ambiguous character, in which boundaries are blurred and absolutes are difficult to determine. In Bowie's *1. Outside*, the endless possibilities of transformation and new life are not available because they are not recognized. Rather, the resulting state after this phase is an unknown one, analogous to the change of the calendar at the end of the millennium. Bowie presents themes of nihilism and darkness, which, coupled with themes of the inhuman progress of technology, serve to reinforce a pessimistic attitude regarding the result of this phase. These themes are particularly clear in the lyrics of "The Heart's Filthy Lesson," and "Strangers When We Meet."

A Barthesian, Fragmental Approach to Lyric Analysis

Bowie explains how many of the lyrics were conceived:

> I'd been writing in a style that I copped from Brion Gysin and William Burroughs, the cut-up/cutting-into sections of prose and then sort of resorting them and recombining them in different ways.... So at the start, when the band started improvising, I'd put all the paper all over the table and just sort of read.[22]

The presentation of the lyrics, constructed through random cut-up techniques, lends itself to a thematic reading through a kind of fragmental analysis. Although lyrics presented in the listener may also consume a narrative fashion in fragments, lyrics which are constructed as "segments" may be even more easily analyzed.

Simon Frith criticizes lyric analyses that attempt to delineate those lyrics that are "real" from those that are "fairy tale." He suggests that this distinction is arbitrary to the listener. Also, content analyses assume that the "content" (or "meaning") of song lyrics are the same for all listeners. Frith suggests that "song words are not about ideas ('content') but about their expression."[23] In his book *The Experience of Songs*, Mark Booth cites Edward Doughtie regarding the tendency of song lyrics to contain images which may be related to a central theme, but tend to be isolated from each other: "they accumulate rather than develop."[24] Consider also Dave Laing's approach to analysis, which in turn draws from the principle of "intertextuality" from literary criticism. Terry Eagleton explains:

> All literary texts are woven out of other literary texts, not in the conventional sense that they bear the traces of "influence" but in the more radical sense that every word, phrase or segment is a reworking of other writings which precede or surround the original work. There is no such thing as literary "originality," no such thing as the "first" literary work: all literature is "intertextual."[25]

In other words, no text can be read outside its relation to other texts. Texts relate to other texts; meanings emerge from a web of interrelated texts. Laing approaches the analysis of lyrics by exploring "networks of connotations" rather than autonomous narratives.[26]

5. An Analysis of 1. Outside

Roland Barthes provides a framework for the analysis of texts. In his book *S/Z*, Barthes describes tools that an author uses to delay the revelation of truth; Barthes' case study is the text of Balzac's short story, *Sarrasine*. Barthes segments the text into various elements; the first category of segments for delaying the revelation of truth is the partial answer, which he officially names the "equivocation": Barthes identifies a point in the narrative where a character provides an answer to one of the central questions of the story up to this point. Yet, this answer is only partial: "the truth is submerged in a list whose parataxis sweeps it along, hides it, holds it back, and finally does not reveal it at all." Here, "parataxis" refers to the placing of phrases in sequence without any indication as to their importance (the passage to which Barthes directly refers is as follows: "The beauty, the wit, the charms of these two children, came solely from their mother"). Consider, then, Bowie's lyrical segments as "parataxes," phrases or fragments in sequence.[27] In addition to the "equivocation," Barthes identifies other categories, including the snare ("a kind of deliberate evasion of the truth" which ultimately acts as a delay).[28] Barthes calls the snare and the equivocation "dilatory morphemes," part of his "hermeneutic code." In addition to the snare and the equivocation there are the partial answer, the suspended answer, and jamming, all working to "*arrest* the enigma, to keep it open."[29]

The hermeneutic code is the first of five codes which Barthes introduces to aid in his (post)structuralist analysis of the text. He writes, "Let us designate as *hermeneutic code* all the units whose function it is to articulate in various ways a question, its response, and the variety of chance events which can either formulate the question or delay its answer; or even, constitute an enigma and lead to its solution."[30] Though Barthes' methods might appear scientific (under the guise of attempting to find structure through the codification of segments of text), it is more playful than clinical; for Barthes, a code is a "perspective of quotations, a mirage of structures; we know only its departures and returns."[31]

In addition to the hermeneutic code, the cultivation of enigma, Barthes adds: semes (signifiers that are special because of their connotations, that is, they seem to strongly connote a common idea universally); symbolic groupings (terms or phrases that move the narrative along from one place or moment to another, through the presentation of binary oppositions or antitheses); the proairetic code (actions, which lead to consequences); and cultural codes (the greater discourse upon which the text relies; he also uses the term "reference codes" for these).[32] Again, Barthes notes that the codes are not meant to be tools of scientific or clinical analysis; rather, the codes are "associative fields": "the codes are certain types of already-seen, of already-read, of already-done: the code is the form this *already* takes, constitutive of the writing of the world."[33]

Barthes contends that an enigma is like a *fugue*:

> Both contain a *subject*, subject to an *exposition*, a *development* (embodied in the retards, ambiguities, and diversions by which the discourse prolongs a mystery), a *stretto* (a tightened section where scraps of answers rapidly come and go), and a *conclusion*.[34]

Barthes also considers the narrative to be like the "gradual order of melody" in a *fugue*, polyphonic, with various "voices" occurring at the same time. Barthes goes as far as setting up a kind of musical table, with rows of music notes indicating "events" which occur throughout the narrative, divided temporally into columns. This is an interesting analogy considering the subject matter of this book, that of a musician and also of the multi-faceted discourse which surrounds him.

Therefore, like music, "the classic text ... is actually tabular (and not linear), but its tabularity is vectorized, it follows a logico-temporal order."[35] For Barthes, the "classic text" is one which can be read but not written, as opposed to "what can be written (rewritten) today"; he calls the "classic text" a "readerly text," while the other is called a "writerly text."[36] Bowie, though, is a writerly text, a text that is constantly rewritten. The discourse of Bowie is that he is a chameleon, constantly changing who he is in terms of his persona, and how he appears to the world. And in 1995, with the release of *1. Outside*, he again reinvents himself as the artist who embraces new, younger popular musical genres, and attempts to tap into a younger audience. He is the artist that writes an Internet-like narrative that moves back and forth through time, referencing both real and fictional events, full of both real and fictional characters. But the narrative of *1. Outside*, though, makes it quite clear that, like the narrative itself, Bowie is a writerly text. The reader is able to take the fragments in "The Diary of Nathan Adler" and "rewrite" the text. In it, Bowie breaks the "logico-temporal order," even though the text is literally printed on a page (the ultimate medium in arresting the logico-temporal order). And in rewriting the text, the reader then creates new meaning, a meaning that is projected onto David Bowie himself.

However, Bowie is not necessarily the chameleon that is constantly changing, nor is he necessarily the celebrity who, like a good art director, picks and chooses approaches that are brought to him by a knowledgable and talented group of collaborators. Instead, he changes because the reader rewrites him. Furthermore, while David Bowie is being rewritten, he disappears: Bowie moves from the spotlight as the artist, and becomes a "writerly" text, the object-sign that generates meaning. Bowie becomes a piece of fashion. As Barthes suggests, the reader is not a consumer of the text but is a producer of the text. While Bowie destroys himself, the reader (re)creates him.

Barthes suggests that there are two ways to read a text. The first way is formally, establishing a "structure or a grammar of Narrative" which always looks back ("each particular narrative will be analyzed in terms of its departures"), a readerly text. The second way is to read a narrative as part of a "text," that is, as a space in which there is a continual "process of significations under way," a writerly text. Barthes calls this space *signifiance*.[37] He discusses this space in the context of the "grain of the voice," the physical, bodily presence that the listener hears in the voice. Barthes writes about an "individual thrill that I constantly experience in listening to singing."[38] He attempts to give materiality to this thrill in what he calls the "grain of the voice," which refers to not only the sound of the voice, but a space which the voice opens: "the *signifiance* it opens cannot be better defined, indeed, than by the very friction between the music and something else," that is, language.[39] It is between music and language, both media of meaning, that this *signifiance* emerges. S*ignifiance* suggests a continuing process of some kind. He states:

What is listened to here and there (chiefly in the field of art, whose function is often utopian) is not the advent of a signified, object of a recognition or of a deciphering, but the very dispersion, the *shimmering* of signifiers, ceaselessly restored to a listening which ceaselessly produces new ones without ever arresting their meaning: this phenomenon of meaning is called *signifying* [*signifiance*], as distinct from signification.[40]

Although Barthes recognizes that a framework of desire is in place when one reads some kind of text, he suggests that such a framework only exists for a moment: the text is an "'object' only long enough to put the 'subject' into question."[41] It is in the reading of the text that the subject ultimately loses his or her sense of self, and thus experiences this pleasure. When Barthes talks about the "grain" of the voice, he is referring to the "very precise space ... of *the encounter between a language and a voice*."[42] There is an attempt on the part of the listener to "stabilize" or "decipher" the voice, but there is also a willingness to become "destabilized" by it, or to lose one's subjectivity within it. About the voice, Barthes says:

> But what interests me the most in the voice, to begin with, is that this very cultural object is, in a certain way, an absent object (much more absent than the body, which is represented in a thousand ways by mass culture): we rarely listen to a voice *en soi*, in itself, we listen to what it says. The voice has the very status of language, an object thought to be graspable only through what it transmits; however, just as we are now learning, thanks to the notion of the "text," to read the linguistic material itself, we must in the same way learn to listen to the voice's text, its meaning, everything in the voice which overflows meaning.[43]

In his "Translator's Note" to Barthes' text, Stephen Heath sheds some light on the term: "*Signifiance* is a *process* in the course of which the 'subject' of the text, escaping the logic of the *ego-cogito* [a sense of self constructed through thought] and engaging in other logics ... struggles with meaning and is deconstructed ('lost')."[44] There is a pleasure associated with such a loss, and Barthes attempts to clarify this pleasure that comes with the reading of a text: he suggests that a reader is involved in a "dialectic of desire," and is thus erased. The subject in this pleasure vanishes. Barthes expresses the difficulty in articulating this pleasure, as there is no word in French—Barthes' language of writing—which encompasses both the concepts of "pleasure" and "bliss"—the "mode of vanishing"—and also the complexity of its effects. He writes of the dispersions of the subject, where the reader moves from contentment (a state he calls "consistence"), for instance, to annulment or bliss (or loss).[45]

According to Barthes, a textual analysis is not about describing the

5. An Analysis of 1. Outside

structure of a work, but rather working through its *signifying process*: "how the text explodes and scatters." He writes, "Our goal is ultimately to conceive, to imagine, to experience the plurality of the text, the open-endedness of its *signifying process*." To this end, Barthes gives instructions for the analysis of a text. He first advises that the text be segmented into very short numbered fragments; he calls these fragments "units of reading" or *lexias*. Barthes continues: "our segmentation need not be theoretically founded ... dictated by a concern for convenience: the lexis is an arbitrary product." Next, Barthes looks for the *connotations* of the text, the secondary meanings. These can be associations, a kind of lax denotation, or relations, juxtapositions in the text. Barthes continues, "Our lexias will be, we may say, the finest possible sieves, by which we shall 'skim off' the meanings, the connotations." In other words, the analysis need not be *very deep*.

The third step for Barthes is to embark in a gradual analysis through the text: "follow the text *as read*; quite simply, this reading will be *filmed in slow motion*." Finally, Barthes mentions that it is not a concern if the analysis "forgets" some meanings, something that occurs as a part of reading: "what matters to us is to show certain *departures*, not arrivals, of meaning (actually, what is meaning but a departure?)."[46] This lyric analysis will focus on the first two singles released, "The Heart's Filthy Lesson," and "Strangers When We Meet." In Barthes' analyses, each lexia is numbered and listed: this will not be done in this present analysis, but rather, the analysis will attempt to *follow the text as read*.

"The Heart's Filthy Lesson"

In a personal email to the author dated 23 January 2000, Reeves Gabrels provides some context as to how "The Heart's Filthy Lesson," the first single from *1. Outside*, came to be. During March of 1994, the band spent a couple of hours every day in improvisation based on three ideas: there was a "manifesto" that was meant to dictate how the instrumentalists would play; they were to provide musical atmosphere and mood for spoken word pieces (the "segues" of the album); and they improvised, simply inspired by the desire to play. It was in the context of one of these "free" sessions that the song emerged and was committed to tape. Later, Gabrels, co-producer David Richards and Bowie edited the piece into something with a more conventional form. Gabrels added a new rhythm guitar part and Bowie created new lyrics. Gabrels suggests that these new lyrics were about English Landscape painting, to which he objected, and was able to convince Bowie to return to the darker (though incomplete) lyrics of the improvisation session. Gabrels then moved and reinforced the musical hooks to be more "hook-like."

The title itself marks the very beginning of the text, and works in two ways: to link what it says to what follows it and to announce that a "piece of literature" will follow it.[47] The song is set up as a kind of disjointed conversation: the lyrics are "to be sung by Detective Nathan Adler" (as indicated on the lyric sheet of the Japanese double compact disc version of the album) and include personal reflection, one-sided conversation directed to Ramona (probably referring to the female cyborg, quasi-villainous character, Ramona A. Stone) and pleading with another character called Paddy. The first section, what will be called Adler's "personal reflection," is a rather ambiguous passage of four short lines, in which Adler's disjointed verbiage refers to a Diamond (the capitalization is in the lyric sheet), a Laugh Motel (perhaps a reference to another song on the album, "The Hotel"), and a kind of personification of the title of the song, with a reference to it as a female: accompanying this "Lesson"—accompanying *her*—is a long distance or long time, which leads only to destruction and despair. It is unclear as to what the capitalized "Diamond" refers, although it could refer to a person, the "Lesson."

Vocally, this section features Bowie with a closed, almost sneering, voice; this is a similar vocal delivery as the spoken word pieces listed as "segues" attributed to Nathan Adler in the track listing of the album. His voice is not sinister *per se*, but evokes a hardened individual, one that is, in particular, closed to the influences of the outside world, calloused from years of being exposed to injury and negativity. Bowie's sneer is symptomatic of a closed singing voice, a delivery contrasted by his more open voice used on tracks such as "The Motel."

At the end of the section, the singer stresses the last word, singing a slightly elongated "hell" with much air being released, giving a sense

5. An Analysis of 1. Outside

of growling rather than singing. Coupled with this delivery, the sung word is liberally treated sonically with reverb, and Bowie's voice cross-fades with the vocalizations from the next section of the song, creating an elision between the two lines and two sections.

The second section will be referred to as a one-sided conversation with Ramona. As mentioned above, the vocalization, an "Oh," comes in as an extension of the previous line, leading to this conversation. Adler wonders if there might be any feelings between him and Ramona A. Stone apart from the physical clothing that are between them, the clothing that separates them. His question, in the form of a one-sided conversation, suggests longing and points to a kind of absence or lack. The listener knows little, at this point of the album, regarding the relationship between these two characters; the music itself, with its harsh sound, does little to encourage sympathetic feelings or wishes on the part of the listener for reconciliation between these figures. As one listens to the album, Ramona is revealed as otherworldly and not particularly attractive. It is unclear what would attract Adler to Stone in any case.

The phrases in this section carry with them a sense of violation and pollution, suggesting that there exists some contamination in Adler and Stone's blood and skies. If there is something in the blood, there is often an infection of the bloodstream or some other medical problem. This phrase could also be thought of as a euphemistic reference to ingrained cultural ideas or an instinctual urging; for instance, one may have "flying in their blood" and decide to become a pilot. Also, blood is often thought of as the most intimate thing that can be shared (as in "blood brothers," for instance, where a pact is sealed by the mingling of their blood). Kim Hewitt adds:

> The act of shedding blood is perhaps the most universally powerful example of crossing the barrier between the external and internal body. Although different cultures have different levels of alarm at seeing blood shed, all recognize bleeding as precious fluid leaving the body.... Fear of AIDS has caused blood and other body fluids to be thought of even more frequently as sources of possibly fatal contamination.[48]

Something in the blood is pervasive of a person, as the blood flows throughout the body. Blood is an essential part of a living person; without it one dies. The idea that there is an infection throughout the body, or that this intimate fluid is permeated with "something," suggests longing for some kind of healing or resolution of this "infection."

At the start of this one-sided conversation is the question whether there is "something" between the two characters, commonly a sense of attraction or "chemistry." The next few lines, though, refer to that "something," that "chemistry," as an infection, something that is not to be desired and something to be ultimately cured. While Adler suggests "only if…," a indicator of his desiring of a sort of relationship with Stone, the lyrics suggest that this relationship is nothing other than pollution and infection.

Adler's continued litany of "something" makes clear that the character is confused, that the unknown is involved in this infection. The tone of the music is very dark and dense, with various voices and disparate unnatural sounds coming to the listener from various aural directions. These various elements contribute to an atmosphere of confusion and fear. They also suggests longing and depression—the inability to change the present situation.

The third section introduces another character, a person named "Paddy"; this figure does not return in the loose narrative, only appearing as the subject of address in this particular song. Adler asks who might have been wearing the clothing of another character, Miranda (also not mentioned again). These lyrics are ambiguous, for certain, but it is clear that the concept of wearing another's clothes is linked with deception and, again, violation. Bowie as Adler changes his mode of address and sings again of the contaminated lessons to which the title of the song refers. He suggests here that no one pays attention to these lessons; alternately, he suggests that no one pays attention to the *personification* of these lessons and the voyage to destruction that ultimately accompanies "her." If one cannot hear an important message, then one is doomed to live without it; in this context, those who cannot hear—or choose not to hear, and instead choose to ignore—are without hope, fated to meet whatever doom may come. The final lyric suggests that some who cannot hear such warnings—or ignore such warnings—do so because of already being victims, of living life full of nihilism and of regret, and of passing years already wasted and gone.

Adler then returns in the fourth section to the one-sided conver-

5. An Analysis of 1. Outside

sation with Stone: while previously he wondering if there might be any "chemistry" between the two, here he wonders if there is any possible future. The first lines of this section suggest nihilism and extreme pessimism. Interestingly, Adler observes the deep blue color of the clear sky. This term is rather ambivalent, although it is interesting that its connotations are not generally pessimistic, as they would be when referring to a grey or "dirty" sky, for instance. But juxtaposed with this suggestion of a deep blue sky is the proclamation of something invading the skies and the blood, a repeated cry of violation and infection.

Directly following is an aurally striking moment in the song, a moment when all the music stops and all that is heard is a sigh. In this climactic portion of the song, Adler pleads to Paddy to support him and to guide him. In Adler, Bowie presents a speaker who has lost all his strength and bearings, pleading with a partner to help him continue on his way; time has lost its meaning as well, in that Adler suggests that he is instantly older, that he has aged and has died.

In the written narrative, Adler claims that he was born in 1947, which happens to be the same year as Bowie himself. One could then conclude that, of all the characters in the narrative, Adler would be the character most closely associated with Bowie himself. The idea of time passing too quickly seems a common one in contemporary Western society, and particularly at the time the album was made—toward the end of the twentieth century, with the twenty-first century quickly approaching. Even with the advent of computers and other supposedly time-saving appliances, many concede that there seems to be less time. Time no longer seems to be in abundance, even for Bowie himself, who was approaching the age of 50 when the album was made. Barthes would suggest that this is an instance of the "chronological code," and that it appears here with the sole purpose to confuse the reader.

The loss of time—that is, the statement by Adler/Bowie regarding the sudden contraction and passing of time, and the sudden death of himself, suggests the loss of opportunity. Such lyrics further contribute to the sense of sadness and longing for more time. This section of the lyrics is stressed by a "sigh" at its opening and also features Bowie registering his highest delivered pitch of the song. Following this marked moment, Bowie ceases to sing and simply speaks the lyrics, referring to death and darkness in a rather insistent and excited voice.

Barthes' analytical method, considering a text as a tissue of fragments, offers the opportunity to read the lyrics of a song not as a linear narrative but as a variety of segments. Barthes' model as applied here allows the connotations of the lyrics to be come to the forefront. Lyrics and phrases such as hell, blood, deaf ears, and so forth, convey feelings of hopelessness, nihilism and confusion. Musically, this feeling is supported by Bowie's own sneering vocalization, the cold and distorted accompaniment and his various declamatory stresses on certain words.

Applying Barthes' model takes into account the process of reading, and takes the form of a "gradual" analysis, something to which Barthes would be sympathetic. It also takes into account the pleasure of reading, or in this case, hearing. But it is difficult to ascertain any sort of narrative here, or an inherent "chronological code" in this text, that is, that time passes in the text.[49] The text as sequence is non-apparent; the text as *tissue* is. Barthes states: "Textual analysis actually needs to represent the text as a *tissue* ... as a braid of different voices, of many codes, at once interlaced and incomplete." Finally, Barthes states, regarding the *tissue* nature of a text: "the characteristic of narrative, once it achieves the quality of a *text*, is to constrain us to the *undecidability* of the codes."[50]

"Strangers When We Meet"

The second single from the album, "Strangers When We Meet," is to be sung by Leon Blank, the prime suspect in the murder of Baby Grace Blue. The song begins with the narrator observing how his friends have seemingly wasted away: he sings of sought out secrets. He uses a French word (perhaps a result of Bowie's cut-up technique for lyric creation) to (obscurely) refer to the lack of fashionable reheating, paired up with the lack of overly positive prayers (perhaps the fervency of the prayer, a fashionable practice, is being or has been abandoned). Along with these seemingly random lyrics, the narrator complains (or affirms) that, because he is staying with the addressee of the song (perhaps a companion or a lover), he cannot go further, or move on with his life.

5. An Analysis of 1. Outside

These fragments connote a lukewarm relationship that has no hope (no prayer or attempt to rekindle the flames of passion will be successful). And the narrator is stuck in this situation. He seems to describe violent outbursts of crying all because of disbelief that he and the object of the song are "strangers" to each other; that is, they no longer know each other as they have drifted apart in their relationship. The narrator seems to be suffering in his own depression.

The next section of the lyrics refers to a television displaying a blank screen: the next line sung seems to suggest a memory of the narrator and his companion fixing themselves (that is, grooming themselves), in the "snow" of the static of a television that is receiving no signal. The narrator fixes himself in the reflection that he sees in a broken or dysfunctional television: this is a pathetic image. And though he does not understand why he and his companion are "strangers," he seems to have accepted this state and is ready to move on. But he does mention that, while he was confused in the past, he is now resentful. Not only is the narrator depressed, but he feels he was treated unfairly and is bitter. All of these fragments of images and phrases point to depression, to memory and nostalgia for a time that has passed and resentment toward the other.

There is also another group of segments referring to technology. The narrator refers to the television that displays the "snow" of a television that is receiving no signal. The notion of a television that is tuned to "snow" or static suggests a television that is not working properly. The image of a television tuned to a dead station conjures up relationships between televisions and future technology. One needs only to think of such culturally influential films as *Blade Runner*, where televisions are often shown with static or "noisy" images being broadcast, or perhaps television programs like *Max Headroom*, in which televisions could not be turned off. William Gibson's extremely influential novel *Neuromancer* begins with the phrase "The sky above the port was the color of television, tuned to a dead channel."[51] A television tuned to a dead channel broadcasts visual and aural distortion; it is also a distorted image.

The idea of the television taking over a person's attention to the extent that one cannot do anything but peer into the screen, is a very negative one, and this idea has often moved concerned parents to encourage their children to spend less time watching it. The mention of a static television set in the lyrics evokes historical concerns of television taking attention from a person. The fact that the television is transmitting essentially nothing suggests that it is not working properly. Thus, the advanced technology has not helped the narrator of the song, by perhaps informing or educating, or even entertaining, but has instead contributed to his pathetic character. The character, like a static television, is not working properly either. The loss of humanity in technology results in a distorted image of the self, or one that is not "working" properly. Perhaps the modification of the body, because of its resulting awareness of "something" real through pain, serves to correct this distorted self-image.

Bowie continues to refer to technology. He sings of remembering events and typing these memories on a keyboard, while feeling cold and tired. This fragment is emphasized by its musical context, as it comes after a piano solo culminating in a descending line down to the dominant, where the vocal line comes in, presumably leading the listener back to the tonic, an anticipated musical resolution which does not happen. Bowie's voice reaches the same pitch levels as in the previous verse, but the entry is much more emotionally charged because of the solo occurring directly before it. The narrator continues to describe the relationship and trading by using the French word for "sold," a strange combination of words: a trade is often a transaction during which equal parts are exchanged. If something is sold, there is less the sense of bartering—trading two items of equal value—but rather a relationship in which one sells the to the other for currency. The latter is not necessarily a relationship based on mutual respect, need or equality: one party serves the other, or one party controls the other. Something in this relationship has been lost.

The narrator sings of losing any sort of motivation for finding a resolution to his situation, and instead wallowing in his own inaction. The lyrics refer to one losing motivation, deciding to remain inactive, being overcome by another's perceived guilt and experiencing a strange contentment in loneliness. The lyrics suggest a very loose narrative: a confused narrator who feels strongly about a relationship; then a bitter narrator able to move on from that relationship; and finally a passive

5. An Analysis of 1. Outside

and nostalgic figure, somehow thankful that the relationship is truly over.

In a personal email to the author, dated 23 February 2000, Gabrels suggests that the emotional energy of the song came from the melody. The song and its lyrics, especially those regarding the dysfunctional television, seemed to resonate during the *Earthling* tour, a highlight of the songs performance for Gabrels.

A fragmental analysis of the lyrics suggests an atmosphere of longing, hopelessness, darkness and of technological advancement that is cold and not advantageous to humanity. Furthermore, the lyrics do not point to any redemption or positive event in the future. These themes contribute to a space that could be called liminoid, not quite reaching the ideal liminal as presented by Turner. It is a place of limbo without the range of possibilities afforded by the liminal, and no sign of the transformative as a result of the struggle in this "in-between" phase.

It is unclear as to why Bowie includes apparently positive lyrics within this context. A possible reading when first hearing this song is that the narrator has decided to resign to the hopelessness of his situation (whatever that might be), that "it is better this way." Such a reading is certainly not optimistic. Nevertheless, Bowie's inclusion of apparent optimism offers the opportunity for various readings of the song, as well as opening other avenues of possibility for what Bowie is conveying through it.

As a final note, Bowie and his band played the song on a *Top of the Pops* performance in 1995. The performance featured Bowie's actually singing (rather than pretending to a vocal track) with the band accompaniment being mimicked over a prerecorded track. A curious visual characteristic of this performance is that most of the band members, including Bowie, are wearing dark sunglasses within a darkened studio (complete with dancing fans and swirling spotlights). Some characteristics of a conventional *Top of the Pops* performance are present here: the band attempts to look convincing as they play their instruments to a prerecorded track. Usually the singer also feigns singing to a prerecorded track: Bowie actually sings here, which is made clear by his additions of various extraneous vocalizations and changes to the melody line. But he also covers his eyes with dark glasses (as do many of the band members). Barthes suggests that dark glasses function to hide the wearer. He recounts the hypothetical situation in which he has wept, but he does not want anyone (particularly his romantic partner) to notice this fact. Thus, Barthes puts on dark glasses ("to darken the sight in order not to be seen"). He continues to suggest that concealment is not the only goal of the dark glasses: "contradictorily, I want to provoke the tender question ('But what's the matter with you?')."[52] The act of wearing dark glasses not only deflects the desiring gaze of the other by concealing Barthes' incident; the act of wearing dark glasses invites the desiring gaze of the other to inquire as to what has happened. Taking this performance into account with some of his other live performance (as in the following chapter), this becomes yet another element in his strategy. He hides himself while being in plain sight.

A Brief Discussion of Album Art

Victor Turner suggests that those living in a postindustrial society are trying to reclaim the numinous. Clearly, there is a common belief that society at the turn of the twentieth century has sped up, due (at least in part) to the proliferation of communications and Internet technologies: information moves at a very quick pace, and thus, those whose lives are dictated by information feel that speed intimately. As Polhemus suggests, many would look to their own bodies as the last item that they can truly control. Bowie reflects on the difficulties that increase in communications technologies and technical advancement bring to society, through the creation of the antagonist of the *1. Outside* text, Ramona A. Stone. In her spoken "segue track," Ramona speaks technologically-themed phrases, referring to her middle-agedness; instead of referring to her age as "midlife," she replaces it with "midi," referring to the acronym for "musical instrument digital interface." She then suggests that she has mocked and shown disregard for her age: this second phrase is elucidated by an image included in the compact disc liner notes: The image suggests that Ramona has reconfigured herself to defy age by some technological modification. In the digitally manipulated image of Bowie himself, Ramona is a green-skinned woman with metallic gear on her

5. An Analysis of 1. Outside

torso and an artificial arm. It is assumed that she has modified her body to become something less human. She wears black fishnet stockings and very large black platform boots. The figure is placed on a background of blurred circular black-and-white, as well as orange, blotches and blurred images of what appear to be internal organs. The text on the right side of the image (to the right of the image of Ramona) is garbled, spelling out her name. Aurally, Bowie has transformed his voice electronically into at least three voices speaking at the same time—using a harmonizing synthesizer—and the accompanying music is cold and mechanical, using synthesizer string pads and various samples of industrial noises. He has transformed himself into something like a character from a video game, much like a science fiction warrior in a simulation: Ramona has become reality in the narrative. The only sound that is not electronically processed in some way in this segue is provided by a piano interjecting various quick successions of notes (O'Leary comes to the same conclusions, and provides some useful technical details as background to this "segue").[53] The piano is a "neutral" instrument, as discussed by Paul Théberge, because of its familiarity and traditional use, as well as the direct connection between bodily gesture and the resulting sound. This relationship can be "completely severed with electronic devices."[54] The image of Ramona coupled with the sound and lyrics of the "segue" suggest a science fiction sense of technology. The dehumanizing nature of progressive technology is revealed in Ramona A. Stone, a green-skinned semi-human manipulator, as revealed in the story; the idea of optimism in technology is nowhere to be found.

Darkness and pessimism are also reflected in the reprinting of the lyrics in the liner notes. The lyrics for "The Heart's Filthy Lesson" are reprinted in fonts of varying size, sometimes blurred and seemingly cut up. They are printed in black within light-colored boxes on a green and black background, an effect which makes successful reading of the complete lyrics almost impossible. Also, the lyrics for "A Small Plot of Land" are listed just beside these in an almost completely illegible state: blurred white printing over the black background, each letter of each word separated from the other. The lyrics for "Strangers When We Meet" are printed in a somewhat clearer manner, but in four thin closely-spaced columns, which is confusing to the reader. The words are difficult to read further to the right of the page due to the "interference" of a tinted photo and more text. In addition to conveying a similar sense of darkness and confusion as the music itself by actually hindering the ability of one to properly read the lyrics, such a presentation also causes one to question why the lyrics are reprinted in the first place. The images blur the lines between reprinted lyrics and artistically manipulated images, and may cause one to question at which point such an image could still be called reprinted lyrics. Bowie contributes to a space between these lines—this liminal space—by suggesting an atmosphere of confusion to the reader.

Musical Analysis: "The Motel"

The themes throughout *1. Outside* intersect with the culture of body modification, as they are generally explored in the previous chapter. The loose album narrative deals with murder as art, and contains references to body play. Is there a way to relate the music of the album with the lyrical (and other) themes? From the Barthesian analyses above, themes of confusion, infection, regret and the influence of technology are made apparent to the listener. The question is, how are these themes reflected in the music of the album, and how do they connect to the culture of body modification, the lack inherent in the Judeo-Christian ethic at the end of the twentieth century, and the strategies employed by Bowie to obfuscate and destroy his celebrity persona at this point in his career? A particularly powerful demonstration of this connection is embodied in the seventh track on the album, "The Motel."

The track begins with background noise and a large number of people talking beneath a jazz-like piano and bass accompaniment. The atmosphere created is suggestive of a club or bar where people congregate for a short time before returning to their previous activities. A bar is a place of leisure outside of the everyday. Similarly, a motel as a transitional place evokes the notion of a liminal space: the limbo atmosphere created in this opening establishes the aural space evoking a transitory location.

The beginning strains of music (the Intro) are sparse and airy, with

5. An Analysis of 1. Outside

scattered piano and bass entering, playing over an accompaniment oscillating between G-flat and F tonal centers, with a string pad providing a pedal of E-flat at the back of the mix. Bowie begins to sing at the downbeat of the eleventh bar of 4/4 time with a melody line that follows the oscillations of the accompaniment (this can be called an A section). After a short interlude at measure 21, Bowie repeats the melodic material at measure 27 (an A' section). At m. 39, he begins singing on different pitches (a B section), oscillating between B-flat and A corresponding to the G-flat and F of the accompaniment (that is, a third to the accompaniments tonic), at the same time that the drums enter to solidify the quarter note pulse. It is at this point in the song that the vocals provide the mediant in relation to the accompaniment's tonic; the harmonic progression of V—flat-VI—V—etc. (F—G-flat—F—etc.) in B-flat is suggested. At m. 47, the beginning of a C section, Bowie sings a C4 (middle-C on a piano), the highest pitch thus far (the lyrics here suggest a call to turn on lights) with the listener expecting a resolution to a tonic, which does not happen. Rather, the accompaniment returns to the G-flat/F oscillation in an instrumental interlude. At m. 59, the vocals return to the pitches B-flat/A using different lyrics than before (a B' section), but then repeating the previous B section from mm. 39–46. The vocals continue upwards to C as in the previous case, but then continue to D-flat and finally hitting E-flat while the accompaniment lands decidedly on the tonic, accentuated by distorted power chords in the accompanying guitars (a D section). The song finishes without vocals, with the instruments playing the static tonic harmony as an Outro, while the song fades to an end.

There is no real sense of arrival or resolution for the listener until m. 83 when the vocals reach E-flat and the accompaniment cadences on the tonic. This arrival on the tonic is emphasized by highly distorted power chords, the only appearance of distortion in the song so far. Walter Everett, discussing power chords, comments, "the listener is forced to hear ... an assertion of tonic based solely on non-pitch factors: 'a tonic is likely to ... receive an attack more emphasized ... than that of its temporal neighbors.'"[55] In this case, the assertion of a tonic *is* based on pitch factors—in other words, there is a cadence immediately before the arrival on the tonic—but the tonic comes rather unexpectedly. The piece does not begin on a tonic, and a dominant is not recognized until its resolution to the tonic emphasized by distorted power chords. It is also through non-pitch factors, heavy distortion in this case, that the tonic is established. In his discussion of heavy metal music, Robert Walser discusses power chords and distortion "as a sign of extreme power and intense expression." This "overflowing of channels" is a characteristics of power rather than failure, as "intentional transgression rather than accidental overload" firmly in the realm of music, not just noise.[56] The resolution on the tonic is accentuated by the distorted power chords, and thus the resolution is a sign of extreme power. The song traces a movement from airy and scattered accompaniment, treated vocals and oscillations to an intensely expressive arrival at a tonic, complete with Bowie's highest sung pitch and distorted power chords, outlining a chord progression of I—V—flat-VII—I—etc. This could be thought of as an arrival to a settled structure from a very loose structure, achieved through the inclusion of drums to solidify the quarter note beat to the playing of a progression rather than an oscillation of chords. One cannot help but draw a parallel between this reading of the song and the process of a rite of passage ritual as discussed by Turner and the culture of body modification as explored in the previous chapter. The initiands are in a liminal state, basically undefined and generic in their cultural role; the music is atmospheric and impersonal without reaching any resolution. After an unsuccessful ascent to C, hoping to reach E-flat, the music suddenly returns to a stable place, marked by order and confidence, which could be an analog of the resulting phase of a rite of passage (perhaps a "cut" or "piercing" occurs at m. 83, with the sudden appearance of distorted power chords). Reinforcing this feeling, during the final strains of the song, guitarist Gabrels plays a melody that basically harmonizes the tonic of the key. His melody line, played clearly with little distortion, provides closure to the song. No longer is there any tonal confusion or uncertainty; Gabrels' melodic outlining of the tonic chord further establishes this arrival at balance and stability.

    Through such a reading, the song's form can be recognized as pointing to certain behaviors explored in the previous chapter. The notion of body modification as a transformative event is certainly reflected in this piece. The moment of transformation, at m. 83, corresponds to lyrics that point to violence, explosions happening to the narrator and explosions occurring to the subject of the song. But instead of a negative view of violence, perhaps an explosion could be seen in a positive light, as in a sudden strong outburst of emotion; in this light, an explosion could be thought of as an emancipation rather than a destructive and violent event. Read in this way, this song suggests an analog to Turner's liminal phase: the transformation occurs with a feeling of order and stability following. Bowie moves from the general sense of the liminal, conveyed in the album as a whole, to a song analogous to the middle phase of a rite of passage. Bowie's intention with this positive presentation is unclear. In an album that is rife with negative themes contributing to an atmosphere suggesting a dark and fear-filled liminal phase, this analog to Turner's liminal, with its "storehouse of possibilities," is unexpected. "The Motel" may represent Bowie giving body modification its chance; this is the one song that says, "Yes, the behaviour works. Be transformed." However, it could also be perceived that Bowie does not put his faith in the activity as a force of change, as is made evident by the other elements of the album, forcibly by the music videos for "The Heart's Filthy Lesson" and his live performance.

6

Bowie in Video and Live Performance

As has been explored in the previous chapters, *1. Outside* engages with issues including body modification and extreme acts of violence—towards the self and/or others—as art, all of which Bowie has suggested, in his comments to Penman in particular, is a manifestation of the search for a new spirituality different from Judeo-Christianity. Similarly, Bowie expresses the anxiety he perceives as follows:

> There's the idea that there's a great brick wall and we can't possibly get past—that on December 31, 1999—I think it's egotistic—we'll all suddenly not be here. I think this is a feeling of panic and desperation that produces a massive momentum, as it does at the end of every century. It's only an exaggerated version, coming to the end of the millennium.[1]

Through his comments in *Seconds* magazine, as well as through the accompanying narrative (as it takes place on 31 December 1999), Bowie is engaging with the idea of the state of society at the end of the millennium. He suggests that Western society suffers a certain anxiety toward the end of a century. He may also be suggesting that the liminal space that is represented in the album is a characteristic of society at this time; the liminal is not simply a fictional construction, but a reflection of an actual societal state. Furthermore, the album is representative of Bowie that is increasingly "writerly": in creating the liminal space, he also enters into it and is lost.

This chapter will focus on the visual aspects of the album, particularly exploring the music video for "The Heart's Filthy Lesson," and Bowie's live performance of "A Small Plot of Land." Through a study of the music video, various juxtapositions will be revealed. Bowie uses these juxtapositions to create a sense of ambiguity, contributing to the creation of a liminal space.

Video Analysis: "The Heart's Filthy Lesson"

Alf Björnberg, in his article "Structural Relationships of Music and Images in Music Video," introduces an extensive model for the study of music video. Björnberg comments that "the specific characteristics of (the visual dimension of) music video attracting the attention of writers and scholars may be summarized as the breakdown of linear narrativity, of causal logic, and of temporal and spatial coherence."[2] Various writers, such as Aufderheide and Kaplan, suggest that these traits are due to the "postmodern condition," the development of technology (including the ability to produce music videos) and various explanations regarding the nature of the audience. Björnberg points out that what these authors and scholars have overlooked is the significant role of music in the context of music video, suggesting that the music is somehow "dominated" by the visual aspect.[3] Will Straw also suggests that rock journalists have made a similar claim, "that music video had made 'image' more important than the experience of music itself," and "that music video would result in a diminishing of the interpretive liberty of the individual music listener."[4]

Björnberg proposes a list of "analytical dimensions" used in his analysis of music video. The list includes discursive repetition/structure of lyrics/function; demarcation; symmetry; musematic repetition; directionality (or pitch-related directionality); motorial flow; dynamics; sound processes; and individuality predominance factor (referred to as IPF, being a measure of the signification of "individuality" in a piece). This analysis will begin with an exploration of some general characteristics of Bowie's video "The Heart's Filthy Lesson."

To begin, the video's visual content will be arranged according to its corresponding musical sections, as in Björnberg's analyses.[5] The video utilizes quick editing of images and consists of mainly brown, yellow, red or black hues; everything is presented as through a rust or sepia lens. The scenes take place indoors and the "world" is very much in decay, with waste and litter scattered throughout the set. The video opens with an image of a white mannequin against a beige background, followed by various images of the environment in which the video is taking place, presumably an artist's studio. Bowie is shown in a black t-shirt and pants, smoking, followed by an image of a dancing person wearing a Minotaur mask. As all the instruments begin to play, a group of men and women, many of them tattooed and pierced, walk down a flight of stairs. Also, there is a marionette playing a set of drums. As the verse begins, Bowie, wearing black, is shown singing, while images of the group throwing sand and other substances onto a mannequin, are quickly cut to, mixed with close-up shots of a female member of the group.

Bowie begins to sing about Ramona, as members of the group are shown wheeling a cart around, while Bowie is shown "playing" with a mannequin and dancing. Bowie has his arm around its shoulder and sings to it, smiles at it, puts his hand on the figure's chest and head, and so forth. A tattooed and bald female walks toward a bath in a light robe.

As Bowie begins to sing of the skies, there are more shots of the women moving closer to the bath. Bowie, not shown singing, dances, thrusting his arms into the air and moving quickly. Members of the group "adorn" the mannequin with various substances and are shown sawing into its torso. At the bath, the woman drops her robe revealing her bare back and buttocks at the very start of the instrumental section.

During the instrumental interlude, shots of the woman submerging herself in the water of the bath—being "baptised"—are intermingled with quick shots of a male getting needles pierced through his brow. Images of Bowie's face making exaggerated gestures—putting his hands on his face and opening his mouth, for instance—are cut with projected images of gaping mouths on a wall. The woman is lifted out of the bath by a circle of her colleagues. This is followed by various close-ups of individual members of the group in front of swinging suspended light bulbs; others are then shown pulling and hanging from large ropes in a larger room. Shots of Bowie wearing white—"artist" Bowie—are then shown.

As Bowie sings the chorus, repeating the title of the song, Bowie as "artist" is shown singing briefly, and then sketching or painting some-

6. Bowie in Video and Live Performance

thing on the floor. Members of the group are pulling on ropes that are attached to mannequins: the group is lifting mannequins by ropes attached to the mannequins' heads, suspending them over the floor of the studio. "Artist" Bowie is shown in a small circular metal cage-like enclosure, applying red paint to his white shirt and his face. Images of a man being covered in red paint and other substances and accessories are presented, intermingled with shots of a woman drinking or spilling liquids on her face. More sawing of the mannequin's torso is shown here. The viewer at this point can become confused as to which object is being decorated or worked on: the man or the mannequin.

Returning to the subject of Ramona, Bowie is featured singing while images of the adorned man—now completely covered in red paint—destroying boxes and small items are shown. The dancing Minotaur is shown again, while a mannequin is decapitated. Bowie is then shown sitting in a chair with a Minotaur mask in his hand, with various Bowie face shots and quickly edited images of the events recounted above.

The bridge section begins with the sound of a sigh interrupting the music for just a moment; Bowie is in the chair reaching upward. The mannequin is then drenched with liquid, and its head is removed. Bowie is shown in the chair with the Minotaur mask on. In a climactic sequence, members of the group walk slowly with a large bull head and place it on the mannequin, encircling the figure and then walking away from it. During this sequence, there are many images of Bowie singing the song.

In what might be called the Outro (though extended), the camera iris opens on the image of the group gathered at a table, not unlike the traditional image of Christ's Last Supper. Various close images of members of the group eating are shown, and then the group is shown in front of the table violently dancing and throwing mud or paint at each other. Bowie is shown singing, again "playing" with the mannequin, and there are three consecutive shots of the word "OUTSIDE" on the set walls. Bowie is shown sitting in the chair, and the marionette playing the drums makes its final appearance, as does the dancing Minotaur. The final scene is of the minotaur sitting in the chair, unmasking itself to reveal Bowie as the music fades. As he pulls the mask off, his face is happy, but gradually turns sorrowful as his head falls to his chest (the figure of the

Minotaur appears in the album's accompanying narrative—he/it is the murderer).

In her article "Music Video: The Popular Pleasures of Visual Music," Cathy Schwichtenberg begins by breaking the genre of music video into three formal categories: performance videos, in which a concert atmosphere is recreated by the visual images; narrative videos; and conceptual videos. Conceptual music videos present sets of images which, by their interrelationships with the editing and music, develop a concept. Schwichtenberg suggests that "this type of visual music proffers suggestive resonances to be linked together in our musical experience of a concept."[6] Contributing to the conceptual nature of the video are brief moments of action that suggest linearity. For instance, there are distinct sequences of events, such as the "baptism" of the woman in the tub, the adornment of the mannequin and the feast. Through the barrage of images that assault the senses during this video, the viewer experiences a sense of disorientation and confusion. The dynamism of the images makes a linear narrative nearly impossible to perceive. The video could be seen as conceptual, while following a rough narrative sequence; it can be divided into four parts, the actions culminating in the adornment with the bull's head and ending with the feast. The video begins with a "preparation" scene, where the group is introduced, moving from a flight of stairs through the artists' studio environment. A woman is then shown being "baptised," while a man is shown being pierced. Following this is a sequence of "preparation," where both a mannequin and a man are adorned with various objects and liquids. The third part is a climactic section in which the mannequin's head is removed and replaced with that of a bull. Finally, the video ends with a scene depicting a feast.

Schwichtenberg's discussion of conceptual videos may suggest another reading: "Visual fragments are related as metaphorical equivalents for a 'feeling' evoked by 'moving' music."[7] The visual images in this video are often disparate though seemingly occurring in the same enclosed "world." The video's dark and dull hues, quick edits, and images of violence and dirt serve to reflect the aggressive timbre of the music—particularly emphasized by the sound of the electric guitar—and the nihilistic sense transmitted by the lyrics (for instance, Bowie's sung phrases that question whether there is any hope in the future). The

6. *Bowie in Video and Live Performance*

sound of the electric guitar hook is dense, noisy and extremely processed, contributing to the uneasy atmosphere created by the images. Combined with extremely quick edits, the visuals and sound of the video contribute to a sense of insecurity and anxiety. The constant changing of images and the lack of linearity presents the viewer with nothing upon which to focus. Also, among the various elements in the video are those that seem to be contradictory, and others that are more complex than simple contradictory pairs. These various elements, along with the conceptual character of the video, contribute to its ambivalent quality. These elements will be referred to as *juxtapositions*.

Juxtapositions

Carol Vernallis, in her article "The Aesthetics of Music Video: An Analysis of Madonna's 'Cherish,'" suggests that both music and image create large sectional divisions, thus taking into account the information culled by Alf Björnberg's discussion of discursive repetition/structure of lyrics/function.[8] Björnberg's discussion of discursive repetition refers primarily to the determination of the form of a piece, breaking it down into subsections according to function, including verse, chorus, bridge, solo, and so forth.[9] As mentioned, this video can be divided into roughly four major sections: an introduction/opening scene; the preparation and adornment of the mannequin and person; the completion of the mannequin/Minotaur; and the feast. Between the introduction and the preparation scenes is an "interlude," consisting of images of the piercing of the man and the "baptism" of the woman. Also, between the preparation of the mannequin and its final adornment is an extremely disruptive musical event. At this particular moment in the piece, all the instruments are absent and a sound akin to a sigh is heard before the music begins again (marking the beginning of the third section). Vernallis comments that "in music video, the shape of the musical line can correlate to the shape of the visual image."[10] The most striking characteristic of this "break" is not only its suddenness but also the contour of the visual image accompanying it. Generally, one would think of a downward motion when hearing a sigh. Often, in one's own experience, with a sudden exhale of breath, the upper body seems to descend releasing all the air in the lungs. In this case, the visual image is of Bowie sitting in a chair, suddenly reaching upward with his hands and head, contrary to the expected contour. This opposition causes the event to be disruptive to the viewer, audibly as well as visually, and leads the viewer into the climactic scene of the video: the final adornment of the mannequin. This event is aptly named as a sigh because of its role in breaking the motorial flow of the piece, which involves a constant G-flat pedal, and is reinforced by a constant rhythm of drums and bass as well as flowing, virtuosic piano and aggressive guitar lines. In addition, the event serves as an element of juxtaposition, contributing to a sense of ambiguity in the video.

Björnberg's discussion of demarcation generally refers to a division not determined necessarily by repetition, but by "the number of musical dimensions exhibiting change."[11] For Björnberg, demarcation is contributed to by changes in lyrics, melody, harmony, and so forth. These changes would support the broader reading of form above, but act to break the piece into further subsections. The most obvious musical change is in the mode of the melody line. Throughout the piece there is a constant G-flat pedal, with Bowie's opening melody suggesting a D-flat minor tonality. When he begins singing about Ramona, the key in the melody has changed to G-flat-Lydian, which moves to G-flat minor when Bowie sings about something infecting the skies. With the beginning of the chorus, the key of the melody has again changed to F-flat-Lydian (a transposition down a tone from the mode of the previous section). Simplified, the piece is an oscillation between G-flat (the starting and ending tonal area) and F-flat. A more complete map of the tonal areas of the piece follows: G-flat pedal—d-flat—G-flat Lydian—g-flat—F-flat Lydian—G-flat Lydian—g-flat—F-flat Lydian—G-flat pedal. These changes in tonal area do correspond to changing lyrical "sections," and contribute to the musical narrative of the piece; the sections in F-flat arguably demand a return to the framing mode of G-flat. This last statement would come under the rubric of Björnberg's notion of "directionality." Björnberg explains the concept of directionality as "an attempt to summarise the effects both of parametric dimensions such as mode ('tonal language') and of non-parametric aspects of tonal organisation."[12]

6. Bowie in Video and Live Performance

This tension between the two tonalities is another example of juxtaposition, which serves to keep the song in a state of harmonic limbo. This tension again serves to give the video another element of ambiguity. An important recurring element in this video is a moment when Bowie is shown singing the song (rather than simply posing or moving). Björnberg uses the term, Individuality Predominance Factor (IPF), which is "based on a reading of the dualism of lead vocal melody and instrumental accompaniment in terms of the individual/background relationship."[13] For the purpose of this analysis, Björnberg's notion of IPF will be slightly altered: the discussion of this element will revolve around instances of the appearance of the featured artist as singer. Björnberg discusses the different presentations of the featured artist in Bruce Springsteen's "Human Touch" video, but concludes only that the presence of three "different" artists and their apparent synthesis mirrors the form of the piece, which ends in an extended coda section (a musical synthesis). The use of the term in this discussion stresses the presence of the "individual," that is, the featured artist. This reading of a modified Individuality Predominance Factor, indicating the attention given to the individual as opposed to the "background," suggests a privileging of certain lyrics in the piece. One is likely to be drawn to a segment of a music video that showcases the featured artist predominantly, and will arguably pay more attention to the musical and lyrical events occurring during this time. The image of the featured artist is one of the only constant elements in the context of this music video, and as such, it serves as an anchor for the viewer's attention. In "The Heart's Filthy Lesson," Bowie is shown many times while the mannequin/Minotaur is finally adorned, singing about losing his way. This is the only section of the video where Bowie is often shown singing the lyrics. The instances of Bowie singing the lyrics privilege those lyrics, and enhance the visual images that surround him. The privileging of these particular lyrics stresses their sense of confusion, a cry of dependence and the rapid passage of time. The sense of confusion contributes to the atmosphere of insecurity and desperation. These various juxtapositions ultimately contribute to a sense of the liminal in the video.

Although the idea of anonymity or limbo is a characteristic of the liminal phase, the context is one of passage and movement. Those that are involved in a rite of passage are considered set apart and enlightened, and gain a certain stature as a result of the rite. With the many elements of juxtaposition that create a sense of ambiguity and confusion, there is no enlightenment for the participants, nor does there seem to be any result at the end of the rite. The juxtapositions serve to confuse the viewer and support the video's apparent purpose of projecting ambivalence. The constant oppositions and juxtapositions call into question to the effectiveness of the video as a representation of a liminal state, by casting it into a state of limbo, without any hope of closure or finality.

Further reinforcing the idea that the video is a representation of a strange liminal state is the presentation of familiar elements in new combinations. Most notably, images of Christian ritual and iconography are intermingled with those of the *carnivalesque*.

Iconic Images

In "The Heart's Filthy Lesson" video, there are at least two kinds of iconic imagery presented to the viewer: images of primarily Christian ritual and those of the *carnivalesque*. Through the use of these images, the video can be read as the depiction of a rite of passage or a transformative event. The *carnivalesque* imagery serves to reinforce the video as a transformative vehicle, much like Rabelais' books, as analyzed by Mikhail Bakhtin.

The major types of ritual images in this video are as follows: the "baptism" of a woman, the piercing of a man's forehead (reminiscent of Christ's crown of thorns), the preparation of a mannequin through adornment and modification, and the decapitation and attaching of a bull's head to the mannequin, with the group then encircling the completed figure. The video also contains images that invoke Christ's crucifixion as well as the traditional image of the Last Supper. This discussion will begin with the significance of the "baptism" of a woman in the context of the video.

After the first verse of the song, the images of a woman disrobing, uncovering her bare back and buttocks, are shown. Interwoven with

6. Bowie in Video and Live Performance

images of Bowie's face and of the piercing of a man, the woman lowers herself into a tub of water, where she fully submerges herself and is later raised out of it by a group surrounding the tub. They put their arms beneath her and lift her out of the water with her remaining in the same lying position as she was in the tub. She is subsequently lifted above their heads, and thus this sequence of images ends.

Of course, the idea of baptism is primarily a Christian one. In describing the transmutation of rituals due to social circumstances, Catherine Bell provides a concise outline of the development of the Christian ritual of baptism. Originally fashioned after the experience of Christ, which is described in Matthew 3:13–17, Christian baptism was a marker of the entrance of a person into the Christian community. Bell comments,

> As befits an alternative sectarian group outside mainstream Judaism and critical of Judaism's accommodations to a worldly ethos and political necessities, Christians made a sharp distinction between insiders and outsiders—the "way of life" and the "way of darkness"—and ritually guarded it with rites rich in the symbolism of death and rebirth.[14]

With the conversion of Emperor Constantine and the Edict of Milan in 313 CE, in which Christianity was deemed legal and made the official religion of the Roman Empire, the religion moved from being a sect to being a recognized church. Institutionalization followed: the Church became involved in all areas of life, including marriage, death, and appropriating Roman festivals as Christian holidays. Bell comments:

> Hence, the elaborate initiation of the adult catechumen [or initiand] ultimately divided into a rite of infant baptism, confirmation, and communion. In this ethos, the Christian community was no longer a marginal schismatic Jewish-Gentile sect nursing millennial expectations of the end of the world. It was now in a position to be quite at home in the world, closely tied to the major political institutions of the early medieval period, with a growing understanding of its role in the world and its history.[15]

Interestingly, most present evangelical Protestant churches, developing from the Protestant Reformation movements of the sixteenth century, return to the idea of baptism as a commemorative act, imitating Christ's own baptism. In certain evangelical circles, the baptism in water is an act of identifying with Christ, and is often recognized as an initiand's public display as a follower of Christ.

The use of the image of a woman appearing to be baptized is interesting. Bowie may be invoking the evangelical church here, which in itself is critical toward institutionalized Christianity in the form of Roman Catholicism in particular, with what is sometimes perceived as its extra-biblical liturgical rituals. But the action depicted in the video is certainly outside of any kind of conventional Christian sensibility. For instance, the baptism occurs in a tub, into which the woman enters by herself. She is nude upon entering the water, a state which would not be tolerated in an orthodox Christian setting, especially during the public ritual of baptism. Finally, the images of her baptism are intercut with those of Bowie's grotesque facial gesturing and a man being pierced in the forehead. This clash of images is not conducive to any pacifying religious experience or positive transformative event in the traditional sense.

The images of a man being pierced by needles through his forehead, the criss-cross of pins appearing like a "crown" of sorts, also conjures up images of Christ's crown of thorns. The intent here might be similar to that of O'Conner's character, Hazel Motes, and the belief that in order to become closer to Christ, one must identify with him and his pain. This path to Christ is not an orthodox one, but rather an access to God through the self-harm and one's own actions. Why is the piercing image shown in the video, and at this particular spot in the video, intercut with the images of the baptism? The piercing of the head is suggestive of the biblical Passion narrative, during which Christ's head is adorned with a piercing crown of thorns. Consider one member of the group in the video as an icon of Christ: at the end of the video, the man presents himself with arms outstretched as if crucified. His gaunt figure supports a popular image of Christ on the cross, suffering, weak and frail. The inclusion of this image in the video can be read as another evocation of Christ and His crucifixion. The mutilative and ritual nature of Christ's crucifixion is undeniable, but its icons present in the video serve as familiar elements in unfamiliar contexts, which is characteristic of a liminal space.

Further suggesting the image of Christ, the final section of the video

6. Bowie in Video and Live Performance

consists of a feast. While much of the subsequent images of consumption lean toward a more *carnivalesque* reading, the opening of this section with the camera iris revealing the frontal view of the complete table is reminiscent of traditional paintings of the Last Supper, as described in the biblical text, during which Christ partakes in a final meal with his followers before his betrayal and crucifixion. It is also in this setting that Jesus introduces the phrases and actions that have become the basis of the Eucharist, an important Christian ritual seen by some as an act of remembrance of Christ's redeeming sacrifice, and by others as a grace-imparting act in its repeating. Christ is often a focal point at the center of the table, surrounded by His disciples. This first view is not in focus, further adding to the possibility that this is a direct evocation of Christ's Last Supper; it is no longer clear that the viewer is observing a promotional music video showcasing David Bowie. For a moment, the video seems to call up a religious image from antiquity.

Intermingled with these Christian images are images of non–Christian ritual, such as the adornment of the mannequin and its adornment with a bull's head and worshipful encircling of it by the group. This takes place after the disruptive event of the "sigh," which serves both to draw the attention of the viewer in the direction of what follows, and as an instance of juxtaposition contributing to ambiguity in the video. Obviously, the action of adorning a mannequin and then encircling the representation of a Minotaur is not a ritual that is even remotely rooted in Christianity. The encircling of the mannequin invokes an Other ritual in the fact that it is not recognizable as traditionally Christian, although the worshipful encircling of the completed mannequin suggests the worship or adoration of inanimate objects or of idols. But why the emphasis on this portion of the video and its images? The ritual does not involve conventional religion, nor does it "praise" the classical body. As will be discussed in more detail later, the "classical body" as presented in Renaissance statuary also represents rationality itself and everything "high" and intellectual. The minotaur is not an example of the classical body; this new minotaur body represents the "low," the marginalized and the physical.

The reasoning for the *appearance* of Christian ritual is even more difficult to establish. Walser, in his discussion of the use of mystical and religious themes in the music of Heavy Metal groups such as Iron Maiden and Led Zeppelin, comments that religious imagery, along with myth and other types of images, are imbued with a sense of mystery and power. Apart from Christianity, heavy metal bands like Iron Maiden draw upon various traditions, including the Occult, Romantic poetry and even Egyptian civilization. Speaking specifically about Iron Maiden, he suggests that fans attending a concert participate in an experience that empowers them, particularly due to the ritualistic images that proliferate the concert. These images imbue the experience with luminosity. Additionally, Iron Maiden takes these notions of the sacred and inserts them in the music, performances and artwork and thus sets that material apart from the "everyday." Their music becomes sacred, embodying a sense of empowerment and freedom, something Other than the mundane.[16] Walser's suggestions can be easily applied to Bowie's use of Christian images in the video. These images invoke historical depth and depict ritual that is outside of the "everyday." The use of Christian images in the video serves to draw attention to ritual and sacrifice as possible methods to engage with the spiritual. As such, they are empowering, providing the listener with new resources to make sense of his or her own social experience. The Christian images may work in this way, but their effectiveness is changed by their interaction with other types of familiar images.

What then is the purpose of presenting an apparent baptism, the many invocations of Christ as well as the Last Supper, with images of ritual and also the *carnivalesque*? An explanation can be found by referring again to Victor Turner's theory of liminality. Turner states:

> Liminality may involve a complex sequence of episodes in sacred space-time, and may also include subversive and ludic (or playful) events....
> Then the factors or elements of culture may be recombined in numerous, often grotesque ways, grotesque because they are arrayed in terms of possible or fantasied rather than experienced combinations—thus a monster disguise may combine human, animal, and vegetable features in an "unnatural" way.... In other words, in liminality people "play" with the elements of the familiar and defamiliarize them. Novelty emerges from unprecedented combinations of familiar elements.[17]

By combining various familiar elements, including a "baptism" and those of Christian iconography, as well as the *carnivalesque*, the video may represent, in itself, a liminal space. Turner's comments fit the video almost perfectly, even with the statement regarding the recombination of human and animal elements in the creation of a monster; in this case, a bull's head is combined with a human body to create a Minotaur, which is an example of the many juxtapositions in the video.

As a familiar element, the *carnivalesque* serves its purpose in the establishment of a kind of liminal space, but it also serves as an example of transgression. The *carnivalesque* overturns the official; it is a statement against the status quo. The discussion will now turn to an exploration of the *carnivalesque* as transgression.

Transgression

Peter Stallybrass and Allon White, in their book *The Politics and Poetics of Transgression*, shed some light on the *carnivalesque* as a move against the "high" and "official," but not simply in behavior or appearance but in all areas of culture. They begin by discussing the notion of the "high" and "low" in culture: the "high" is constructed in relation to the "low." Each discourse depends on certain historical moments for its definition. These discourses are also inherently political, in terms of aesthetics and morality. Through their discussion, the authors also explore the contradiction inherent in the "low," being both reviled and desired. There is a political imperative to reject and eliminate the "low" by the "high," but there is also a desire by the "high" for this Other. The "top" attempts to eliminate the "bottom" for reasons of prestige and status, only to discover that it is dependent upon the low–Other, but also that the bottom is *included* in the top, as an eroticized element in the top's construction of fantasy. While being an integral part of the fantasies and collective imagination of the high, the low–Other is denied by the dominant culture both politically and socially.[18] Bakhtin's *carnivalesque* has moved from a study of Rabelais' work to the development of the notion into a critical inversion of all hierarchies and official realms. Stallybrass and White note that the "grotesque realism" of Bakhtin's *carnivalesque*, prevalent in Europe of the Middle Ages, functioned in three ways. First, it provided an example of an ideal of a heterogeneous and free community. Second, it provided festive and comic images that stand in start contrast to the official and oppressive "high" culture. Third, it provides a representation of the "grotesque" elements of the imagination as creator of the world. In other words, the world is constructed by these grotesque elements and ruled by them. But the authors also point out that some critics question whether the "licenced release" of carnival activity might deem it as simply a form of social control of the low by the high. They reply that such is essentially a non-issue: mostly, carnivals are cyclical rituals devoid of political transformation, but they often act as a catalyst of and for actual struggle. At the very least, the *carnivalesque* enacts the symbolic struggle between the classes.[19]

Bakhtin's concept of high/low inversion is referred to as "symbolic inversion." Barbara Babcock defines "symbolic inversion" as "any act of expressive behaviour which inverts, contradicts, abrogates, or in some fashion presents an alternative to commonly held cultural codes, values and norms be they linguistic, literary or artistic, religious, social and political."[20]

It is in this spirit that Stallybrass and White wish to use the term "transgression." This notion can be directly applied to the behavior of body modification. The behavior, in many cases, not only transgresses mainstream cultural codes of appearance, but it also transgresses the very notion of the "classical" body as held in Western society.

Stallybrass and White also discuss Bakhtin's notions of the "classical" body and the "grotesque" body, and their contrary nature. The "classical" body, as presented by Renaissance statuary, is generally on a pedestal, placing the observers in a state of admiration, gazing upon a moment of time: the statuary reflects on a heroic past, a "*momento classici*," which the present can only hope to imitate. The grotesque body stands in opposition to the ideal "high" conception of the body, which is based on this heroic past. Thus, "the grotesque body stands in opposition to the bourgeois individualist conception of the body, which finds *its* image and legitimation in the classical." The classical body became the identity of rationality itself, representing the "high" discourses of philosophy, theology, law, and so forth, in opposition to the grotesque, low and marginal. Stallybrass and White advocate

6. Bowie in Video and Live Performance

that one should not treat the *carnivalesque* as nothing more than a political binary, but rather that one should take a wider view of transgression: the *carnivalesque* is a space between the "classical" body and its opposite. Nonetheless, the physical body is central in the *carnivalesque*.[21]

Stallybrass and White also discuss the marketplace as a bounded enclosure and a site of open commerce:

> At the market centre of the polis we discover a commingling of categories usually kept separate and opposed: centre and periphery, inside and outside, stranger and local, commerce and festivity, high and low.... The market square ... is only ever an *intersection*, a crossing of ways.[22]

From the authors' comments, a parallel can be made between the marketplace and Bowie's liminal space, as both of these spaces are rife with juxtaposition. Stallybrass and White further suggest that the marketplace is like the body.

> The tangibility of its boundaries implies local closure and stability, even a unique sense of belonging, which obscure its structural dependence upon a "beyond" through which this "familiar" and "local" feeling is itself produced. Thus in the marketplace "inside" and "outside" (and hence identity itself) are persistently mystified. It is a place where limit, centre and boundary are confirmed and yet also put into jeopardy.[23]

The marketplace, both as a site of juxtaposition and as an analog for the body, leads to another observation. The marketplace as a site of the *carnivalesque* is also a site of the liminal, "with respect to role reversal" as a space "betwixt and between."[24] If one will accept the idea of the marketplace as liminal, then the body also constitutes the liminal with the display of transgression through the *carnivalesque*. The images also serve to overturn the official, and to call for transformation. Thus, the video's display of *carnivalesque* images serves to reinforce the idea that it is creating a liminal state. This state is a problematized construction of the liminal, since its infusion with ambiguity and confusion caused by juxtaposition results in a loss of hope for any sort of positive transformation.

Carnivalesque Images

"The Heart's Filthy Lesson" is saturated with images of the *carnivalesque*, primarily in the form of Bowie's various poses and the feast. Pam Morris comments on the effect of the *carnivalesque*: "it always simultaneously ridicules and celebrates, crowns and decrowns, elevates and debases. The grotesque exaggeration of the body in carnivalesque forms, and especially the persistent emphasis upon the belly and genitals, mocks Medieval religious repudiation of the flesh."[25] Bakhtin states, "Minor occasions were also marked by comic protocol, as for instance the election of a king and queen to preside at a banquet 'for laughter's sake' (*roi pour rire*)."[26] The preparation of the man, and later the mannequin (in some scenes being sawed and finally decapitated) recalls the carnival "king." Bakhtin comments, "Debasement and interment are reflected in carnival uncrownings…. The king's attributes are turned upside down in the clown; he is king of a world 'turned inside out.'"[27] The attaching of the bull's head to the mannequin could be thought of as a crowning of a sort, creating a Minotaur, the mythic monster shaped half like a man and half like a bull, given a pacifying tribute of youths and maidens as food. This contradiction is another example of a juxtaposition contributing to a sense of ambiguity in the video.

The preparation of the man, as well as other images within the video, suggest the presence of bodily fluids. The covering with human waste or other bodily fluids is essentially degrading: "To degrade is to bury, to sow, and to kill simultaneously, in order to bring forth something more and better."[28] Bakhtin continues, "It can be said that excrement represents bodies and matter that are mostly comic; it is the most suitable substance for the degrading of all that is exalted."[29] Through the degradation of an object, Bakhtin suggests that a new birth takes place. He is suggesting that debasement is a precursor to a transformative event, not unlike the loss of individuality in a rite of passage.

The pierced man could also be thought of as a *carnivalesque* figure, "crowned" both literally, with pins in his forehead, and figuratively, being empowered and made different. The attention given to the act of piercing

6. Bowie in Video and Live Performance

in the video suggests its intention as an act against the religious repudiation of the flesh. Piercing can be an attack on what might be perceived as forced social conformity, as society dictates what defines correct appearance. With the previous discussions regarding the culture of body modification, this is only one possible motivation for the behavior, but one that supports the notion of piercing as power. Power, in this sense, stems from one's ability to choose one's own appearance, or to choose one's own expression of transgression.

Throughout the video, Bowie himself is presented as a grotesque figure, often with a gaping mouth and/or protruding eyes. Bakhtin comments:

> Of all the features of the human face, the nose and mouth play the most important part in the grotesque image of the body; the head, ears, and nose also acquire a grotesque character when they adopt the animal form or that of inanimate objects.... The grotesque is interested only in protruding eyes.... It is looking for that which protrudes from the body, all that seeks to go out beyond the body's confines. Special attention is given to the shoots and branches, to all that prolongs the body and links it to other bodies or to the world outside. Moreover, the bulging eyes manifest a purely bodily tension. But the most important of all human features for the grotesque is the mouth. It dominates all else. The grotesque face is actually reduced to the gaping mouth; the other features are only a frame encasing this wide-open bodily abyss.[30]

These gestures are particularly stressed when they are supported by the lyrics, as is the case toward the end of the song. Bowie repeatedly sings about the abyss, a vague term which Bowie explicitly links to death. In the video, those lyrics are paired with facial expressions suggesting madness or exhibiting extreme changes in emotion; these elements contribute to the grotesque in Bowie's mannerisms. Bakhtin suggests that the grotesque is concerned with that which protrudes from the body, or reaches out of the confines of the body. Bowie, exhibiting bodily tension, attempts to cross the boundary of his body and its surroundings by reaching out, whether it is through his sharp and quick movements of his arms or through his protruding eyes and exaggerated emotional faces.

The "abyss" of the open mouth is also prevalent in the feast scene. Bakhtin states:

> Eating and drinking are one of the most significant manifestations of the grotesque body. The distinctive character of this body is its open unfinished nature, its interaction with the world. These traits are most fully and concretely revealed in the act of eating; the body transgresses here its own limits: it swallows, devours, rends the world apart, is enriched and grows at the world's expense. The encounter of man with the world, which takes place inside the open, biting, rending, chewing mouth, is one of the most ancient, and most important objects of human thought and imagery. Here man tastes the world, introduces it into his body, makes it part of himself.... Man's encounter with the world in the act of eating is joyful, triumphant; he triumphs over the world, devours it without being devoured himself.[31]

The video features a raucous feast scene, with a particular sequence of images consisting of a woman (again, a member of the group) devouring a piece of meat, her gaping mouth particularly noticeable. Along with this image is that of a projected mouth on the set walls throughout the video. Around the eating woman and the other participants in the feast, her colleagues dance in a violent manner. Referring to acts such as this, Bakhtin comments: "We have shown the essential link of blows and abuses with uncrowning. In Rabelais abuse never assumes the character merely of personal invective; it is universal, and when all is said and done it always aims at the higher level."[32] Morris suggests that these *carnivalesque* images bring attention to that which is material and corporeal: "The upward impulse of official ideology rejects all that is earthly and material. But the downward thrust of grotesque realism affirms the material life of the body and of the earthly world."[33]

Just as the novels of Rabelais showcase the exaggerated body, emphasis on eating and excrement, and frequent beating and debasing, the grotesque body represents all of humanity: "it is the undying body of all the people, comically debased so that it may be festivally reborn."[34] And like the novels of Rabelais, Bowie's video is a representation of humanity through its presentation of particular grotesque images; it is no mistake that the young people in this video appear as members of a subculture with an affinity for piercing and other body modification. The video is a statement against the terror of the "official" world. Bakhtin's *carnivalesque* works against such terror:

6. Bowie in Video and Live Performance

> In the sphere of imagery cosmic fear (as any other fear) is defeated by laughter. Therefore dung and urine, as cosmic matter that can be interpreted bodily, play an important part in these images. They appear in hyperbolic quantities and cosmic dimensions. Cosmic catastrophe represented in the material bodily lower stratum is degraded, humanized, and transformed into grotesque monsters. Terror is conquered by laughter.[35]

The notion that "terror is conquered by laughter" is applicable also to the narrative of Nathan Adler discussed earlier. The presentation of the narrative in a humorous manner is a method of defeating the terror of the event being described. The notion of cosmic fear—perhaps the approach of a millennium, a boundary to be crossed—being defeated by laughter, in the form of the grotesque and the transgressive is interesting. The suggestion that this "laughter" conquers the unknown fear might support Bowie's suggestion that the behavior of body modification is a manifestation of tension at the end of the millennium. What the behavior does suggest is a transgression against what society deems as normal and proper, and a crossing of societal aesthetic lines.

The combination of *carnivalesque* images with those of Christian iconography and ritual serve to establish the video as a kind of liminal space. But through its many presentations of juxtapositions, the video also suggests a sense of overwhelming ambiguity. The video does not fit into Turner's description of the proper liminal phase. This notion of a liminal space, though, does not only apply to the video or to the music and lyrics as were explored in the last chapter, but also to Bowie's live performance. Juxtaposition in his performance is notable and effective in continuing the establishment of a liminal space.

Bowie in Live Performance

Christopher Sandford describes Bowie's first appearance on David Letterman's late night television show in September 1995:

> The disparity showed between his dark clothes and the puce-red stage. After a perfunctory "Heart's Filthy Lesson"—shorn of the studio

effects, no more than a slab of bristling art-noise—he gave a wolflike leer and bared his teeth. Bowie looked seriously ill. The lights picked out the disconcerting colours of his eyes. For the first time in twenty years, he was physically reproaching his audience, turning his back even before the song ended. His grim "Thanks" was an irony.[36]

Sandford's description certainly conveys the spirit of the evening. Bowie was presented in a shiny black jacket and pants, a cream colored T-shirt, with matching black nail polish and eye liner, appearing angry and gaunt. Sanford fails to mention that the music actually started before Bowie even appeared on stage, and he appeared highly agitated when he began to sing, with his arms flailing and his gestures extreme and sudden. The multitude of technical blunders throughout the performance contribute to the overall feeling of confusion and loss of control, although it is unclear as to whether they were planned or whether they were simply early performance glitches. Sanford suggests that this performance shocked the audience into rethinking who Bowie was and what he was doing. The performance was presented like an accident, furious and volatile. Recorded the day before the release of his album, this performance of the first single was probably the first exposure of Bowie's new material to a wide American audience, and would certainly make an impression on the audience for any future performances. Sanford continues:

> The tour took the same frequently antisocial line. On some nights concert-goers were confronted by a bare set, on others by a backdrop of torn drapes, a few chairs, a kitchen table and stark, operating-theatre lighting. Scrolls were rolled down to indicate changes in mood. The whole thing rested on Bowie's frozen presence, broken only by his ambling to the wings or slumping at the table.[37]

Bowie presents himself, to use Sandford's words, as antisocial and also strange and frightening. Bowie sets up yet another juxtaposition of being both exposed to an audience, needing them to buy his albums or attend his concerts, but then presenting himself in an antisocial manner, as if his dependence was not an actuality. Symbolically, Bowie separates himself from his audience by the dropping of banners on stage in the live performance of the song "A Small Plot of Land."

6. Bowie in Video and Live Performance

"A Small Plot of Land"

In November 1995, Bowie performed at the Wembley Arena in London. The concert stage set for the *Outside* tour featured a large scaffold-type marquee holding large letters forming the words "OPEN THE DOG" over the stage. As Sanford mentions, the stage itself was covered with drop cloths, with some stacked chairs and other various forms which appear to be mannequins draped in drop cloths toward the back of the stage. Toward the front of the stage was a small table surrounded by some chairs, just immediately behind and to the left of Bowie's microphone position. Bowie wore a white/grey t-shirt and same-colored pants with a white long-sleeved button-up shirt draped around his waist, all stained with dark blotches of what appeared as dark paint. At one point in the concert, a mannequin in a fetal position, encased in circular metal bars, was positioned high above the stage as Bowie knelt at the table in a prayerful position, as if praying to this human moon.

In "A Small Plot of Land," an event occurs which stands out among the rest of the performance. The song begins with a spotlight only on Bowie, the rest of the stage in darkness, while Bowie speaks some words accompanied by piano beginning the introduction. As the other musicians begin playing, the stage is washed with a blue light and Bowie proceeds to sit at the table with his back to the audience; he turns only as he begins to sing. As the performance continues, Bowie walks in a limited area slowly, often making quick but smooth gestures with his hands and arms. He then visits a lower portion of the stage, a few feet away from the audience, making slow graceful movements, although he does not make any physical contact with the fans only a few feet away. He walks slowly to a hanging cord and pulls on it, causing a large rectangular banner to unfold above the stage, and repeats this action three more times at various locations around the stage. For the first banner, he reaches up to grab the cord with his right hand, while grabbing his right wrist with his left hand and then sliding it down to his elbow. He rests his head on his forearm as if in a state of sorrow, and then proceeds to pull the cord downward slowly but forcefully. The pulling of the cords occurs during Gabrels' guitar solo. This action in the performance is one of the only instances of Bowie doing anything other than singing and wandering within a relatively small area. Bowie is acting like a person separating himself from the audience, much like a person pulling down a window blind to avoid having to see a pesky neighbor. Sanford suggests that the banners served to change mood, but here they do not seem to serve such a simple purpose. In a personal email to the author dated 19 March 2000, Gabrels states that the practice of dropping the banners did not go on for very long, and he does not recall the purpose of the action. He suggests that it was simply to give Bowie something to do during the guitar solo and to change the scenery a bit—he suggests the term "functional theatricality."

Bowie alienates himself from the audience by his physical presentation, as Sanford suggests, but also by the literal dropping of divisive banners, which constitutes yet another example of juxtaposition. Bowie is supposedly alienating himself although he is performing in front of crowds night after night on tour. Why this constant juxtaposition? It stresses the idea of the liminal, presenting a state of ambiguity and confusion, which is limbo-like without absolutes. It reflects both Bowie's own confusion regarding the function and results of body modification, but also reflects some of Bowie's comments regarding society at the end of the millennium. Furthermore, Bowie is stressing the tension between being in performance for a paying audience while being separated from that very audience.

The video and live performance exhibit many juxtapositions. In the video, there are those who are adorning a mannequin, sawing it in half and covering it with fluids, but there is also the piercing and adornment of an actual person. The lyrics referring to the deep blue color of a clear sky are juxtaposed into a lyric that is laden with themes of infection and pollution, and a video with no sign of blue sky anywhere. In live performance, Bowie pulls down blinds for no practical reason (except for something for him to do), his clothes stained with paint or perhaps some other substance. Bowie pulls the blinds down to be alienated from his audience, although he is performing in front of them. He turns his back to the audience on television although his album is being released the next day. He wears sunglasses in a darkened studio while performing a single. In the narrative, the idea that a horrible murder of a young girl could be investigated with such humor

6. Bowie in Video and Live Performance

and nonchalance, and that this murder could be investigated as art, is an intriguing juxtaposition, as is the notion of body modification as a method of internal transformation—that through physical transformation comes a kind of spiritual rebirth. These contradictions and juxtapositions serve to surround the work with ambiguity, confusion, the unknown.

There is no multitude of positive possibilities available in this limbo state, as suggested by Turner's notion of the liminal stage of a rite of passage. Bowie does suggest that the date of 31 December 1999 is like a great brick wall.[38] *1. Outside* is a reflection of the late 1990s as a kind of liminal state, with the "transformative event" at the end of it all, the turning of the clock—like some kind of grand body modification, destroying the old and bringing in the new—leads to the unknown. As is generally the case with most things that are unknown, they are responded to with fear; it is easy to be fearless of what is known or expected. There is no sense of stature or social office for the participants at the end of this grand rite of passage, but only a fear of greater disparity in society and nihilism in technology as is evident in some of the lyrics for the album. With the unknown comes fear, and fear is rarely accompanied by optimism. Generally, there is only a confusion and dread of what the future will hold.

Is it possible to say that Bowie, through *1. Outside*, is constructing a true reflection of society (or at least some part of it) at the end of the millennium? It is difficult to say, especially when time has in fact gone on and midnight on 31 December was not so much of a brick wall as some people thought. What this discussion does support is that Bowie and his creation of a sense of the liminal is a metaphor for the despair of some portion of society at this period of time. The liminal not only reflects Bowie's own confusion regarding the act of body modification, but perhaps the confusion of a segment of Western society at a point in time when their own future was unclear.

In an interview with *Musician* magazine, Bowie shares a fascinating personal reflection: "Imagine what a wonderful optimistic freeing experience January the first 2000 is gonna [sic] be, psychologically.... One has to remain optimistic. And I do; even though the album is seemingly very dark, it actually pleads for an understanding that there is a through road to the next century."[39] Bowie's later career, and the *1. Outside* album, do not suggest optimism. Throughout this study, what has been made clear is the complexity of Bowie's album and, in fact, the later part of his career.

Postscript

Along with the new musical material mentioned at the end of Chapter 1, there has been a wealth of new literature on Bowie. Wendy Leigh's *Bowie: The Biography* (Gallery Books, September 2014), is a chronicle of the singer's life, focusing on his personal and business relationships, and his struggles with drugs and his sexual exploits, though it does not provide new insights into Bowie's creative process. According to the publisher's description listed on the Canadian version of the Amazon online store, Roger Griffin's *David Bowie: The Golden Years* (Overlook Press, 2015) "chronicles Bowie's creative life during that decade in a year by year, month by month, day by day format, placing his works in their historical, personal and creative contexts." Sean Egan's *Bowie on Bowie: Interviews and Encounters with David Bowie* (Chicago Review Press, 2015) collects Bowie interviews in order to paint a more complete picture of the celebrity. Chris O'Leary, who provides much useful commentary in this present work, published his own exploration of the earlier songs of Bowie, entitled *Rebel Rebel*, published by Zero Books in March 2015. It has been announced that O'Leary will publish a second volume, presumably covering songs from 1977 onwards, continuing from the end of the first volume.

In terms of academic studies of Bowie, there are some exciting works that have not yet been released at the time of printing. Edited by Eoin Devereux, Aileen Dillane and Martin Power, *David Bowie: Critical Perspectives* (Routledge, 2015) is a collection of essays covering six broad areas, such diverse topics such as psychoanalytical approaches to his music and persona, the Other in his music and critical readings of musical texts. Shelton Waldrep's *Future Nostalgia: Performing David Bowie* (Bloomsbury, 2015) promises to explore key time periods in Bowie's career through the lenses of sub-culture theory, gender/sexuality studies, post-colonial theory and more. Also from Bloomsbury in 2015 is *Enchanting David Bowie: Space/Time/Body/Memory*, edited by Sean Redmond and Toija Cinque: Bloomsbury's own description states, "He [Bowie] requisitions and challenges his audiences, through frequently indirect lyrics and images, to critically question sanity, identity and essentially what it means to be 'us' and why we are here."[1] This is not an exhaustive list of new literature on Bowie, but these works do demonstrate the renewed interest generated by Bowie's own resurgence.

As recounted earlier in this book, Martin Roth calls Bowie an "instigator ... of a particular zeitgeist that is uniquely his and yet resonates with enormous numbers of people around the globe." Part of that zeitgeist seems to emerge from Bowie's move as a young person from suburbia into the creative milieu of the city of London and the neighborhood of Soho in particular. For Geoffrey Marsh, Bowie's career can be mapped geographically, a kind of "psychogeography" that corresponds to the evolution of his career—and early life—in post–World War II London. Bowie began his life in the suburbs, nine miles away from the center of London, as a member of the growing middle class in the postwar period. His early life consisted of a visible and moral conformity, deeply entrenched in an almost homogeneous whiteness. Bowie himself had three older half-siblings, and thus lived his life like a single child. But he had a good relationship with his older brother Terry, nine years David's senior, who introduced Bowie to "Beat" writing, jazz and the Soho clubs in the heart of London. Bowie comments, "Terry was into all the Beat writers ... and he'd come back home to Bromley with the latest paperbacks tucked away in a coat pocket."[2]

Bowie's eye for all things visual, as well as his ability to create his own visual personae, were honed during his time working at an advertising agency when he was 16 years old.[3] In fact, Bowie obtained his first record deal with Decca Records in May of 1964, when he was seventeen, and released his first single, "Liza Jane," in June 1964. His first album of songs was released in 1967, on the same day as The Beatles' *Sgt. Pepper's Lonely Hearts Club Band*. Bowie's album was not commercially successful, and he was subsequently dropped from the record label.

Bowie's transformation into a performer would follow: he became

Postscript

a member of Lindsay Kemp's mime and dance troupe and began to explore the act of living as a complete performance: "Kemp's total commitment to his art introduced Bowie to an edgy world of make-up, camp and sexual ambiguity."[4] George Tremlett quotes Bowie as saying that Kemp introduced him to "the whole idea of restructuring and going against what people generally expect."[5] Bowie also began to explore what Marsh calls "inner space," originally conceived by science-fiction writer J. G. Ballard as "the internal landscape of tomorrow that is a transmuted image of the past ... concerned with the discovery of images in which the internal and external reality meet and fuse."[6] Bowie began to manifest what he was exploring, particularly in the persona of the narrator of his first hit single, "Space Oddity": "fear, envy, madness, self-loathing and isolation." It is often suggested that Bowie's interest in alienation and dystopia stems from the depressing and economic state of Britain in the early 1970s, though "Space Oddity" was released in 1969, thus predating the 1970s by half a year.

As his career developed, he began to show "the conflation of common representations of gender, as well as common conceptions of presentations of gendered sexualities." Camille Paglia notes that the cover of *The Man who Sold the World* features Bowie as a sort of "man-dress character," and that the back cover of *Ziggy Stardust and the Spiders from Mars* features Bowie possessing "the bare chest and bulging crotch of a male hustler." But his presentation of the male hustler was not exactly right either: "Bowie created something entirely new in this taunting yet fey street tough" instead of portraying the stereotypically masculine sailor, motorcyclist or cowboy of the male hustlers of that period. Paglia describes the visual representation of Ziggy Stardust, with its amalgamation of Western and Eastern expressions of gender (and gender bending) as well as male homosexuality, as "the Ziggy gender mirage."[7] Michael Bracewell makes a direct link between Bowie's gender presentation and the move to the city: "From the platform of Bowie's groundbreaking androgyny, the ragged history of English dandyism's nervous flirtation with actual homosexuality can be seen as an elderly branch line on England's counter-cultural Underground map."[8]

Seemingly foreshadowing the subject matter of some of his later period material, Paglia explores the cover of *Aladdin Sane* from 1973:

"the inflamed creases of Ziggy's armpits, which look like fresh surgical scars as well as raw female genitalia." Also, the iconic lightening make-up looks, to Paglia, initially like a wound on his face.[9] Paglia suggests that *Young Americans* is the last album cover that Bowie used as a "gender canvas," though this is debatable.[10] Consider the cover for *'hours...'* in 1999 in which Bowie becomes Mary holding a past version of himself as a type of dead Christ.

Furthermore, the cover of *'hours...'* is an atopia. Roland Barthes, in his study of the language of lovers, explores *atopos*, referring to attributes that Socrates' interlocutors attributed to him: he was "unclassifiable, of a ceasingly unforeseen originality." The cover is evocative of the *Pietà* by Michelangelo. O'Leary writes, "This new album would be his severance from his Nineties obscurantist period: to make it obvious, he had the cover of 'Hours' [sic] play on Michelangelo's Pietà, with his new, somber curator persona cradling the dying 'rave uncle' of Earthling. Both videos for the album would set Bowie in surreal domestic situations, with muted colors and lighting; the actor looking his age for once."[11] The Bowie that cradles his mid–1990s persona appears younger, more effeminate and more artificial. He wears a white parka-like coat, whereas the dead Bowie wears a white linen shirt and pants. If Bowie's career can be illustrated in a psychogeography, consisting early on of a move from suburbia into the city, this cover suggests something akin to a move back to suburbia, but through a tunnel. That is, the move is one done in secret, cloaked by the appearance of nostalgia and commercial intent (O'Leary points out that Bowie enjoyed a more conventional songwriting process during the sessions that led to *'hours...'*). The cover betrays the sense, though, that the nostalgia is not genuine: nostalgia is expressed even while Bowie cradles an older version of himself, dead in his arms. The new Bowie confounds the listener: O'Leary suggests that Bowie is looking his age (52 at the time of the album), but he looks much younger if one considers the "live" Bowie of the cover. He moves back to the suburbs not to get away from "creative milieu" of his career, not necessarily to forsake his musical forays of the 1990s (he is too ingenious for that), but to confuse, to obfuscate, to become unclassifiable.

Barthes considers *atopos* as the Other whom he loves; he writes, "I cannot classify the other, for the other is, precisely, Unique, the singular

Postscript

Image which has miraculously come to correspond to the specialty of my desire. The other is the figure of my truth, and cannot be imprisoned in any stereotype (which is the truth of others)."[12] He goes on to describe seeing a "certain tremendous innocence" on the face of the loved or desired other, which is their *atopia*. He suggests that the other does not realize the harm that he or she has committed toward him. On the cover of '*hours…*,' a younger Bowie seems also to display this atopia on his face, a young and smooth face (tremendously innocent) free from any indication that he realizes the harm that he has inflicted on the older Bowie. Barthes continues: "Being Atopic, the other makes language indecisive: one cannot speak *of* the other, *about* the other; every attribute is false, painful, erroneous, awkward: the other is *unqualifiable*."[13] In other words, the Atopic is, for all intents and purposes, hidden. Who, in fact, is the figure that holds the older Bowie's seemingly lifeless body (though with eyes wide open, but with limp arms and hands)? He appears to be a younger version of Bowie, though he is also somewhat alien (seemingly continuing with the "space" theme even this late in his career) and effeminate (seemingly continuing with the "blurring of gender and sexualities" theme here as well). But this figure is not from the same *space* as the older Bowie: he is wearing different clothing for different conditions. As he is Atopic, he appears innocent, not knowing how his creation has inevitably killed off the older Bowie. And his appearance from elsewhere does nothing to afford the viewer a way to speak *of* or *about* him. Bowie of '*hours…*' deflects all discourse by his atopia. If *1. Outside* constructs a dark dystopian liminoid space, then '*hours…*' is an atopic space: it kills the old and then deflects any exploration of the new. If Bowie returns, then, to a theoretical suburbia with the album, he returns also with new clothing and an unreadable expression, able to then sink back into psychogeographic obscurity.

Mark Paytress puts it another way. In exploring Bowie's foray into Ziggy Stardust, he writes, "Was not the entire Ziggy escapade the fruition of Bowie's own quest … an embrace of the Other that lurked within himself? Inhabiting an alter ego that propelled him into the eye of the kind of self-destructive stardom he found so mesmerizing was Bowie's ultimate venture into the unknown."[14] In a way, the '*hours…*' album is his Other embracing his older self, the impossibly young and effeminate

Postscript

thing from elsewhere (somewhere cold) holding on to him. Christopher Sandford suggests that *1. Outside* was an instance of Bowie not so much "ignoring his past as wilfully killing it"; *'hours...'* was the funeral.[15]

But there is a further layer here. About English suburbia, Michael Bracewell writes, "[it] has become simultaneously synonymous with the sinister and the sad."[16] He suggests that the suburbs are rife with "felt absence," with nostalgia and a mixture of potential and loss, and "proposing romance in the midst of an unreal reality."[17] Bracewell describes the band The Cure as a musical expression of his conception of the English suburbs: "a dense and repetitious sound, carrying a mesmeric dirge of infinitely transferable songs, all of which sound as though they could go on for ever—like endless avenues, crescents and drives."[18] Bowie's move back to a theoretical suburb is foreshadowed by "No Control," from *1. Outside* in 1995.

"No Control," the ninth track on the album, directly references the later song "I'm Deranged," the sixteenth song on the album. The narrator names the latter song in the lyrics at the end, which suggests that the songs are, at the least, closely linked, and quite possibly part of the same composition (or formed from the same compositional material). O'Leary suggests that "No Control" came together quickly; for O'Leary, the interesting elements of the song are revealed in the bridge portions. He writes, "It's as if a minor character from [the musical] Oklahoma! has turned up in Oxford Town [the fictional locale of the *1. Outside* narrative], trying to impart some homespun common sense."[19] Eno puts it another way:

> There's a stunning section in which [Bowie] alludes to that style of singing you get in Broadway musicals, when the hero looks up into the sun, one arm extended to the future, and sings in this gloriously open-throated, honest, touchingly trusting way. It's a style of singing that belongs to the middle of the century, the time of great dreams for the future.[20]

O'Leary suggests that this is a vocal strategy for Bowie, and that he strips away the artifice of the moment, for a moment: "setting up a lyrical scenario ... and then pulling back to reveal the stage lights and scrim." O'Leary also suggests that "No Control" is a microcosm of Bowie's career.[21] If "No Control" is so closely related to "I'm Deranged," the move back to theoretical suburbs is further solidified.

Postscript

Eno writes that "I'm Deranged" is a "poorly organized song with no meaningful structure. It goes something like ABBBBBBBB-BCBBBBBBBB, but the hook is A. I've had relationships like that, where the bit you liked never happens again."[22] To reinforce the idea that "I'm Deranged" touches on Bracewell's "repetitious sound," O'Leary points out that the track was used by director David Lynch in his film, *Lost Highway*: "The track's harmonic stasis and ominous mood better suited the … scoring [of] a driver's-eye shot of a sped-up stream of highway center lines, a loop of ceaseless, violent motion." O'Leary links the song to Bowie and Eno's trip to the Maria Gugging Psychiatric Clinic on the outskirts of Vienna in 1994. Gugging is a facility which encourages its patients to paint and create art; Bowie and Eno claim that they wanted to "recreate that state of grace" with *1. Outside*. For Bowie, the Gugging visit revealed artists that were quite honest about their shortcomings: none of them considered themselves artists. They stayed away from what Eno calls "ideological arguments," for or against certain artistic movements or philosophies. Eno adds, "It's like you could suddenly meet people who didn't care whether there was a God." It is this sense of innocence (and grace) that propelled the pair to create the music on *1. Outside*. In many ways, *1. Outside* is meant to be "delinear" (Bowie remarks that, in the 1980s, "I went all linear," and that in the process of collaborating with Gabrels, he broke away from that; Gabrels is "a delinearist," says Eno).[23] Bowie recounts his experience meeting a patient who he calls the Angel Man (who, in fact, appears in the lyrics of "I'm Deranged"). The Angel Man claims that he became an angel at a specific time of his life: before that time, the Angel Man was a man, but after that time, he was an angel. Bowie concludes, "from that point, he believes that his old person disappeared and this angel took over him, he was totally reborn at that moment." Again, the innocence of the artist compels Bowie, the sheer abandonment is what is ultimately most attractive to Bowie. He continues, though, to suggest that the subject matter of *1. Outside* also "has something to do with alienation." It is about being an Other.[24]

But there is something also lost in that "delineation," more than simply the constraints of ideology or order. Eno states that "No Control" was poorly organized, a song that perhaps closely resembles the suburbs of Bowie's early life, mediated through The Cure, and Bracewell's conception of the English suburbs as songs which go on forever. In fact, "No Control" *is*, in terms of lyrical connection, the very same song as "I'm Deranged." "No Control" (and, by extension its delineated and poorly organized companion, "I'm Deranged") is a microcosm of Bowie's career. O'Leary punctuates this song (and, by extension, Bowie's career) with the following: "Bowie defaces his melody, weighing and sounding each word as if he can't recall how it's pronounced, getting mired in each syllable, building up to the last repeats of 'I'm deraaanged,' where he bloats and strangles the latter word."[25]

On the cover for '*hours…*,' Bowie is killed by an Other Bowie, who has come in from the cold and is willing to dole out sympathy, though he does not realize the harm that he has done. The old Bowie (before his death), encourages his listeners to cruise him (in "I'm Deranged"), using Barthes' term for his own text: he is an image-sign and a readerly text. Bowie invites exploration in this way, and in doing so, also abandons himself from the constraints, not only of ideology and (perhaps) sanity (like the Angel Man of the Gugging visit), but of a properly defined sense of self as well. It is not that Bowie loses his identity completely: there is still as sense that he is able to slink out of the white room on the cover of '*hours…*' and return to those theoretical suburbs. He does so under a cloak of darkness, a cloud that hides him as he moves. The cloud is a sinister cloud, in that it destroys in its quest to create. It sweeps away the old and introduces the new, but a new that is less decipherable. Bowie asks the listener to cruise him, to search him out for pleasure, but the listener is left with a white room and an alien staring back. The Bowie we know is gone, sitting in his childhood home, under the cover of darkness.

Chapter Notes

Introduction

1. Martin Roth, "David Bowie Is What Follows: Foreword," *David Bowie Is*, Victoria Broackes and Geoffrey Marsh, eds. (London: V&A, 2013), 17.
2. Matt McAllester, "Where Is He Now? David Bowie Is Back to His Mysterious Best," *Time* 181:10 (18 March 2013), 52.
3. Ibid., 55.
4. Chris O'Leary, "Everyone Says 'Hi,'" *Pushing Ahead of the Dame* (15 August 2014); available at http://bowiesongs.wordpress.com/2014/08/15/everyone-says-hi/; Internet; accessed 15 August 2014.

Chapter 1

1. Ben Slater, "The Up Escalator Forever: Bowie in Singapore," *"Clearly, You've Never Been..."* (27 October 2010); available at http://sporeana.blogspot.ca/2010/10/up-escalator-forever-bowie-in-singapore.html; Internet; accessed 23 October 2014.
2. Jon Pahl, "The Shopping Mall as 'Stairway to Heaven,' Leading Nowhere," *Shopping Malls and Other Sacred Spaces: Putting God in Place* (Grand Rapids: Brazos Press, 2003), 71–72.
3. Walter Benjamin, "M [The Flâneur]," *The Arcades Project*, Howard Eiland and Kevin McLaughlin, trans. (Cambridge: The Belknap Press of Harvard University Press, 1999), 422.
4. Ibid., 429.
5. Tom Gunning, "From the Kaleidoscope to the X-Ray: Urban Spectatorship, Poe, Benjamin, and *Traffic in Souls* (1913)," *Wide Angle* 19:4 (1997), 36.
6. Benjamin, "The Flâneur," 416.
7. Ibid., 417.
8. Ibid., 422.
9. Ibid., 418.
10. Ibid., 419.
11. Ibid., 425.
12. Anke Gleber, "Flanerie, of The Redemption of Visual Reality," *The Art of Taking a Walk: Flanerie, Literature, and Film in Weimar Culture* (Princeton: Princeton University Press, 1999), 152.
13. Benjamin, "The Flâneur," 420.
14. Ibid., 429.
15. Ibid., 444.
16. Bowie's dance is a visual representation of the metaphor used by Jesus in the biblical passage: "Let them alone; they are blind guides of the blind. And if one blind person guides another, both will fall into a pit" (Matthew 15:14 NRSCV). Often, the saying is used colloquially to describe when those not knowledgeable in a subject are instructing others who similarly are not knowledgeable in a subject.
17. Roland Barthes, "On *The Fashion System* and the Structural Analysis of Narratives," *The Grain of the Voice: Interviews 1962–1980*, Linda Coverdale, trans. (Evanston: Northwestern University Press, 2009), 43.

18. Billy Donald, "Interview with Reeves Gabrels," *MusicDish* (21 May 2003); available at http://musicdish.com/mag/?id=8017; Internet; accessed 27 October 2014.

19. Chris O'Leary, "Jewel," *Pushing Ahead of the Dame* (31 January 2014); available at http://bowiesongs.wordpress.com/2014/01/31/jewel/; Internet; accessed 27 October 2014.

20. Chris O'Leary, "Look Back in Anger," *Pushing Ahead of the Dame* (22 July 2011); available at http://bowiesongs.wordpress.com/?s=Look+back+in+anger; Internet; accessed 27 October 2014.

21. David Buckley, *Strange Fascination: David Bowie: The Definitive Story* (London: Virgin, 2000), 450.

22. See Numbers 21:8, "And the Lord said to Moses, 'Make a poisonous serpent, and set it on a pole; and everyone who is bitten shall look at it and live,'" and John 12:32, "'And I, when I am lifted up from the earth, will draw all people to myself'" (NRSVCE). See also John 3:14 for the link between the two scriptural passages.

23. Roland Barthes, "History and Sociology of Clothing: Some Methodological Observations," *The Language of Fashion*, Andy Stafford, trans., Andy Stafford and Michael Carter, eds. (London: Bloomsbury, 2013), 14.

24. Barthes, "On *The Fashion System*," 43.

25. Ibid., 45.

26. Michael Moriarty, *Roland Barthes* (Stanford: Stanford University Press, 1991), 19–21.

27. Jazmin Rodger, "Critically Assess Barthes' Notion That Signs Are Ideological," *University of Essex Department of Sociology Undergraduate Journal* 4 (Summer 2010); available at https://www.essex.ac.uk/sociology/documents/pdf/ug_journal/vol4/2010SC301_JazminRodger.pdf; Internet; accessed 27 October 2014.

28. Barthes, "On *The Fashion System*," 49.

29. Roland Barthes, "The Fashion System," *The Grain of the Voice: Interviews 1962–1980*, Linda Coverdale, trans. (Evanston: Northwestern University Press, 2009), 57.

30. Barthes, "On *The Fashion System*," 50. Emphasis added.

31. Judith Butler, *Bodies That Matter: On the Discursive Limits of "Sex"* (New York: Routledge, 1993), x.

32. Ibid., 2.

33. Judith Butler, *Undoing Gender* (New York: Routledge, 2004), 1.

34. Roland Barthes, "Showing How Rhetoric Works," *The Language of Fashion*, Andy Stafford, trans., Andy Stafford and Michael Carter, eds. (London: Bloomsbury, 2013), 110.

35. Roland Barthes, *The Fashion System*, Matthew Ward and Richard Howard, trans. (Berkeley: University of California Press, 1990), x.

36. Ibid., xi–xii.

37. Ibid., 5.

38. Ibid., 13.

39. See Nicholas P. Greco, "Cruising in Prime Time," *Rush and Philosophy*, Jim Berti and Durrell Bowman, eds. (Chicago: Open Court, 2011), 211–221.

40. Roland Barthes, "Twenty Key Words for Roland Barthes," *The Grain of the Voice: Interviews 1962–1980*, Linda Coverdale, trans. (New York: Hill and Wang, 1985), 231.

41. Roland Barthes, "Preface to Renaud Camus' *Tricks*," *The Rustle of Language*, Richard Howard, trans. (New York: Hill and Wang, 1986), 294.

42. Nicholas de Villiers, "A Great Pedagogy of Nuance: Roland Barthes' The Neutral," *Theory & Event* 8:4 (2005), para. 11; available at http://lion.chadwyck.com.libaccess.lib.mcmaster.ca/display/printView.do?area=abell; Internet; accessed 22 May 2009.

43. Gary Burns, "A Typology of 'Hooks' in Popular Records," *Popular Music* 6:1 (January 1987), 1.

Notes—Chapter 1

44. Devin McKinney, "Cruising a Road to Nowhere: Mechanics and Mysteries of the Pop Moment," *Popular Music* 24:3 (October 2005), 319.

45. Ibid., 312.

46. Ibid., 320.

47. Victor Turner, "Are There Universals of Performance in Myth, Ritual, and Drama?" *By Means of Performance: Intercultural Studies of Theatre and Ritual*, W. Schechner and W. Appels, eds. (New York: Cambridge University Press, 1990), 12. Emphasis added.

48. Buckley, *Strange Fascination*, 500.

49. Ian Maxwell, "The Ritualization of Performance (Studies)," *Victor Turner and Contemporary Cultural Performance*, Graham St John, ed. (New York: Berghahn Books, 2008), 60.

50. Victor Turner, *The Ritual Process* (New York: Aldine De Gruyter, 1969), 96–97.

51. Maxwell, "The Ritualization of Performance (Studies)," 62. Victor Turner writes of "an instant of pure potentiality" in *From Ritual to Theatre: The Human Seriousness of Play* (New York: PAJ, 1982), 44.

52. Ibid., 65.

53. Elias Canetti, *Crowds and Power*, Carol Stewart, trans. (New York: Continuum, 1981), 29.

54. Turner, *The Ritual Process*, 97.

55. James W. Flanagan, "Space," *Handbook of Postmodern Biblical Interpretation*, A.K.M. Adam, ed. (St. Louis: Chalice Press, 2000), 242–243.

56. Graham St. John makes a more concrete, albeit theoretical, link between Turner's *limen* and Foucault's heterotopia, querying whether the result of his study is communitas or heterotopia. See Graham St. John, "Alternative Cultural Heterotopia and the Liminoid Body: Beyond Turner at ConFest," *The Australian Journal of Anthropology* 12:1 (2001), 47–66.

57. Chris O'Leary, "Thursday's Child," *Pushing Ahead of the Dame* (21 January 2014); available at http://bowiesongs.wordpress.com/2014/01/21/thursdays-child/; Internet; accessed 31 October 2014.

58. Michel Foucault, "Of Other Spaces," Jay Miskowiec, trans., *Diacritics* 16:1 (Spring 1986), 24.

59. Ibid., 22.

60. Ibid., 24–25.

61. Ibid., 26–27.

62. Ibid., 24.

63. Ibid., 25.

64. Ibid., 27.

65. Ibid.

66. Rosalind E. Krauss and Dennis Hollier, "Translator's Preface," in Roland Barthes, *The Neutral*, R. E. Krauss and D. Hollier, trans. (New York: Columbia University Press, 2005), xiv.

67. Roland Barthes, *Roland Barthes by Roland Barthes*, Richard Howard, trans. (Berkeley: University of California Press, 1977), 87.

68. Sir Christopher Freyling, Philip Hoare and Mark Kermode, "David Bowie Then ... David Bowie Now ...," *David Bowie Is*, Victoria Broackes and Geoffrey Marsh, eds. (London: V&A, 2013), 293.

69. Roland Barthes, "In the Ring," *Mythologies*, Richard Howard, trans. (New York: Hill and Wang, 2012), 3.

70. Ibid.

71. Ibid., 13–14. See Roland Barthes, "The World of Wrestling," *Mythologies*, Annette Lavers, trans. (New York: Hill and Wang, 1972), 25.

72. David Pattie, "4 Real: Authenticity, Performance, and Rock Music," *Enculturation* 2:2 (Spring 1999); available at http://www.enculturation.net/2_2/pattie.html; Internet; accessed 17 November 2014.

73. Richard Dyer, "*A Star Is Born* and the Construction of Authenticity," *Stardom: Industry of Desire*, Christine Gledhill, ed. (London: Routledge, 1991), 137.

74. Paul Virilio, *The Administration*

of Fear, Ames Hodges, trans. (Los Angeles: Semiotext(e), 2012), 15.

75. Roland Barthes, *How to Live Together*, Kate Briggs, trans. (New York: Columbia University Press, 2013), 9.

76. David Pattie, *Rock Music in Performance* (New York: Palgrave Macmillan, 2007), 40–45.

77. Paul Virilio, *The Futurism of the Instant: Stop-Eject*, Julie Rose, trans. (Cambridge: Polity Press, 2010), 2–6.

78. Ibid., ix.

79. Virilio, *The Administration of Fear*, 10.

80. Ibid., 20–21.

81. Ibid., 15.

82. Ibid., 25.

83. Ibid., 28.

84. Ibid., 61.

85. Ibid., 30–33.

86. Ibid., 27.

87. Ibid., 38.

88. Ibid., 43.

89. Ibid., 56.

90. Roland Barthes, *The Preparation of the Novel*, Kate Briggs, trans. (New York: Columbia University Press, 2011), 4–5.

91. Ibid., 7.

92. Ibid., xx.

93. Ibid., 10.

94. Ibid., 11–12.

95. Scott Esposito, "Four Questions for Kate Briggs on Roland Barthes' Preparation of the Novel," *Conversational Reading* (7 April 2011); available at http://conversationalreading.com/four-questions-for-kate-briggs-on-roland-barthes-preparation-of-the-novel/; Internet; accessed 18 November 2014.

96. Maarten De Pourcq, "'The *Paideia* of the Greeks': On the Methodology of Roland Barthes's *Comment vivre ensemble*," *Paragraph* 31:1 (2008), 24.

97. Austen Rosenfeld, "Can We Live Together, Roland Barthes?," *The Daily Beast* (19 December 2012); available at http://www.thedailybeast.com/articles/2012/12/19/can-we-live-together-roland-barthes.html; Internet; accessed 18 November 2014.

98. Barthes, *How to Live Together*, xxii.

99. Rosenfeld, "Can We Live Together," n.p.

100. Barthes, *How to Live Together*, xxii.

101. Ibid., 6.

102. Ibid., 5.

103. Virilio, *The Administration of Fear*, 43.

104. Ivan Hewett, "David Bowie's jazz song shows his genius for self-reinvention," *The Telegraph* (16 October 2014); available at http://www.telegraph.co.uk/culture/music/worldfolkandjazz/11163556/David-Bowies-jazz-song-shows-his-genius-for-self-reinvention.html; Internet; accessed 18 November 2014.

Chapter 2

1. Roland Barthes, "The Grain of the Voice," *Image—Music—Text*, Stephen Heath, trans. (New York: Hill and Wang, 1977), 188.

2. Roland Barthes, "The Phantoms of the Opera," *The Grain of the Voice: Interviews 1962–1980*, Linda Coverdale, trans. (New York: Hill and Wang, 1985), 183–184.

3. Roland Barthes, "Listening," *The Responsibility of Forms: Critical Essays on Music, Art, and Representation*, Richard Howard, trans. (Berkeley: University of California Press, 1985), 259.

4. Paul Sinclair, "Bowie Collaborator Erdal Kizilcay on Glass Spider and Never Let Me Down," *Super Deluxe Edition* (11 December 2013); available at http://www.superdeluxeedition.com/interview/bowie-collaborator-erdal-kizilcay-on-glass-spider-and-never-let-me-down/; Internet; accessed 27 October 2014.

5. Christopher Sandford, *Bowie: Loving the Alien* (London: Warner, 1997), 125.

6. Chris O'Leary, "Future Legend," *Pushing Ahead of the Dame* (14 September 2010); available at http://bowiesongs.wordpress.com/2010/09/14/future-legend/; Internet; accessed 27 October 2014.

7. Christopher Breward, "For 'We are the Goon Squad': Bowie, Style and the Power of the LP Cover, 1967–1983," *David Bowie Is*, Victoria Broakes and Geoffrey Marsh, eds (London: V & A, 2013), 198.

8. Nick Stevenson, *David Bowie: Fame, Sound and Vision* (Cambridge: Polity Press, 2006), 72–73.

9. Lorne Murdoch, "Hitting an All-Time Low," *The Bowie Companion*, Elizabeth Thomson and David Gutman, eds. (New York: Da Capo Press, 1996), 151.

10. Eric Tamm, "Soul Robots: Eno and Fripp with Bowie," *The Bowie Companion*, Elizabeth Thomson and David Gutman, eds. (New York: Da Capo Press, 1996), 144.

11. Chris O'Leary, "Sense of Doubt," *Pushing Ahead of the Dame* (20 May 2011); available at http://bowiesongs.wordpress.com/2011/05/20/sense-of-doubt/; Internet; accessed 27 October 2014.

12. Stevenson, *Fame, Sound and Vision*, 75.

13. Chris O'Leary, "Outside Tour: The Nine Inch Nails Duets," *Pushing Ahead of the Dame* (2 May 2013); available at http://bowiesongs.wordpress.com/2013/05/02/outside-tour-the-nine-inch-nails-duets/; Internet; accessed 27 October 2014.

14. Buckley, *Strange Fascination*, 512.

15. Eric R. Danton, "Trent Reznor Praises David Bowie's 'The Next Day' Album," *Rolling Stone* (19 December 2013); available at http://www.rollingstone.com/music/news/trent-reznor-praises-david-bowies-the-next-day-album-20131219; Internet; accessed 27 October 2014.

16. Marc Spitz, *Bowie: A Biography* (New York: Crown, 2009), 362.

17. Jason J. Hanley, "'The Land of Rape and Honey': The Use of World War II Propaganda in the Music Videos of Ministry and Laibach," *American Music* 22:1 (Spring 2004), 158–164.

18. Ian Penman, "The Resurrection of Saint Dave," *Esquire Magazine* (October 1995); available at http://www.algonet.se/~bassman/articles/95/e.html; Internet; accessed 31 October 2014.

19. Buckley, *Strange Fascination*, 499–500.

20. "The Year in Review: The Insider," *Groove Culture*; available at http://models.com/life_style/groove/bowie/bowie3.html; Internet; accessed 31 October 2014.

21. Buckley, *Strange Fascination*, 501.

22. Brian Eno, *A Year with Swollen Appendices* (London: Faber and Faber, 1996), 373–374.

Chapter 3

1. David Toop, *Ocean of Sound* (London: Serpent's Tail, 1995), 279–80.

2. Brian Eno and Russel Mills, *More Dark Than Shark* (London: Faber and Faber, 1986), 138.

3. Colin Larkin, ed., "Brian Eno," *The Encyclopedia of Popular Music*, 3d ed. (London: Muze UK, 1998), Vol. 3, 1764.

4. Eric Tamm, *Brian Eno: His Music and the Vertical Color of Sound* (Cambridge, MA: Da Capo Press, 1995), 4.

5. Larkin, ed., "Brian Eno," 1765.

6. Tamm, *Brian Eno*, 16.

7. Ibid., 17.

8. Jim Aikin, "Brian Eno," *Keyboard* 7 (July 1981), 62; available at http://music.hyperreal.org/artists/brian_eno/interviews/keyb81.html; Internet; accessed 2 November 2014.

9. Tamm, *Brian Eno*, 18.

10. Ibid., 19.

11. John Cage, "Composition as Pro-

cess: I. Changes," *Silence* (Middletown: Wesleyan University Press, 1967), 18–23.

12. John Cage, "Erik Satie," *Silence* (Middletown: Wesleyan University Press, 1967), 76.

13. Ibid., 79.

14. Bobby DeVito, "'But is it MUSAK????' Ambient Music—from Satie through Cage to Eno," *The Hyperreal Music Archive*; available at http://music.hyperreal.org/epsilon/info/devito.html; Internet; accessed 3 November 2014.

15. Rob Tannenbaum, "A Meeting of Sound Minds: John Cage and Brian Eno," *Musician* 83 (September 1985), 67.

16. Eno and Mills, *More Dark Than Shark*, 43.

17. Tamm, *Brian Eno*, 40.

18. Ibid., 41.

19. Ibid., 42.

20. Frank Rose, "Eno: Scaramouche of the Synthesizer," *Creem* 7 (July 1975), 70; available at http://music.hyperreal.org/artists/brian_eno/interviews/creem75c.html; Internet; accessed 2 November 2014.

21. Brian Eno, "Generating and Organizing Variety in the Arts," *Breaking the Sound Barrier: A Critical Anthology of the New Music*, Gregory Battcock, ed. (New York: E.P. Dutton, 1981), 137, 140.

22. Lester Bangs, "Eno," *Musician, Player & Listener* 21 (November 1979), 40.

23. Tamm, *Brian Eno*, 30.

24. Brian Eno, "Pro Session: The Studio as Compositional Tool—Part II," *Down Beat* 50 (July 1983), 52.

25. Ibid., 56.

26. Tamm, *Brian Eno*, 64.

27. Cynthia Dagnal, "Eno and the Jets: Controlled Chaos," *Rolling Stone* 169 (12 September 1974), 21.

28. Brian Eno, "The Revenge of the Intuitive," *Wired* 7.01 (January 1999); available at http://archive.wired.com/wired/archive/7.01/eno_pr.html; Internet; accessed 5 November 2014.

29. Tamm, *Brian Eno*, 56.

30. Ibid., 36.

31. Steven Grant, "Brian Eno Against Interpretation," *Trouser Press* 9 (August 1982), 29; available at http://music.hyperreal.org/artists/brian_eno/interviews/troup82a.html; Internet; accessed 3 November 2014.

32. Douglas Rushkoff, *Cyberia: Life in the Trenches of Hyperspace* (New York: HarperCollins, 1995), 161.

33. Eno, "Generating Variety," 130.

34. Eno, *A Year with Swollen Appendices*, 344.

35. Eno, "Generating Variety," 140–141.

36. Glenn O'Brien, "Eno at the Edge of Rock," *Andy Warhol's Interview* 8:6 (June 1978), 31; available at http://music.hyperreal.org/artists/brian_eno/interviews/unk-78b.html; Internet; accessed 3 November 2014.

37. Toop, *Ocean of Sound*, 123.

38. Tamm, *Brian Eno*, 144.

39. Toop, *Ocean of Sound*, 129.

40. O'Brien, "Eno At the Edge," 31.

41. Ibid.

42. Ibid.

43. Allan Jones, "Eno—Class of '75," *Melody Maker* 50:48 (29 November 1975), 14.

44. Eno and Mills, *More Dark Than Shark*, 101.

45. O'Brien, "Eno at the Edge," 31.

46. Eno and Mills, *More Dark Than Shark*, 98–99.

47. Brian Eno, "Games for Musicians," *Raygun* 30 (October 1995), n.p.

48. Tamm, "Soul Robots," 145–146.

49. Ibid., 148.

50. Mark Rowland, "The Outside Story," *Musician* 204 (November 1995), 40.

51. Tamm, "Soul Robots," 149.

52. Toop, *Ocean of Sound*, 280.

Chapter 4

1. Rowland, "The Outside Story," 39.

2. Kim Hewitt, *Mutilating the Body: Identity in Blood and Ink* (Bowling

Notes—Chapter 4

Green, OH: Bowling Green State University Popular Press, 1997), 1.

3. Ted Polhemus and Housk Randall, *The Customized Body* (London: Serpent's Tail, 1996), 7–9.

4. Clinton R. Sanders, *Customizing the Body: The Art and Culture of Tattooing* (Philadelphia: Temple University Press, 1989), 2.

5. Armando R. Favazza and Barbara Favazza, *Bodies Under Siege: Self-Mutilation in Culture and Psychiatry* (Baltimore: Johns Hopkins University Press, 1987), 10–20.

6. Richard Leppert, *Art and the Committed Eye: The Cultural Functions of Imagery* (Boulder: Westview/HarperCollins, 1996), 115–6.

7. Favazza, *Bodies Under Siege*, 24–44.

8. Polhemus, *The Customized Body*, 93–94.

9. Jean-Chris Miller, *The Body Art Book: A Complete, Illustrated Guide to Tattoos, Piercings, and Other Body Modifications* (New York: Berkley Books, 1997), 120.

10. Ibid., 114–116.

11. Polhemus, *The Customized Body*, 11.

12. Rufus C. Camphausen, *Return of the Tribal: A Celebration of Body Adornment* (Rochester: Park Street Press, 1997), 47.

13. Sanders, *Customizing the Body*, 4; also Polhemus, *The Customized Body*, 11.

14. Polhemus, *The Customized Body*, 50.

15. Turner, "Are There Universals of Performance," 12–13.

16. V. Vale and Andrea Juno, "Fakir Musafar," *Modern Primitives: An Investigation of Contemporary Adornment & Ritual*, V. Vale and Andrea Juno, eds. (San Francisco: Re/Search Publications, 1989), 13.

17. V. Vale and Andrea Juno, "Introduction," *Modern Primitives: An Investigation of Contemporary Adornment & Ritual*, V. Vale and Andrea Juno, eds. (San Francisco: Re/Search Publications, 1989), 4.

18. John Clark, Stuart Hall, Tony Jefferson and Brian Roberts, "Subcultures, Cultures and Class: A Theoretical Overview," *Resistance Through Rituals: Youth Subcultures in Post-War Britain*, S. Hall and T. Jefferson, eds. (New York: Holmes & Meier, 1976), 61–62.

19. Polhemus, *The Customized Body*, 38.

20. Miller, *The Body Art Book*, 121.

21. Camphausen, *Return of the Tribal*, 86–89.

22. Marilee Strong, *A Bright Red Scream: Self-Mutilation and the Language of Pain* (New York: Viking Penguin, 1998), 144–146.

23. Ibid., 155.

24. Favazza, *Bodies Under Siege*, 191–192.

25. Ibid., 195–198.

26. Miller, *The Body Art Book*, 1.

27. Ibid., 4–5.

28. Ibid., 29–30.

29. Camphausen, *Return of the Tribal*, 79.

30. Miller, *The Body Art Book*, 31.

31. Sanders, *Customizing the Body*, 6–8.

32. Camphausen, *Return of the Tribal*, 55.

33. Ibid., 65.

34. Ibid., 96–100.

35. Bruce Lambert, "Unlikely AIDS Sufferer's Message: Even You Can Get It," *New York Times* (11 March 1989); available at http://www.nytimes.com/1989/03/11/nyregion/unlikely-aids-sufferer-s-message-even-you-can-get-it.html; Internet; accessed 11 November 2014.

36. Camphausen, *Return of the Tribal*, 83.

37. Strong, *Bright Red Scream*, 141–150.

38. Camphausen, *Return of the Tribal*, 86.

39. Dominic Wells, "Boys Keep Swing-

ing," *Time Out* 48 (23–30 August 1995); available at http://music.hyperreal.org/artists/brian_eno/interviews/Bowieno.html; Internet; accessed 11 November 2014.

40. Frank C. Senn, "Epilogue: Postmodern Liturgy," *Christian Liturgy: Catholic and Evangelical* (Minneapolis: Fortress Press, 1997), 696.

41. Senn points the reader to Harold Bloom, *Omens of Millennium: The Gnosis of Angels, Dreams, and Resurrection* (New York: Riverhead Books, 1996), 27. See also Bloom, *The American Religion* (New York: Chu Hartley, 2006), 15–16.

42. Senn, "Epilogue: Postmodern Liturgy," 698. For further reading, Senn suggests Philip J. Lee, *Against the Protestant Gnostics* (Oxford University Press, 1987).

43. Wolfgang Wunderlich, *Hermann Nitsche: The O.M. Theatre 80th Action*, Andrew Clegg Littler, trans. (München: Verlag Fred Jahn, 1988), 31.

Chapter 5

1. Douglas Coupland, *Microserfs* (New York: HarperCollins, 1995), 139.

2. Axel Rüger, "54. *Figures with Horses by a Stable*," 334, and Michiel C. Plomp, "122. *Deer in the Wood*," 482, Walter Liedtke, *Vermeer and the Delft School* (New York: The Metropolitan Museum of Art, 2001).

3. K. Sememova, "21. *The Watchdog*," *Dutch and Flemish Paintings from the Hermitage* (New York: The Metropolitan Museum of Art, 1988), 44.

4. Arthur C. Danto, *Mark Tansey: Visions and Revisions* (New York: Harry N. Abrams, 1992), 16–17.

5. Ibid., 17–18.

6. Thomas De Quincey, "Supplementary Paper on Murder Considered, as One of the Fine Arts," *On Murder as a Fine Art* (London: Philip Allan & Co., 1925), 56.

7. Ibid., 73–76.

8. Richard Schechner, "Toward a Poetics of Performance," *Performance Theory* (New York: Routledge, 1988), 169.

9. Anthony Haden-Guest, "The Return of Guy Bourdin," *The New Yorker* 70 (7 November 1994), 143.

10. Penman, "Saint Dave," n.p.

11. Catherine Bell, *Ritual Theory, Ritual Practice* (New York: Oxford University Press, 1992), 172–3.

12. Turner, "Are There Universals of Performance," 11.

13. Victor Turner, "Liminal to Liminoid, in Play, Flow, and Ritual," *From Ritual to Theatre: The Human Seriousness of Play* (New York: Performing Arts Journal Publications, 1982), 24.

14. Ibid., 26.
15. Ibid., 27.
16. Ibid., 34.
17. Ibid., 36.
18. Ibid., 40.
19. Ibid., 52.
20. Ibid., 54.
21. Ibid., 54–55.

22. Moon Zappa, "David Bowie," *Raygun* 30 (October 1995), n.p.

23. Simon Frith, *Performing Rites: On the Value of Popular Music* (Cambridge: Harvard University Press, 1996), 163–164.

24. Edward Doughtie, "Words for Music: Simplicity and Complexity in the Elizabethan Air," *Rice University Studies* 51 (1965), 4–6; quoted in Mark W. Booth, *The Experience of Songs* (New Haven: Yale University Press, 1981), 24.

25. Terry Eagleton, *Literary Theory: An Introduction* (Minneapolis: University of Minnesota Press, 1996), 119.

26. Dave Laing, *One Chord Wonders: Power and Meaning in Punk Rock* (London: Open University Press, 1985), 74.

27. Roland Barthes, *S/Z*, Richard Miller, trans. (New York: Hill and Wang, 1974), 38.

28. Ibid., 75, 32.
29. Ibid., 75–76. Barthes also adds the "false reply" to the hermeneutic code; the false reply differs from the snare because the former emerges from error rather than from a lie or the intention to mislead (42).
30. Ibid., 17.
31. Ibid., 20. Barthes makes a similar statement in his later essay "Textual Analysis of a Tale by Edgar Allan Poe" from 1973.
32. Ibid., 18–20.
33. Roland Barthes, "Textual Analysis of a Tale by Edgar Allan Poe," *The Semiotic Challenge*, Richard Howard, trans. (New York: Hill and Wang, 1988), 288.
34. Barthes, *S/Z*, 29.
35. Ibid., 30.
36. Ibid., 4.
37. Barthes, "Textual Analysis of Poe," 261.
38. Barthes, "The Grain of the Voice," 181.
39. Ibid., 185.
40. Barthes, "Listening," 259.
41. Roland Barthes, "The Adjective is the 'Statement' of Desire," *The Grain of the Voice: Interviews 1962–1980*, Linda Coverdale, trans. (New York: Hill and Wang, 1985), 173.
42. Barthes, "The Grain of the Voice," 181.
43. Barthes, "The Phantoms of the Opera," 183–184.
44. Stephen Heath, "Translator's Note," in Roland Barthes, *Image—Music—Text*, S. Heath, trans. (New York: Hill and Wang, 1977), 10.
45. Barthes, "The Adjective is the 'Statement' of Desire," 173.
46. Barthes, "Textual Analysis of Poe," 262–265.
47. Ibid., 267.
48. Hewitt, *Mutilating the Body*, 16–17.
49. Barthes, "Textual Analysis of Poe," 273.
50. Ibid., 292–293.

51. William Gibson, *Neuromancer* (New York: Ace, 1987), 3.
52. Roland Barthes, *A Lover's Discourse: Fragments*, Richard Howard, trans. (New York: Hill and Wang, 2010), 43.
53. Chris O'Leary, "I Am with Name/Segue: Ramona A. Stone," *Pushing Ahead of the Dame* (31 January 2013); available at https://bowiesongs.wordpress.com/2013/01/31/i-am-with-name-segue-ramona-a-stone/; Internet; accessed 14 November 2014.
54. Paul Théberge, *Any Sound You Can Imagine: Making Music/Consuming Technology* (Hanover: Wesleyan University Press, 1997), 199.
55. Walter Everett, "Confessions from Blueberry Hell, or, Pitch Can Be a Sticky Subject," *Expressions in Pop-Rock Music*, W. Everett, ed. (New York: Garland, 2000), 332. Everett is quoting Allan Moore, "Patterns of Harmony," *Popular Music* 11:1 (1992), 77.
56. Robert Walser, *Running With the Devil: Power, Gender, and Madness in Heavy Metal Music* (Hanover: Wesleyan University Press, 1993), 42.

Chapter 6

1. George Petros and Steven Blush, "I Don't Feel as Though I Hold a Torch for One Particular Style of Music, I Find that Absolutism Outmoded," *Seconds* (August/September 1995); available at http://www.algonet.se/~bassman/articles/95/s.html; Internet; accessed 15 November 2014.
2. Alf Björnberg, "Structural Relationships of Music and Images in Music Video," *Popular Music* 13:1 (1994), 51.
3. Ibid., 53.
4. Will Straw, "Music Video in its Contexts: Popular Music and Postmodernism in the 1980s," *Popular Music* 7:3 (1988), 247.

5. Björnberg, "Structural Relationships," 61.
6. Cathy Schwichtenberg, "Music Video: The Popular Pleasures of Visual Music," *Popular Music and Communication*, James Lull, ed. (Newbury Park, CA: Sage, 1992), 124.
7. Ibid.
8. Carol Vernallis, "The Aesthetics of Music Video: An Analysis of Madonna's 'Cherish,'" *Popular Music* 17:2 (1998), 153–154.
9. Björnberg, "Structural Relationships," 57.
10. Vernallis, "Aesthetics of Music Video," 157.
11. Björnberg, "Structural Relationships," 57.
12. Ibid., 58.
13. Ibid., 59.
14. Catherine Bell, *Ritual: Perspectives and Dimensions* (New York: Oxford University Press, 1997), 213.
15. Ibid., 216.
16. Walser, *Running With the Devil*, 151–155.
17. Turner, "Liminal to Liminoid," 27.
18. Peter Stallybrass and Allon White, *The Politics and Poetics of Transgression* (Ithaca: Cornell University Press, 1986), 3–6.
19. Ibid., 10–14.
20. Barbara Babcock, *The Reversible World: Symbolic Inversion in Art and Society* (Ithaca: Cornell University Press, 1978), 14; quoted in Stallybrass and White, *Transgression*, 17.
21. Stallybrass and White, *Transgression*, 21–26.
22. Ibid., 27.
23. Ibid., 28.
24. Ibid., 18.
25. Pam Morris, "Introduction," *The Bakhtin Reader*, Pam Morris, ed. (London: Edward Arnold, 1994), 21.
26. Mikhail Bakhtin, *Rabelais and his World*, H. Iswolsky, trans. (Cambridge: M.I.T. Press, 1968), 5.
27. Ibid., 370.
28. Ibid., 21.
29. Ibid., 151–152.
30. Ibid., 316–317.
31. Ibid., 281.
32. Ibid., 212.
33. Mikhail Bakhtin, "The Banquet, the Body and the Underworld," *The Bakhtin Reader*, Pam Morris, ed. (London: Edward Arnold, 1994), 227.
34. Mikhail Bakhtin, "Folk Humour and Carnival Laughter," *The Bakhtin Reader*, Pam Morris, ed. (London: Edward Arnold, 1994), 195.
35. Bakhtin, *Rabelais*, 336.
36. Sandford, *Loving the Alien*, 325.
37. Ibid., 325–326.
38. Rowland, "The Outside Story," 39.
39. Ibid.

Postscript

1. "Enchanting David Bowie: Space/Time/Body/Memory," *Bloomsbury*; available at http://www.bloomsbury.com/uk/enchanting-david-bowie-9781628923063/; Internet; accessed 18 November 2014.
2. George Tremlett, *David Bowie: Living on the Brink* (New York: Carroll & Graf, 1997), 19.
3. Geoffrey Marsh, "Astronaut of Inner Spaces: Sunridge Park, Soho, London ... Mars," *David Bowie Is*, Victoria Broackes and Geoffrey Marsh, eds. (London: V&A, 2013), 27–30.
4. Ibid., 38.
5. Tremlett, *Living on the Brink*, 293.
6. J.G. Ballard, "Time, Memory and Inner Space," *The Woman Journalist* (1963); available at http://www.jgballard.ca/non_fiction/jgb_time_memory_innerspace.html; Internet; accessed 21 January 2015.
7. Camille Paglia, "Theatre of Gender: David Bowie at the Climax of the Sexual Revolution," *David Bowie Is*, Vic-

toria Broackes and Geoffrey Marsh, eds. (London: V&A, 2013), 70.

8. Michael Bracewell, *England is Mine: Pop Life in Albion from Wilde to Goldie* (London: HarperCollins, 1997), 195.

9. Paglia, "Theatre of Gender," 78.

10. Ibid., 80.

11. Chris O'Leary, "Survive," *Pushing Ahead of the Dame* (1 November 2013); available at https://bowiesongs.wordpress.com/2013/11/01/survive/; Internet; accessed 21 January 2015.

12. Barthes, *A Lover's Discourse*, 34.

13. Ibid., 35.

14. Mark Paytress, *The Rise and Fall of Ziggy Stardust and the Spiders from Mars: David Bowie (Classic Rock Albums)* (New York: Schirmer Books, 1998), 91.

15. Sandford, *Loving the Alien*, 6.

16. Bracewell, *England is Mine*, 110.

17. Ibid., 113.

18. Ibid., 116.

19. Chris O'Leary, "No Control," *Pushing Ahead of the Dame* (8 April 2003); available at http://bowiesongs.wordpress.com/2013/04/08/no-control/; Internet; accessed 22 January 2015.

20. Eno, *A Year with Swollen Appendices*, 29.

21. O'Leary, "No Control," n.p.

22. Eno, *A Year with Swollen Appendices*, 24.

23. Tim De Lisle, "Immaculate Conceptions," *The Independent* (10 September 1995); available at http://www.independent.co.uk/arts-entertainment/immaculate-conceptions-1600363.html; Internet; accessed 23 January 2015.

24. Zappa, "David Bowie," 35.

25. Chris O'Leary, "I'm Deranged," *Pushing Ahead of the Dame* (26 March 2013); available at http://bowiesongs.wordpress.com/2013/03/26/im-deranged/; Internet; accessed 23 January 2015.

Bibliography

Aikin, Jim. "Brian Eno." *Keyboard* 7 (July 1981). Available at http://music.hyperreal.org/artists/brian_eno/interviews/keyb81.html. Internet. Accessed 2 November 2014.

Babcock, Barbara. *The Reversible World: Symbolic Inversion in Art and Society*. Ithaca: Cornell University Press, 1978.

Bakhtin, Mikhail. "The Banquet, the Body and the Underworld." *The Bakhtin Reader*. Edited by Pam Morris. London: Edward Arnold, 1994. 226-244.

_____. "Folk Humour and Carnival Laughter." *The Bakhtin Reader*. Edited by Pam Morris. London: Edward Arnold, 1994. 194-206.

_____. *Rabelais and his World*. Translated by H. Iswolsky. Cambridge: M.I.T. Press, 1968.

Ballard, J.G. "Time, Memory and Inner Space." *The Woman Journalist* (1963). Available at http://www.jgballard.ca/non_fiction/jgb_time_memory_innerspace.html. Internet. Accessed 21 January 2015.

Bangs, Lester. "Eno." *Musician, Player & Listener* 21 (November 1979). 38-44.

Barthes, Roland. "The Adjective is the 'Statement' of Desire." *The Grain of the Voice: Interviews 1962-1980*. Translated by Linda Coverdale. New York: Hill and Wang, 1985. 172-176.

_____. *The Fashion System*. Translated by Matthew Ward and Richard Howard. Berkeley: University of California Press, 1990.

_____. "The Fashion System." *The Grain of the Voice: Interviews 1962-1980*. Translated by Linda Coverdale. Evanston: Northwestern University Press, 2009. 56-62.

_____. "The Grain of the Voice." *Image—Music—Text*. Translated by Stephen Heath. New York: Hill and Wang, 1977. 179-189.

_____. "History and Sociology of Clothing: Some Methodological Observations." *The Language of Fashion*. Translated by Andy Stafford. Edited by Andy Stafford and Michael Carter. London: Bloomsbury, 2013. 3-19.

_____. *How to Live Together*. Translated by Kate Briggs. New York: Columbia University Press, 2013.

_____. "In the Ring." *Mythologies*. Translated by Richard Howard. New York: Hill and Wang, 2012. 3-14.

_____. "Listening." *The Responsibility of Forms: Critical Essays on Music, Art, and Representation*. Translated by Richard Howard. Berkeley: University of California Press, 1985. 245-260.

_____. *A Lover's Discourse: Fragments*. Translated by Richard Howard. New York: Hill and Wang, 2010.

_____. *The Neutral*. Translated by R. E. Krauss and D. Hollier. New York: Columbia University Press, 2005.

_____. "On *The Fashion System* and the

Bibliography

Structural Analysis of Narratives." *The Grain of the Voice: Interviews 1962-1980*. Translated by Linda Coverdale. Evanston: Northwestern University Press, 2009. 43-55.

———. "The Phantoms of the Opera." *The Grain of the Voice: Interviews 1962-1980*. Translated by Linda Coverdale. New York: Hill and Wang, 1985. 183-187.

———. "Preface to Renaud Camus' *Tricks*." *The Rustle of Language*. Translated by Richard Howard. New York: Hill and Wang, 1986. 291-295.

———. *The Preparation of the Novel*. Translated by Kate Briggs. New York: Columbia University Press, 2011.

———. *Roland Barthes by Roland Barthes*. Translated by Richard Howard. Berkeley: University of California Press, 1977.

———. *S/Z*. Translated by Richard Miller. New York: Hill and Wang, 1974.

———. "Showing How Rhetoric Works." *The Language of Fashion*. Translated by Andy Stafford. Edited by Andy Stafford and Michael Carter. London: Bloomsbury, 2013. 108-111.

———. "Textual Analysis of a Tale by Edgar Allan Poe." *The Semiotic Challenge*. Translated by Richard Howard. New York: Hill and Wang, 1988. 261-293.

———. "Twenty Key Words for Roland Barthes." *The Grain of the Voice: Interviews 1962-1980*. Translated by Linda Coverdale. New York: Hill and Wang, 1985. 205-232.

———. "The World of Wrestling." *Mythologies*. Translated by Annette Lavers. New York: Hill and Wang, 1972. 15-25

Bell, Catherine. *Ritual: Perspectives and Dimensions*. New York: Oxford University Press, 1997.

———. *Ritual Theory, Ritual Practice*. New York: Oxford University Press, 1992.

Benjamin, Walter. "M [The Flâneur]." *The Arcades Project*. Translated by Howard Eiland and Kevin McLaughlin. Cambridge: The Belknap Press of Harvard University Press, 1999. 416-455..

Björnberg, Alf. "Structural Relationships of Music and Images in Music Video." *Popular Music* 13:1 (1994). 51-74.

Bloom, Harold. *The American Religion*. New York: Chu Hartley, 2006.

———. *Omens of Millennium: The Gnosis of Angels, Dreams, and Resurrection*. New York: Riverhead Books, 1996.

Booth, Mark W. *The Experience of Songs*. New Haven: Yale University Press, 1981.

Bracewell, Michael. *England Is Mine: Pop Life in Albion from Wilde to Goldie*. London: HarperCollins, 1997.

Breward, Christopher. "For 'We are the Goon Squad': Bowie, Style and the Power of the LP Cover, 1967-1983." *David Bowie Is*. Edited by Victoria Broakes and Geoffrey Marsh. London: V & A, 2013. 192-203.

Buckley, David. *Strange Fascination: David Bowie: The Definitive Story*. London: Virgin Books, 2000.

Burns, Gary. "A Typology of 'Hooks' in Popular Records." *Popular Music* 6:1 (January 1987). 1-20.

Butler, Judith. *Bodies that Matter: On the Discursive Limits of "Sex."* New York: Routledge, 1993.

———. *Undoing Gender*. New York: Routledge, 2004.

Cage, John. "Composition as Process: I. Changes". *Silence*. Middletown: Wesleyan University Press, 1967. 18-34.

———. "Erik Satie." *Silence*. Middletown: Wesleyan University Press, 1967. 76-82.

Camphausen, Rufus C. *Return of the Tribal: A Celebration of Body Adornment*. Rochester: Park Street Press, 1997.

Canetti, Elias. *Crowds and Power*. Trans-

Bibliography

lated by Carol Stewart. New York: Continuum, 1981.

Clark, John, Stuart Hall, Tony Jefferson and Brian Roberts. "Subcultures, Cultures and Class: A Theoretical Overview." *Resistance Through Rituals: Youth Subcultures in Post-War Britain.* Edited by S. Hall and T. Jefferson. New York: Holmes & Meier, 1976. 9–72.

Coupland, Douglas. *Microserfs.* New York: HarperCollins, 1995.

Dagnal, Cynthia. "Eno and the Jets: Controlled Chaos." *Rolling Stone* 169 (12 September 1974). 16–17, 21.

Danto, Arthur C. *Mark Tansey: Visions and Revisions.* New York: Harry N. Abrams, 1992.

Danton, Eric R. "Trent Reznor Praises David Bowie's 'The Next Day' Album." *Rolling Stone* (19 December 2013). Available at http://www.rollingstone.com/music/news/trent-reznor-praises-david-bowies-the-next-day-album-20131219. Internet. Accessed 27 October 2014.

De Lisle, Tim. "Immaculate Conceptions." *The Independent* (10 September 1995). Available at http://www.independent.co.uk/arts-entertainment/immaculate-conceptions-1600363.html. Internet. Accessed 23 January 2015.

De Pourcq, Maarten. "'The *Paideia* of the Greeks': On the Methodology of Roland Barthes's *Comment vivre ensemble*." *Paragraph* 31:1 (2008). 23–37.

De Quincey, Thomas. "Supplementary Paper on Murder, Considered as One of the Fine Arts." *On Murder as a Fine Art.* London: Philip Allan & Co., 1925. 56–77.

de Villiers, Nicholas. "A Great Pedagogy of Nuance: Roland Barthes' *The Neutral*." *Theory & Event* 8:4 (2005). Available at htttp://lion.chadwyck.com.libaccess.lib.mcmaster.ca/display/printView.do?area=abell. Internet. Accessed 22 May 2009.

DeVito, Bobby DeVito. "'But is it MUSAK????' Ambient Music—from Satie through Cage to Eno." *The Hyperreal Music Archive.* Available at http://music.hyperreal.org/epsilon/info/devito.html. Internet. Accessed 3 November 2014.

Donald, Billy. "Interview with Reeves Gabrels." *MusicDish* (21 May 2003). Available at http://musicdish.com/mag/?id=8017. Internet. Accessed 27 October 2014.

Doughtie, Edward. "Words for Music: Simplicity and Complexity in the Elizabethan Air." *Rice University Studies* 51 (1965). 1–12.

Dyer, Richard. "*A Star is Born* and the Construction of Authenticity." *Stardom: Industry of Desire.* Edited by Christine Gledhill. London: Routledge, 1991. 132–140.

Eagleton, Terry. *Literary Theory: An Introduction.* Minneapolis: University of Minnesota Press, 1996.

"Enchanting David Bowie: Space/Time/Body/Memory." *Bloomsbury.* Available at http://www.bloomsbury.com/uk/enchanting-david-bowie-9781628923063/. Internet. Accessed 18 November 2014.

Eno, Brian. "Games for Musicians." *Raygun* 30 (October 1995). n.p.

_____. "Generating and Organizing Variety in the Arts." *Breaking the Sound Barrier: A Critical Anthology of the New Music.* Edited by Gregory Battcock. New York: E.P. Dutton, 1981. 129–141.

_____. "Pro Session: The Studio as Compositional Tool—Part II." *Down Beat* 50 (July 1983). 50–52.

_____. "The Revenge of the Intuitive." *Wired* 7.01 (January 1999). Available at http://archive.wired.com/wired/archive/7.01/eno_pr.html. Internet. Accessed 5 November 2014.

_____. *A Year with Swollen Appendices.* London: Faber and Faber, 1996.

Eno, Brian, and Russel Mills. *More Dark*

Bibliography

Than Shark. London: Faber and Faber, 1986.

Esposito, Scott. "Four Questions for Kate Briggs on Roland Barthes' Preparation of the Novel." *Conversational Reading* (7 April 2011). Available at http://conversationalreading.com/four-questions-for-kate-briggs-on-roland-barthes-preparation-of-the-novel/. Internet. Accessed 18 November 2014.

Everett, Walter. "Confessions from Blueberry Hell, or, Pitch Can Be a Sticky Subject." *Expressions in Pop-Rock Music*. Edited by W. Everett. New York: Garland, 2000. 269–346.

Favazza, Armando R., and Barbara Favazza. *Bodies Under Siege: Self-Mutilation in Culture and Psychiatry*. Baltimore: Johns Hopkins University Press, 1987.

Flanagan, James W. "Space." *Handbook of Postmodern Biblical Interpretation*. Edited by A.K.M. Adam. St. Louis: Chalice Press, 2000. 239–244.

Foucault, Michel. "Of Other Spaces." Translated by Jay Miskowiec. *Diacritics* 16:1 (Spring 1986). 22–27.

Freyling, Sir Christopher Freyling, Philip Hoare and Mark Kermode. "David Bowie Then…. David Bowie Now …." *David Bowie Is*. Edited by Victoria Broackes and Geoffrey Marsh. London: V&A, 2013. 282–301.

Frith, Simon. *Performing Rites: On the Value of Popular Music*. Cambridge: Harvard University Press, 1996.

Gibson, William. *Neuromancer*. New York: Ace, 1987.

Gleber, Anke. "Flanerie, of The Redemption of Visual Reality." *The Art of Taking a Walk: Flanerie, Literature, and Film in Weimar Culture*. Princeton: Princeton University Press, 1999. 151–168.

Grant, Steven. "Brian Eno Against Interpretation." *Trouser Press* 9 (August 1982). 27–30. Available at http://music.hyperreal.org/artists/brian_eno/interviews/troup82a.html. Internet. Accessed 3 November 2014.

Greco, Nicholas P. "Cruising in Prime Time." *Rush and Philosophy*. Edited by Jim Berti and Durrell Bowman. Chigaco: Open Court, 2011. 211–221.

Gunning, Tom. "From the Kaleidoscope to the X-Ray: Urban Spectatorship, Poe, Benjamin, and *Traffic in Souls* (1913)." *Wide Angle* 19:4 (1997). 25–61.

Haden-Guest, Anthony. "The Return of Guy Bourdin." *The New Yorker* 70 (7 November 1994). 136–146.

Hanley, Jason J. "'The Land of Rape and Honey': The Use of World War II Propaganda in the Music Videos of Ministry and Laibach." *American Music* 22:1 (Spring 2004). 158–175.

Heath, Stephen. "Translator's Note." In Roland Barthes, *Image—Music—Text*. Translated by S. Heath. New York: Hill and Wang, 1977. 7–11.

Hewett, Ivan. "David Bowie's jazz song shows his genius for self-reinvention." *The Telegraph* (16 October 2014). Available at http://www.telegraph.co.uk/culture/music/worldfolkandjazz/11163556/David-Bowies-jazz-song-shows-his-genius-for-self-reinvention.html. Internet. Accessed 18 November 2014.

Hewitt, Kim. *Mutilating the Body: Identity in Blood and Ink*. Bowling Green, OH: Bowling Green State University Popular Press, 1997.

Jones, Allan. "Eno—Class of '75." *Melody Maker* 50:48 (29 November 1975). 14.

Krauss, Rosalind E. "Translator's Preface." In Roland Barthes, *The Neutral*. Translated by R. E. Krauss and D. Hollier. New York: Columbia University Press, 2005. xiii–xvii.

Laing, Dave. *One Chord Wonders: Power and Meaning in Punk Rock*. London: Open University Press, 1985.

Lambert, Bruce. "Unlikely AIDS Sufferer's Message: Even You Can Get It."

New York Times (11 March 1989). Available at http://www.nytimes.com/1989/03/11/nyregion/unlikely-aids-sufferer-s-message-even-you-can-get-it.html. Internet. Accessed 11 November 2014.

Larkin, Colin, ed. "Brian Eno." *The Encyclopedia of Popular Music*, 3d ed. London: Muze UK, 1998. Vol. 3. 1764.

Leppert, Richard. *Art and the Committed Eye: The Cultural Functions of Imagery*. Boulder: Westview/HarperCollins, 1996.

Liedtke, Walter. *Vermeer and the Delft School*. New York: The Metropolitan Museum of Art, 2001.

Marsh, Geoffrey. "Astronaut of Inner Spaces: Sunridge Park, Soho, London.... Mars." *David Bowie Is*. Edited by Victoria Broackes and Geoffrey Marsh. London: V&A, 2013. 26–46.

Maxwell, Ian. "The Ritualization of Performance (Studies)." *Victor Turner and Contemporary Cultural Performance*. Edited by Graham St John. New York: Berghahn Books, 2008. 59–75.

McAllester, Matt. "Where Is He Now? David Bowie Is Back to His Mysterious Best." *Time* 181:10 (18 March 2013). 52–55.

McKinney, Devin. "Cruising a Road to Nowhere: Mechanics and Mysteries of the Pop Moment." *Popular Music* 24:3 (October 2005). 311–321.

Miller, Jean-Chris. *The Body Art Book: A Complete, Illustrated Guide to Tattoos, Piercings, and Other Body Modifications*. New York: Berkley Books, 1997.

Moriarty, Michael. *Roland Barthes*. Stanford: Stanford University Press, 1991.

Morris, Pam. "Introduction." *The Bakhtin Reader*. Edited by Pam Morris. London: Edward Arnold, 1994. 1–24.

Murdoch, Lorne. "Hitting an All-Time Low." *The Bowie Companion*. Edited by Elizabeth Thomson and David Gutman. New York: Da Capo Press, 1996. 149–155.

O'Brien, Glenn. "Eno at the Edge of Rock." *Andy Warhol's Interview* 8:6 (June 1978). 31–33. Available at http://music.hyperreal.org/artists/brian_eno/interviews/unk-78b.html. Internet. Accessed 3 November 2014.

O'Leary, Chris. "Everyone Says 'Hi.'" *Pushing Ahead of the Dame* (15 August 2014). Available at http://bowiesongs.wordpress.com/2014/08/15/everyone-says-hi/. Internet. Accessed 15 August 2014.

_____. "Future Legend." *Pushing Ahead of the Dame* (14 September 2010). Available at http://bowiesongs.wordpress.com/2010/09/14/future-legend/. Internet. Accessed 27 October 2014.

_____. "I am with Name/Segue: Ramona A. Stone." *Pushing Ahead of the Dame* (31 January 2013). Available at http://bowiesongs.wordpress.com/2013/01/31/i-am-with-name-segue-ramona-a-stone/. Internet. Accessed 14 November 2014.

_____. "I'm Deranged." *Pushing Ahead of the Dame* (26 March 2013). Available at http://bowiesongs.wordpress.com/2013/03/26/im-deranged/. Internet. Accessed 23 January 2015.

_____. "Jewel." *Pushing Ahead of the Dame* (31 January 2014). Available at http://bowiesongs.wordpress.com/2014/01/31/jewel/. Internet. Accessed 27 October 2014.

_____. "Look Back in Anger." *Pushing Ahead of the Dame* (22 July 2011); available from http://bowiesongs.wordpress.com/?s=Look+back+in+anger; Internet. Accessed 27 October 2014.

_____. "No Control." *Pushing Ahead of the Dame* (8 April 2003). Available at http://bowiesongs.wordpress.com/2013/04/08/no-control/. Internet. Accessed 22 January 2015.

_____. "Outside Tour: The Nine Inch Nails Duets." *Pushing Ahead of the Dame* (2 May 2013). Available at http://bowiesongs.wordpress.com/2013/05/

Bibliography

02/outside-tour-the-nine-inch-nails-duets/. Internet. Accessed 27 October 2014.

———. "Sense of Doubt." *Pushing Ahead of the Dame* (20 May 2011). Available at http://bowiesongs.wordpress.com/2011/05/20/sense-of-doubt/. Internet. Accessed 27 October 2014.

———. "Survive." *Pushing Ahead of the Dame* (1 November 2013). Available at https://bowiesongs.wordpress.com/2013/11/01/survive/. Internet. Accessed 21 January 2015.

———. "Thursday's Child." *Pushing Ahead of the Dame* (21 January 2014). Available at http://bowiesongs.wordpress.com/2014/01/21/thursdays-child/. Internet. Accessed 31 October 2014.

Paglia, Camille. "Theatre of Gender: David Bowie at the Climax of the Sexual Revolution." *David Bowie Is*. Edited by Victoria Broackes and Geoffrey Marsh. London: V&A, 2013. 68–92.

Pahl, Jon. "The Shopping Mall as 'Stairway to Heaven,' Leading Nowhere." *Shopping Malls and Other Sacred Spaces: Putting God in Place*. Grand Rapids: Brazos Press, 2003. 65–82.

Pattie, David. "4 Real: Authenticity, Performance, and Rock Music." *Enculturation* 2:2 (Spring 1999). Available at http://www.enculturation.net/2_2/pattie.html. Internet. Accessed 17 November 2014.

———. *Rock Music in Performance*. New York: Palgrave Macmillan, 2007.

Paytress, Mark. *The Rise and Fall of Ziggy Stardust and the Spiders from Mars: David Bowie (Classic Rock Albums)*. New York: Schirmer Books, 1998.

Penman, Ian. "The Resurrection of Saint Dave." *Esquire Magazine* (October 1995). Available at http://www.algonet.se/~bassman/articles/95/e.html. Internet. Accessed 31 October 2014.

Petros, George and Steven Blush. "I Don't Feel as Though I Hold a Torch for One Particular Style of Music, I Find that Absolutism Outmoded." *Seconds* (August/September 1995). Available at http://www.algonet.se/~bassman/articles/95/s.html. Internet. Accessed 15 November 2014.

Polhemus, Ted, and Housk Randall. *The Customized Body*. London: Serpent's Tail, 1996.

Rodger, Jazmin. "Critically Assess Barthes' Notion that Signs are Ideological." *University of Essex Department of Sociology Undergraduate Journal* 4 (Summer 2010). Available at https://www.essex.ac.uk/sociology/documents/pdf/ug_journal/vol4/2010SC301_JazminRodger.pdf. Internet. Accessed 27 October 2014.

Rose, Frank. "Eno: Scaramouche of the Synthesizer." *Creem* 7 (July 1975). Available at http://music.hyperreal.org/artists/brian_eno/interviews/creem75c.html. Internet. Accessed 2 November 2014.

Rosenfeld, Austen. "Can We Live Together, Roland Barthes?" *The Daily Beast* (19 December 2012). Available at http://www.thedailybeast.com/articles/2012/12/19/can-we-live-together-roland-barthes.html. Internet. Accessed 18 November 2014.

Roth, Martin. "David Bowie is what Follows: Foreword." *David Bowie Is*. Edited by Victoria Broackes and Geoffrey Marsh. London: V&A, 2013. 17.

Rowland, Mark. "The Outside Story." *Musician* 204 (November 1995). 30–32, 34, 38–41, 94.

Rushkoff, Douglas. *Cyberia: Life in the Trenches of Hyperspace*. New York: HarperCollins, 1995.

St. John, Graham. "Alternative Cultural Heterotopia and the Liminoid Body: Beyond Turner at ConFest." *The Australian Journal of Anthropology* 12:1 (2001). 47–66.

Bibliography

Sanders, Clinton R. *Customizing the Body: The Art and Culture of Tattooing*. Philadelphia: Temple University Press, 1989.

Sandford, Christopher. *Bowie: Loving the Alien*. London: Warner Books, 1997.

Schechner, Richard. "Toward a Poetics of Performance." *Performance Theory*. New York: Routledge, 1988. 153–186.

Schwichtenberg, Cathy. "Music Video: The Popular Pleasures of Visual Music." *Popular Music and Communication*. Edited by James Lull. Newbury Park, CA: Sage, 1992. 116–133.

Sememova, K. "21. The Watchdog." In *Dutch and Flemish Paintings from the Hermitage*. New York: The Metropolitan Museum of Art, 1988. 44.

Senn, Frank C. "Epilogue: Postmodern Liturgy." *Christian Liturgy: Catholic and Evangelical*. Minneapolis: Fortress Press, 1997. 693–706.

Sinclair, Paul. "Bowie Collaborator Erdal Kizilcay on Glass Spider and Never Let Me Down." *Super Deluxe Edition* (11 December 2013). Available at http://www.superdeluxeedition.com/interview/bowie-collaborator-erdal-kizilcay-on-glass-spider-and-never-let-me-down/. Internet. Accessed 27 October 2014.

Slater, Ben. "The Up Escalator Forever: Bowie in Singapore." *"Clearly, You've Never Been..."* (27 October 2010). Available at http://sporeana.blogspot.ca/2010/10/up-escalator-forever-bowie-in-singapore.html. Internet. Accessed 23 October 2014.

Spitz, Marc. *Bowie: A Biography*. New York: Crown, 2009.

Stallybrass, Peter, and Allon White. *The Politics and Poetics of Transgression*. Ithaca: Cornell University Press, 1986.

Stevenson, Nick. *David Bowie: Fame, Sound and Vision*. Cambridge: Polity Press, 2006.

Straw, Will. "Music Video in its Contexts: Popular Music and Post-Modernism in the 1980s." *Popular Music* 7:3 (1988). 247–266.

Strong, Marilee. *A Bright Red Scream: Self-Mutilation and the Language of Pain*. New York: Viking Penguin, 1998.

Tamm, Eric. *Brian Eno: His Music and the Vertical Color of Sound*. Cambridge, MA: Da Capo Press, 1995.

_____. "Soul Robots: Eno and Fripp with Bowie." *The Bowie Companion*. Edited by Elizabeth Thomson and David Gutman. New York: Da Capo Press, 1996. 143–149.

Tannenbaum, Rob. "A Meeting of Sound Minds: John Cage and Brian Eno." *Musician* 83 (September 1985). 64–72, 106.

Théberge, Paul. *Any Sound You Can Imagine: Making Music/Consuming Technology*. Hanover: Wesleyan University Press, 1997.

Toop, David. *Ocean of Sound*. London: Serpent's Tail, 1995.

Tremlett, George. *David Bowie: Living on the Brink*. New York: Carroll & Graf, 1997.

Turner, Victor. "Are There Universals of Performance in Myth, Ritual, and Drama?" *By Means of Performance: Intercultural Studies of Theatre and Ritual*. Edited by W. Schechner and W. Appels. New York: Cambridge University Press, 1990. 8–18.

_____. *From Ritual to Theatre: The Human Seriousness of Play*. New York: PAJ Publications, 1982.

_____. "Liminal to Liminoid, in Play, Flow, and Ritual." *From Ritual to Theatre: The Human Seriousness of Play*. New York: PAJ Publications, 1982. 20–60.

_____. *The Ritual Process*. New York: Aldine De Gruyter, 1969.

Vale, V., and Andrea Juno, "Introduction." *Modern Primitives: An Investigation of Contemporary Adornment & Ritual*. Edited by V. Vale and Andrea Juno. San Francisco: Re/Search Publications, 1989. n.p.

Bibliography

_____. "Fakir Musafar." *Modern Primitives: An Investigation of Contemporary Adornment & Ritual*. Edited by V. Vale and Andrea Juno. San Francisco: Re/Search, 1989. n.p.

Vernallis, Carol. "The Aesthetics of Music Video: An Analysis of Madonna's 'Cherish.'" *Popular Music* 17:2 (1998). 153–185.

Virilio, Paul. *The Administration of Fear*. Translated by Ames Hodges. Los Angeles: Semiotext(e), 2012.

_____. *The Futurism of the Instant: Stop-Eject*. Translated by Julie Rose. Cambridge: Polity Press, 2010.

Walser, Robert. *Running With the Devil: Power, Gender, and Madness in Heavy Metal Music*. Hanover: Wesleyan University Press, 1993.

Wells, Dominic. "Boys Keep Swinging." *Time Out* 48 (23–30 August 1995). Available at http://music.hyperreal.org/artists/brian_eno/interviews/Bowieno.html. Internet. Accessed 11 November 2014.

Wunderlich, Wolfgang. *Hermann Nitsche: The O.M. Theatre 80th Action*. Translated by Andrew Clegg Littler. München: Verlag Fred Jahn, 1988.

"The Year in Review: The Insider." *Groove Culture*. Available at http://models.com/life_style/groove/bowie/bowie3.html. Internet. Accessed 31 October 2014.

Zappa, Moon. "David Bowie." *Raygun* 30 (October 1995). n.p.

Index

Abel (biblical figure) 134
Achtung Baby 87
Adler, Nathan 106, 119, 130–131, 133–137, 150–152, 183; *see also* persona
The Administration of Fear 57–61, 64
"The Aesthetics of Music Video: An Analysis of Madonna's 'Cherish'" 169
Aladdin Sane 191–192
"Aladdin Sane (1913–1938–197?)" 70
Alford, Zachary 31
Alomar, Carlos 22, 79
Ambient music 72–73, 85–86, 87, 97, 100
Ambient I: Music for Airports 97
"American Religion" 126
Another Green World 86, 87, 101, 103
Antichrist Superstar 78
Apollo: Atmospheres and Soundtracks 86, 100
"Are There Universals of Performance in Myth, Ritual, and Drama?" 139
Arma Christi 111
"Art Decade" 103
Arts Protectorate of London *see* "The Diary of Nathan Adler"
Ashby, W.R. 97
Athey, Ron 82, 106–107, 119–120, 125, 135–136, 139
atopos 192–193
authenticity 47–48, 52–53, 83
Away from the Flock 135

Babcock, Barbara 178
badaud 17–18; *see also flâneur*
Bakhtin, Mikhail 172, 177–183
Ballard, J.G. 191
Bangkok 12, 13–14, 16–17; *see also* Ricochet (film)
baptism 16, 166, 168, 169, 172–174
Barthes, Roland 5, 6, 24, 27–30, 32–35, 44, 45, 46–47, 53–54, 61–64, 68–69, 145–149, 154, 158, 192–193, 196, 205n29
"Battle for Britain (The Letter)" 30–35; *see also* fiftieth birthday concert (9 January 1997)

Baudelaire, Charles 17
Baudrillard, Jean 133
The Beach Boys 94
The Beatles 94, 190
"The Beautiful People" 78
"The Becoming" 78
Beer, Stafford 97–98
Bell, Catherine 139, 173
Benjamin, Walter 13, 17–21
Berlin 71–72, 73, 87, 104, 135, 136
Berlin (Lou Reed album) 71
Berlin trilogy 8, 11, 71, 72–75, 85, 86, 103–104; *see also* "*Heroes*"; *Lodger*; *Low*
Björnberg, Alf 165, 169–171
Black Tie White Noise 1, 3–4, 66, 67, 69–70
Blade Runner 155
Blank, Leon 135, 154; *see also* persona
Bloom, Harold 126
Blue, Baby Grace 130, 134, 135, 137, 154; *see also* persona
Bodies Under Siege: Self-Mutilation in Culture and Psychiatry 109–110
body modification 4, 6–7, 81–82, 106–109, 114–118, 120–125, 129, 135, 138–139, 142–143, 160, 162, 164, 181, 183, 186–187
"body play" 118–120, 124, 160
Booth, Mark 144
"Born This Way" 115
Bosch, Hieronymus 111
Bourdin, Guy 137
Bowie, Alexandria 5
Bowie: Loving the Alien 71
Bowie on Bowie: Interviews and Encounters with David Bowie 189
Bowie: The Biography 189
Bracewell, Michael 191, 194–196
Brain of the Firm: The Managerial Cybernetics of Organization 97
Brand, Stewart 97–98
Brecht, George 87
Breward, Christopher 71
Briggs, Kate 62
"Bring Me the Disco King" 49

217

Index

Brüken, Claudia 9
Buckley, David 25, 74, 82
The Buddha of Suburbia 69–71, 85
Burden, Chris 82, 106–107, 125, 134–135, 139
Burns, Gary 33
Burroughs, William 69, 144
Bush, George H.W. 76
Butler, Judith 28–29, 41
Byrne, David 99

Cage, John 86, 88, 89–91, 92–93, 96, 104–105
Cain (biblical figure) 134
Camera Lucida 61, 63
Camphausen, Rufus C. 116, 117, 118, 121, 122–123, 127–128
Camus, Renaud 32
Canetti, Elias 37–38, 45
Cardew, Cornelius 87
carnivalesque 45, 172, 175–183; *see also* Bakhtin, Mikhail
Carracci, Annibale 111–112
celebrity 2, 3, 5, 6, 7–10, 20–22, 44–45, 46–47, 50–52, 54, 85; *see also* persona; star image
Chicago 76
Christianity 76–78, 110–111, 121, 123, 125–128, 129, 172–177, 183; *see also* Protestantism; Roman Catholicism
cinéma vérité 19–20, 21
Cinque, Toija 190
Clark, John 117
Cold War 76
communitas 37–38, 45, 199n56; *see also* liminality; Turner, Victor
"Composition as Process" 89
Constantine 173
Construction in Metal 90
Coupland, Douglas 129
Crowds and Power 37
"cruising" 6, 30–35
The Cure 194–195
The Customized Body 108
Customizing the Body: The Art and Culture of Tattooing 109
Cyberia 97
cybernetics 97–98, 121

Danto, Arthur C. 132–133
David Bowie: Critical Perspectives 189
David Bowie Is 7, 8–9
David Bowie: The Golden Years 189
death 2, 49, 50, 61, 67, 77, 111–112, 119, 124, 134, 136–137, 154, 181
the death of the author 45; *see also* Barthes, Roland
de Balzac, Honoré 145
De Pourcq, Maarten 63
De Quincey, Thomas 134

Descartes, René 118
Devereux, Eoin 189
de Villiers, Nicholas 32
Diamond Dogs 71–72
"The Diary of Nathan Adler" 106, 126, 130–138, 146–147
Dillane, Aileen 189
disability 23
Discreet Music 87
Donald, Billy 24–25
Dorsey, Gail Ann 31, 80
Doughtie, Edward 144
The Downward Spiral 78
The Drop 88
Dyer, Richard 47–48, 51, 52
dystopia 53–54, 57, 64, 71, 75; *see also* utopia; Virilio, Paul

Eagleton, Terry 144
Earthing 2, 5, 30, 85, 192; tour 157
Edict of Milan 173
Egan, Sean 189
Enchanting David Bowie: Space/Time/Body/Memory 190
enigma 46–47, 52, 145–146
Eno, Brian 2, 4, 6, 24–25, 33, 70–71, 72–73, 74–75, 83, 85–105, 194–195
Eno, Roger 100
Esquire (magazine) 81, 83, 106, 107
Everett, Walter 161
"Everyone Says 'Hi'" 9
The Experience of Songs 144
Exploding Plastic Inevitable 89

"Fame" 17; *see also* "Fame '90"
"Fame '90" 30–31
The Fashion System 29; *see also* Barthes, Roland
Favazza, Armando 109–111, 113–115, 117, 120, 121, 124
Feist, Leslie 46–47, 50–52
Ferry, Brian 87
fiftieth birthday concert (9 January 1997) 30–33; *see also* "Battle for Britain (The Letter)"
Fils des Etoiles 91
Flanagan, Bob 119, 124, 134
Flanagan, James W. 38–39; *see also* space
flâneur 13, 17–21; *see also* Benjamin, Walter
Foucault, Michel 6, 39, 40–43, 45, 199n56; *see also* heterotopia
"Four Scenes in a Harsh Life" 135
Frampton, Peter 22
Fresh Air (NPR radio program) 9
Freyling, Sir Christopher 45
Fripp, Robert 72, 87, 104
Frith, Simon 144

218

Index

Future Nostalgia: Performing David Bowie 189–190
The Futurism of the Instant: Stop-Eject 55–57, 59

Gabrels, Reeves vi, 3, 5, 6, 11, 24–26, 31, 70, 80, 82, 85, 102, 137–138, 149–150, 157, 162, 185–186, 195
Gallina, Raelyn 119
Garden of Earthly Delights 111
Garson, Mike 31, 36–37, 70
"Generating and Organizing Variety in the Arts" 93, 97
Gertz, Alison 123
Gibson, William 155
Glass Spider tour 11, 22
Gleber, Anke 20
God 118, 125–127, 195
Gould, Glenn 94
the grain of the voice 6, 34–35, 68–69, 147–148; *see also* Barthes, Roland
Greater Bundahisn 113
Griffin, Roger 189
Groove Culture 82
Gross, Terry 9–10
Gunning, Tom 18
Gysin, Brion 144

haiku 62
Halévy, Daniel 21; *see also flâneur*
Hall, Stuart 117
"Hallo Spaceboy" 80, 84
Hanley, Jason 75–76
Hassel, Jon 99
"The Heart's Filthy Lesson" 80, 83, 138, 143, 149–154, 159, 163, 164–177, 180–184
Heath, Stephen 148
Heathen 2, 5, 9
Hendrix, Jimi 94
Here Come the Warm Jets 86, 87, 95, 101
"Heroes" 15, 71, 72, 73–74, 86, 87, 104; *see also* Berlin trilogy
heterotopia 6, 39–43, 45, 199n56; *see also* space
Hewett, Ivan 65
Hewitt, Kim 108, 151
Hirst, Damien 107, 119, 135
Hoffmann, E.T.A. 20
Hong Kong 2, 12, 13–14; *see also Ricochet* (film)
"hook" 33–34, 195
"hours..." 2, 5, 26, 39, 85, 192–194, 196
How to Live Together 61
Howard, Richard 64
"Human Touch" 171
"Hurt" 31, 80, 124; *see also* Nine Inch Nails
hyperreality 133

idiorrhythmy 53–54, 61, 63–64
"I'm Deranged" 194–196
Iman 5
The Importance of Being Morrissey 79–81
India 113
industrial music 36, 75–76, 79, 80, 81
The Innocent Eye Test 131–134
Institute of Contemporary Arts 24
intertextuality 144
An Introduction to Cybernetics 97–98
"Intruders at the Palace" 24–27
Ipswich 87, 92
Iran 113
Iron Maiden 176

Jackson, Michael 12
Jagger, Mick 35
Jefferson, Tony 117
Jesus Christ 3, 26, 77, 110–113, 126, 127, 167, 172–176, 192, 197n16
The Joshua Tree 87
Jourgensen, Al 76
Judaeo-Christianity 81–82, 107, 124–125, 129, 140, 160, 164; *see also* Christianity
Judaism 173
Juno, Andrea 116–117
juxtaposition 14, 42–43, 48, 54–55, 130, 138–139, 149, 153, 164–165, 169–172, 175, 177, 179–180, 183–184, 186–187

Kemp, Lindsay 191
Kizilcay, Erdal 70
Koons, Jeff 135
Kracauer, Siegfried 20

La La La Human Steps 11, 22, 24–27, 35–36; *see also* Lecavalier, Louise
Lady Gaga 115
Laing, Dave 144
Lanois, Daniel 87
The Last Judgement 111
Last Supper 167, 172, 175–176; *see also* Jesus Christ
Lecavalier, Louise 23, 24–27, 30–31
Led Zeppelin 176
Leigh, Wendy 189
Leppert, Richard 111–113
Let's Dance 1, 3, 12, 35, 70, 74
Letterman, David 183–184
"Liminal to Liminoid, in Play, Flow, and Ritual" 140–141
liminality 5–6, 31, 34, 36–39, 42–43, 44, 45–46, 57, 68, 107, 116, 128, 129, 138–143, 157, 160, 162–163, 164–165, 171–172, 174, 176–177, 179, 183, 186–187; *see also* space; Turner, Victor
Lippman, Steven 48

Index

liturgy 126, 174
"Liza Jane" 190
Lock, Edouard 24
Lodger 1, 11, 71, 73–74, 86, 87, 104; *see also* Berlin trilogy
London (Canada) 137
London (England) 48, 87, 185, 190
"The Loneliest Guy" 49
Look at What the Light Did Now 50–52
"Look Back in Anger" 5, 11, 24–27, 31; *see also* "Intruders at the Palace"; La La La Human Steps
Loomis, Roland *see* Musafar, Fakir
Los Angeles 71, 73
Lost Highway 195
Low 69, 71, 73–74, 79, 86, 87, 103, 104; *see also* Berlin trilogy
Lutens, Serge 137
Lynch, David 195

Madonna 83, 169
The Man Who Fell to Earth 73
The Man Who Sold the World 191
Manhattan 135; *see also* New York
Maria Gugging Psychiatric Clinic 195–196
Marilyn Manson 78
Mark Tansey: Visions and Revisions 132–133
Marsh, Geoffrey 190–191
Mary (biblical figure) 5, 26, 111, 192
Masai 116
Max Headroom 155
Maxwell, Ian 37–38, 42–43, 45
The Maxwell Demon 87
McAllester, Matt 8–9
McKinney, Devin 33–34
mediation 21, 28, 31–32, 35, 41, 46–52
Mehndi 115
Merchant Taylor's Simultaneous Cabinet 87
Michelangelo 192
Microserfs 129
Middle Ages 41, 177–179
millennium 4, 6, 45–46, 107, 122, 129–130, 136, 143, 164, 173, 183, 186–187
Miller, Jean-Chris 115, 118, 120–121
Minaker, Clea 51–52
minimalism 86, 88, 89, 91, 93
Ministry (band) 76–78
Minotaur 166–169, 171, 175, 177, 180
Miranda 152; *see also* persona
Miskowiec, Jay 41
"Modern Primitive" 116–117, 121
Monet, Claude 132–133
Morceaux en forme de poire 91
Moriarty, Michael 28
Morris, Pam 180, 182
Morrissey 79–81

"The Motel" 138, 150, 160–163
Motes, Hazel 111, 174
MTV Unplugged 47
Murdoch, Lorne 72
Musafar, Fakir 116, 121, 124, 143
Music for Non Musicians 87
Music of Changes 89–90
"Music Video: The Popular Pleasures of Visual Music" 168
Musician (magazine) 187
Mutilating the Body: Identity in Blood and Ink 108
My Life in the Bush of Ghosts 86, 99
myth 28, 45, 141

Neroli 88
Nerve Net 88
Neuromancer 155
neutral 44, 45, 61; *The Neutral* 61; *see also* "third term"
"Never Get Old" 46, 48–49
Never Let Me Down 3, 11, 70
"New Killer Star" 49
New York 49–50, 71, 73, 89, 130–131
The New Yorker (magazine) 137
New Zealand 12
The Next Day 2, 5, 6, 8, 11, 22, 53, 73, 74–75
Nine Inch Nails 3–4, 31, 35, 36, 74–75, 78, 79–80, 124
1984 (novel) 71
"Nite Flights" 67–69
Nitsch, Hermann 126–127, 134
"No Control" 194–196
No Pussyfooting 87
Nothing Has Changed 66
Nuba 116
"N.W.O." 76–77

Oblique Strategies 72, 86, 87, 98, 102, 104–105; *see also* Eno, Brian
O'Brien, Glenn 98–102
Ocean of Sound 85
O'Connor, Flannery 111, 113, 114, 174
O'Leary, Chris 9, 24–25, 39, 71, 72–73, 74, 159, 189, 192, 194–196
"On Being an Artist" 83; *see also* Eno, Brian
"On Murder Considered as One of the Fine Arts" 134
Ono, Yoko 127
Orlan 115
Orwell, George 71
Osaka 102
Ottawa Citizen 127
Outside tour 31, 75, 184–186; *see also* Nine Inch Nails
Oxford 130–131, 194

Index

Paddy 150, 152–153; *see also* persona
Paglia, Camille 191–192
Pahl, Jon 16
Paris 17–19
Passengers: Original Soundtracks 1 87, 88
Pattie, David 46, 47–48, 51, 52, 54
Paytress, Mark 193
Peelaert, Guy 71
Penman, Ian 81–84, 106, 107, 164
persona 1, 6, 7–10, 12–13, 21, 46, 50–51, 65, 71, 72, 190; *see also* celebrity
Pet Shop Boys 84
Peter (biblical figure) 111
Pietà 26, 111, 192; *see also* "hours..."
Plati, Mark 85
Plomp, Michiel C. 131
Poe, Edgar Allan 17
Polhemus, Ted 108–109, 115–116, 117–118, 124, 158
The Politics and Poetics of Transgression 177–179; *see also* carnivalesque
Pop, Iggy 24–25
Pope, Tim 22; *see also* "Time Will Crawl"
Portsmouth Sinfonia 87
Potter, Paulus 131–134
Power, Martin 189
The Preparation of the Novel 61, 63
Prose Edda 113
Protestantism 113, 173–174
"Psalm 69" (song) 77–78
Psalm 69: The Way to Succeed and the Way to Suck Eggs 76–78
Punk 71–72

Queen (band) 70

Rabelais 177, 182
"Rave" culture 123
"readerly" 146–147, 196; *see also* Barthes, Roland; "writerly"
Reality 2, 5, 6; film 46, 48–50
Rebel Rebel (book) 189
Redmond, Sean 190
Reed, Lou 71
Reich, Steve 91
The Reminder 50, 51–52
"Reptile" 79
Reznor, Trent 74–75, 79–81, 124; *see also* Nine Inch Nails
Richard, Bertrand 57–58
Richard, Cliff 88–89
Richards, David 70, 150
Ricochet (film) 1, 5, 12–22, 23; *see also Serious Moonlight* tour
Rigueda 113
Riley, Terry 91
Rites of Passage 140

ritual 36, 45, 110, 114, 116, 119, 121, 124, 125, 127, 139, 140–142, 162, 172–178, 183
Roberts, Brian 117
Rodger, Jazmin 28
Roeg, Nicolas 73
Roland Barthes by Roland Barthes 61, 63
Rolling Stone 74
The Rolling Stones 12
Roman Catholicism 111, 174
Roman Empire 173
Rose, Julie 56
Roth, Martin 7–8, 190
Rothko, Mark 135–136
Roxy Music 87, 94
Rozzi, Mary 52
Rüger, Axel 131
Rushkoff, Douglas 97

St. John, Graham 199n56
Salma di Cristo 111–113
San Fransisco 119
Sanders, Clinton 109, 116, 121–122
Sandford, Christopher 71, 183–186, 194
Sarrasine 145
Satie, Erik 86, 88, 89, 91, 96, 104
Scandinavia 113
"Scare Crow" 77
"Scary Monsters (and Super Creeps)" 79–80
Schechner, Richard 136
Scheider, Maria 65
Schmidt, Peter 87; *see also* Oblique Strategies
Schwartz, Mark 124
Schwarzkogler 134
Schwichtenberg, Cathy 168
Scratch Orchestra 87
semiotics 27–30; *see also* Barthes, Roland
Senn, Frank C. 125–126
"Sense of Doubt" 15, 72–73, 104
Sgt. Pepper's Lonely Hearts Club Band 190
Serious Moonlight tour 1, 12, 15; *see also Ricochet* (film)
The Shutov Assembly 88
Silence (book) 89–91
Singapore 1, 12, 13, 14–16, 18–21; *see also Ricochet* (film)
Slater, Ben 12, 15- ; *see also Ricochet* (film); Singapore
"A Small Plot of Land" 159, 164, 184–186
Soja, Edward 38–39, 43, 45; *see also* space
Sonatas and Interludes 90
Sound+Vision tour 24, 75
Soviet Union 76
space 5–6, 11, 35–46, 130, 164, 183, 191–192; *see also* Foucault, Michel; heterotopia; liminality; Turner, Victor;
"Space Oddity" 191
Spector, Phil 94

221

Index

speed 53, 56, 59–61, 64
Springsteen, Bruce 171
Stallybrass, Peter 177–179
star image 2, 7–10, 23, 35, 44; *see also* celebrity; persona
Stardust, Ziggy 9, 71, 72, 191–193
Steele, Tommy 89
Stevenson, Nick 72, 73–74
Stone, Ramona A. 82, 130, 135, 136, 137, 150–153, 158–59, 166–167, 170; *see also* persona
"Strangers When We Meet" 83–84, 143, 154–158, 159
Straw, Will 165
Strong, Marilee 118–119, 123–124
"Structural Relationships of Music and Images in Music Video" 165, 170–171
"Subterraneans" 79–80
Sudan 116
"Sue (or in a Season of Crime)" 2, 5, 6, 65–66
Sun Dance 110, 118
surveillance 16, 21; *see also* Virilio, Paul
S/Z 145–146

Talking Heads 99
Tamm, Eric 72, 87, 88–89, 92–93, 95–96, 103
Tansey, Mark 131–134
Tantra 123
technology 4, 30, 53–65, 76, 78, 81, 86, 95, 100, 121, 129, 143, 155–160, 187
television 13, 15, 48, 136, 155–156
Thailand 2
Théberge, Paul 159
"third term" 35, 44; *see also* Barthes, Roland
"Thirdspace" 38–39, 43, 45; *see also* space
Thursday Afternoon 86, 100–101
"Thursday's Child" 6, 39–40, 42, 43, 57
Tibetan Book of the Dead 110
Time Out 125
"Time Will Crawl" 22–23, 67
Tin Machine 3, 70, 85
"'Tis a Pity She's a Whore" 2, 66
Tommy 89
Tonight 3
Toop, David 85–86
Top of the Pops 157–158
Toryna, Gerry 12; *see also* Ricochet (film)
Touchshriek, Algeria 135; *see also* persona
"Toward a Poetics of Performance" 136
"Trance" (musical style) 123
Trans-Fixed 134; *see also* Burden, Chris
transgression 162, 177–179, 181–183
Tremlett, George 191
Tricks (novel) 32
"True Love Waits" 123
Turner, Tina 35
Turner, Victor 5, 36–38, 42–43, 44, 45–46, 107, 116, 130, 138–143, 157, 158, 162–163, 176–177, 183, 199*n*56

U2 86–87, 88, 96
The Unforgettable Fire 87
United States 76–77
utopia 6, 16, 37, 41–43, 44, 53–54, 57, 64, 117; *see also* Foucault, Michel; Virilio, Paul

Vale, V. 116–117
"Valentine's Day" 6, 53–55, 64
van Gennep, Arnold 140–141
Vancouver 15
The Velvet Underground 89
Vernallis, Carol 169
"Very High Building" 53–57; *see also* Virilio, Paul
"VHB" *see* "Very High Building"
Vienna 195; Viennese castrationists 106, 126, 134
violence 12, 23, 26–27, 55, 67, 69, 77, 78, 82, 126, 129, 136, 155, 163, 164, 167
Virilio, Paul 6, 53–61, 64–65, 140
Visconti, Tony 71, 85
Vogue (magazine) 137

Waldrep, Shelton 189
Walker, Scott 67–69
Walser, Robert 162, 175–176
Warhol, Andy 89
"Warszawa" 103
The Watchdog 131–132; *see also* Potter, Paulus
Wells, Dominic 125
Wembley Arena 185
White, Allon 177–179
The Who 89
Winchester Art School 87
Wise Blood 111
Wolff, Christian 87
Woodbridge 87, 88
"writerly" 146–147, 164; *see also* Barthes, Roland; "readerly"

X for Henry Flynt 92

"Y2K" 4
A Year with Swollen Appendices 97–98
Young, La Monte 87, 91–92
Young Americans 192
The Young Bull 131–134
"You've Been Around" 70

Ziggy Stardust and the Spiders from Mars 191; *see also* Stardust, Ziggy
Zoo TV tour 87
Zooropa 87

www.ingramcontent.com/pod-product-compliance
Ingram Content Group UK Ltd.
Pitfield, Milton Keynes, MK11 3LW, UK
UKHW041951140426
5217IPUK00014B/739